Trading in Uncertainty

Esther Horat

Trading in Uncertainty

Entrepreneurship, Morality and Trust in a Vietnamese Textile-Handling Village

palgrave
macmillan

Esther Horat
Universität Zürich
Zurich, Switzerland

This work was accepted as a Ph.D. thesis by the Faculty of Arts and Social Sciences, University of Zurich in the spring semester 2016 on the recommendation of the Doctoral Committee: Prof. Dr. Peter Finke (main supervisor), PD Dr. Kirsten Endres, Prof. Dr. Annuska Derks.

ISBN 978-3-319-55647-5 ISBN 978-3-319-55648-2 (eBook)
DOI 10.1007/978-3-319-55648-2

Library of Congress Control Number: 2017937278

Printed on acid-free paper

This Palgrave Macmillan imprint is published by Springer Nature
The registered company is Springer International Publishing AG
The registered company address is: Gewerbestrasse 11, 6330 Cham, Switzerland

For my Family

Preface

The first time I was exposed to Vietnam (and Asia for that matter) was in 2006 when I went there as a visiting tourist. Having been impressed by the dynamic and forward-looking spirit prevalent among the people I encountered throughout my journey, I developed a profound longing to familiarise myself with the country, its people and their lives. I returned to the country in 2008 and stayed there for a period of six months in order to conduct ethnographic research for my master thesis, and again in 2011 to collect data for another research project on small- and middle-scale private businesses in Hanoi and Ho Chi Minh City. It was during my recurrent sojourns that I first began to take notice of the remarkable pace of transformation in the country.

It was not until July 2012, when officially I arrived in Hanoi for commencing the fieldwork stage of my Ph.D., that I embarked on a much longer ethnographic inquiry. Soon after settling in, I was constantly under the impression that a vibrant atmosphere prevailed wherever I went. This was in large part due to the countless and very-well-frequented shops lined along the streets of the city centre. The locals appeared to be constantly on the move. To my amazement, Hanoi had undergone even further change since my last visit. But this time in addition to the bustling streets filled with even more cars, the painstaking traffic jams, the newly built high-rise buildings in the south-western part of the city, the conspicuous presence of shopping malls also drew my attention.

Scattered across the city, these brand new multi-storey malls now host international luxury labels, food courts and large entertainment areas with cinemas. Traditional marketplaces, which are still the favourite places for most Vietnamese to buy fresh foods and grocery as well as household articles, clothing and other items for daily life, exist next to these shopping malls. However, according to the state's vision of modernity and its developmental model, more and more of these traditional marketplaces are undergoing what the state refers to as an "upgrade", which in reality results either in renovation of the building or in changes made to marketplace ownership and their transformation into commercial centres. This process is not confined to urban areas but extends to places well beyond it. I became aware of this during my first visit to Ninh Hiệp, when I began to appreciate the various indicators of the pace and extent of marketisation. However, it was throughout the course of my fieldwork that I saw more vividly the centrality of the marketisation process to the lives of Ninh Hiệp traders. Although a great deal of this book is about the operation of the marketplace, it also addresses the broader topics of economic restructuring, governance and participation that inform the market.

Zurich, Switzerland Esther Horat

Acknowledgements

Traders are no strangers to debt, and the completion of this book is indebted to the invaluable support I have received from various individuals, not all of whom I can mention here.

This work would never have seen the light of day were it not for the traders in Ninh Hiệp and their families, who not only readily accepted my presence in the village, but also allowed me into their everyday lives, invited me to their houses and shared their stories with me. Their cooperation helped me animate the theoretical arguments with ethnographic descriptions. I am especially grateful to cô Nguyệt and her family for offering me to stay with them, and for their openness towards me. I also appreciate the hospitality and willingness of many other traders in the village as well as their family members who supported the research in the various ways they could. In conversations, they opened up about their lives as well as about the village history. They introduced me to other fellow villagers, showed me the production sites in their homes, took me along to a business trip to China and let me stay at their stalls for long hours. In the interest of preserving their anonymity, their real names have been substituted with pseudonyms.

I am thankful to Mr. Khanh, vice chairman of the People's Committee of Ninh Hiệp, and to Mr. Sơn, chairman of the cooperative of Ninh Hiệp, for supporting my research and providing me relevant information on the commune. I am also grateful to the nine hamlet chiefs, who have invested considerable time in talking to me and introducing me to villagers.

A number of scholars have provided insightful comments on earlier drafts of some chapters. In particular, I would like to thank Minh Nguyễn, Christine Bonnin, Ann Marie Leshkowich, Regina Abrami, Sarah Turner, Helle Rydstrøm, Lynne Milgram, Ben Kerkvliet and David Szanton. I would also like to extend my gratitude to colleagues, either at the University of Zurich or at the Max Planck Institute for Social Anthropology, who assisted me in the writing phase. I would like to thank Daniela Dietz, Jan Patrick Heiss and Anne Breubeck for their friendship and support. I would also like to thank Varsha Patel and Saheira Haliel for their readiness to discuss and comment on my work, and for accompanying me through the inherent ups and downs of a long-term research project.

Special thanks go to my Ph.D. supervisors Peter Finke and Kirsten Endres for their support on the research that laid the foundations for this book. I am deeply grateful to Peter for his continuous encouragement and support for the project. He has provided guidance throughout the different stages and has been an incessant source of inspiration. Kirsten, a Vietnam scholar herself with long-standing experience in the country, has opened many doors and continuously supported me in Vietnam as well as in Halle. It is also thanks to Kirsten that I had the opportunity to meet leading Vietnam scholars whose knowledge of the field provided me with valuable insights. The assistance of Annuska Derks, who became my third supervisor in the later stage of the research, was invaluable to this book project. Her enthusiasm and vigour as well as her professional qualities were fundamental for completing this book.

My research would not have been possible without the funding provided by the Max Planck Institute for Social Anthropology in Halle (Saale). I especially benefited from the conferences organised there, which provided opportunities for interaction and an exchange of ideas with scholars from various fields. I thank Jutta Turner for producing the maps of Ninh Hiệp. Furthermore, I would like to express my thanks to the Vietnam Academy for Social Sciences (VASS) for their cooperation. I am also grateful for the financial and intellectual support that I received during two dissertation workshops in March 2013 and 2014, organised by the Association for Asian Studies (AAS) and the Social Science Research Council (SSRC) and funded by the Henry Luce Foundation. Attending workshops organised by the Swiss Graduate Program in Anthropology was helpful to establish contacts with graduate students at other Swiss universities and discuss my work in a broader setting. I would like to thank Heinz Käufeler for coordinating the programme and enriching the individual modules with his knowledge, experience and good spirits.

I also owe a debt of gratitude to Lưu Văn Hiến, whom I met during my very first research project in Vietnam. Hiến was kind enough to introduce me to his favourite places, as well as his family. I cherish the deep friendship and encounters that developed thanks to him. When I looked for a tandem partner to practice Vietnamese, the university matched me with Mai Trần. This resulted not only in a language exchange, but also in a deep, adventurous, laughter-ridden friendship. Special thanks go to Nguyễn Trường Giang for his tireless help in every step of the research. His contribution is invaluable for this project. In the first months of the research, I lived with bác Dấu and his family in Yên Viên. They treated me like a daughter and sister, respectively, by welcoming me in their midst and caring for me. It is also thanks to them that I came to understand a great deal about Vietnamese families. I would like to thank Vương Tâm, who always had an open ear and supported me in all my endeavours. Trần Thị Cúc and Bùi Thị Ngân helped me in different ways during the research but most of all, blessed me with their friendship. Before starting the research, I took intense language lessons at Bách Khoa University with Vũ Thị Xuyến and Nguyễn Thị Phương Trà, who have patiently helped me to improve my Vietnamese and have deepened my understanding of the Vietnamese culture and people. I had the luck to meet Hoài Trần in Vietnam as well as later in Halle and highly appreciate his feedback on my research. His insights into Vietnamese trade were of great value.

I would like to express my never-ending gratitude for my family, who were a continuous source of encouragement, inspiration and love in life and throughout the research and writing. I would like to thank my parents, Irène and Erwin Horat, for their unconditional support and their faith in me, and my sister, Isabelle, and my brother, Tobias, for always standing by my side. It is to my family that I dedicate this book.

***

All names in this book are pseudonyms. In citations and for names and places, I used Vietnamese characters, except for places that are well known in English, such as Hanoi and Ho Chi Minh City. Citations from conversations and interviews with informants are translated into English. When the original wording seemed relevant, I inserted the Vietnamese terms in brackets. All translations are my own unless stated otherwise. The photographs were taken by the author, and the maps were prepared by Jutta Turner (Max Planck Institute for Social Anthropology).

Contents

List of Figures

1

Introduction: Neoliberal Governance and Market Socialism

"I've been a trader all my life. Since I got married at the age of nineteen, I have been buying and selling", 73-years-old Mrs. *Sửu* told me. Her fragile demeanour was the first noticeable thing about her when she opened the door and let us in the house. And yet her mood seemed to swing instantly towards vivaciousness when she began to tell her grandson Quân and me, in a firm voice, about her past: "Life was so hard back then, and being a trader was risky, because it was prohibited. But I was never afraid—I already went to Saigon in the seventies, to sell herbal medicine (*thuốc bắc*) to Chinese traders and buy cloth to bring back to Ninh Hiệp". Before she could go into detail, the two great-grandchildren she had been taking care of woke up in need of her attention. Promising to come by later, Quân and I left for the old state-owned market to pay his mother, Mrs. Quy, a visit. As we approached her stall, she was sitting in simple but colourful cotton clothes on a stack of wrapped merchandise, reading a newspaper. When I asked how her business had been that day, she replied that there had not been many customers in the market and that making a sale was proving more difficult by the year. With a slight frustration in her voice and nodding towards the new privately owned market, she said

E. Horat, *Trading in Uncertainty*,
DOI 10.1007/978-3-319-55648-2_1

that competition was increasing and that she and her friends at the old market feared a change of market ownership might happen in the near future. Comparing the present to the past, she reminisced about the eighties, when she would frequently go to the market in Phố Lu, Lào Cai province, close to the Chinese border. Later on, she recalled, she would also cross the border in search of cloths. It was when Mrs. Quy explained how she had acquired a stall at the Đồng Xuân market in Hanoi in the nineties that Quân weighed in: "I used to help my mother with her business from early on, starting from the 2000s, when I was around 15 years old. Since 2008, when my mum rented a stall here [in Ninh Hiệp], I would go to China to buy merchandise for her. However, when it came to business, we didn't get along so well and I wanted to do something else, not trading clothes". That "something else" would be a café Quân opened next to the new market. But this, he explained, was not just a café like the ones that already existed, but rather, it was one that took orders from vendors and brought the drinks inside the market. With this business model, he seemed to fare well—so well that one could see his workforce, consisting mostly of adolescents who migrated from faraway places close to the Laotian border, continually growing to meet demand.

This short ethnographic prelude provides a brief glance at the themes that will be covered in this book. Not only the vast spatial reach of trade relations, but also the resourcefulness and the flexibility of Ninh Hiệp people are remarkable. Quân's family is not a single case, but fairly typical in several ways: in many families trading has been an occupation that was passed down from one generation to the next, and along with it knowledge, skills, and networks. Travelling up the vertical ties within families are acts of physical, emotional and financial care. Thus, favours and affects reinforce each other in both directions. As the political and economic environment has undergone considerable transformation in the last couple of decades, the social and spatial organisation of trade has changed as well. Quân, Mrs. Quy and Mrs. Sửu all have or had to deal with challenges embedded in the context of a particular time. To be confronted with situations of risk and uncertainty—albeit different ones—is also what connects their experiences with trade: risking to be caught when trade was banned; fearing to lose one's stall in the wake of the growing trend of privatisation; and not knowing whether the investments in a new business will pay off. This last point needs to be seen in relation to the incertitude adhering to new markets—not only in terms of economic performance, but also regarding the collaboration between investors and state officials, shaping the way the market is managed. Underlying these uncertainties is the state's complicated relation with trade and its effort to maintain control while not suffocating it. Moreover, moral ambiguity of money, boiling down to the question of how to be wealthy and good, looms large in post-reform Vietnam. Attempting to understand the reasons for and the nature of uncertainty that the people in contemporary Vietnam experience in many aspects of their lives, it is not enough to refer to the integration into the world market and its volatility. Instead, I suggest looking closely at the Vietnamese state and its mode of governance, which shifted from socialist to a mix of socialist and neoliberal. Exploring what this entails is the aim of the following pages.

Neoliberalism, a rather vague term with a wide range of usages, is often associated with a particular kind of free market ideology that saw its heyday during the Reagan-Thatcher Era in the 1980s. Although the ascent of neoliberalism seemed inevitable, the ideology of free market supremacy suffered a blow due to the financial crisis of 2007–2008. Neoliberalism, however, is not only about market deregulation, privatisation and minimal state interference. It is also a mode of managing populations. A central rhetorical theme within neoliberalism is the strong emphasis on the individual as entrepreneur. This entrepreneurship is not strictly limited to one's pursuit of economic interest. More broadly, it signifies the incorporation of certain norms related to the optimisation of one's person and one's life. It is through the promotion of these norms and lifestyles, as well as through laws and decrees that the state as well as powerful transnational companies and international organisations secure their influence. Although the neoliberal logic sounds gender-neutral, it is not necessarily the case. Thus, in this book, economic change is seen from a perspective that takes the gendered effects of neoliberal governance into account.

It bears emphasis that much like any other economic model, the image conjured up by "neoliberalism" does not necessarily jibe with the complex real-world in which economic agents interact and operate (Brenner and Theodore 2002). Rather, economic processes are always embedded in particular historical, political and social contexts. Ideology and practice do not only diverge, but there are also distinct forms of neoliberalism; consequently, the Western—or more accurately the American or the British—model should not be seen as the standard from which others deviate (Ong and Zhang 2008). This tension between economic model and lived reality lies at the heart of the ethnographic investigation presented in this book.

Writing about neoliberalism in a Socialist Republic like Vietnam may seem like an inherent contradiction at a first glance. However, when understanding neoliberalism not as a hegemonic system or a stage in an evolutionary sense, but rather as one logic of governance among others (Ong and Zhang 2008; Schwenkel and Leshkowich 2012), neoliberal processes become palpable. In that sense, neoliberal governance is not all-encompassing and does thus not replace socialist governance, but the two are interwoven. I argue that the combination of these two logics leads to ambivalent outcomes not primarily because they are incompatible, but rather because they are applied in an inconsistent manner. Illustrating how the neoliberal logic, in combination with a socialist rhetoric, works in Vietnam, and also how it is being adopted or challenged is one of the main tasks of this book.

Although this book is an attempt to shed light on some of the inner workings of neoliberalism, it does not get bogged down with abstract market principles and formulas. Instead, the centrepiece of this book is people, their actions, stories and perceptions. The people I encountered during my 1-year stay in the village of Ninh Hiệp, the majority of whom work in their own family businesses related to textile trade and who literally make the economy, animate my arguments. It is particularly through the focus on family businesses that the inextricable interweaving of the social and the economic becomes apparent. From the outset, my investigations were inspired and guided not only by a curiosity about the trajectory of market evolution, but also by how traders experience, and navigate through, the changes and challenges brought about by marketisation. The process of "marketisation"—it should be borne in mind—does not automatically imply an external enforcement, but rather, a mix of internal *and* external dynamics.

This book offers an ethnographic exploration of how a long-standing small-scale production and trading community resourcefully adapts to global capitalist formations and actively shapes its local economy. It is, equally, an ethnographic account of the micro-level interactions and processes within the broader context of neoliberal economic reforms that have swept across much of the world, including Vietnam. As the word "ethnography" readily suggests, this body of work offers a perspective "from below", that is, through the lived experiences of people in the village of Ninh Hiệp in northern Vietnam. Strategies employed by traders to cope with changing conditions are central to this study. Particular attention is paid to the social organisation of trade, the centrality of the family for business, the crucial role of trust in the trade system and notions of morality informing actions of traders. In this sense, this project investigates the dynamic relation between state, society and market, and makes a contribution to anthropological understandings of economic restructuring and social change.

Neoliberal Governance in Vietnam

Since the introduction of the Open Door Policy in 1986—known as Đổi mới—Vietnam has been undergoing a thorough process of transformation from central planning to a socialist-oriented market economy (*kinh tế thị trường định hướng xã hội chủ nghĩa*). While the Đổi mới policies aimed at restructuring the economic sector, the political system remained untouched on the face of it, as Vietnam continues to be a one-party state led by the Communist Party. Among the major changes resulting from the economic reforms were de-collectivisation of land, dissolution of cooperatives coupled with the promotion of the family as economic unit and a multisector commodity economy with the newly permitted private sector as a thriving motor for growth.

Along with the launch of economic reforms, restrictions on trade and physical mobility were loosened, leading to a sudden multiplication of commercial activities at different levels and with different scopes. In the mid-1990s, however, in an attempt to re-regulate the economic sector, a new set of policies aimed towards a strong regulatory state and the construction of "civilised" markets was introduced. Following up on this, the Vietnamese government issued a decree in 2003 aimed at developing the country's marketplaces by upgrading existing markets while at the same time establishing new ones. This trend has been reinforced in rural areas since the passing of the resolution "Building a New Countryside" (*Xây dựng nông thôn mới*) in August 2008. As a consequence, many marketplaces throughout Vietnam underwent substantial renovation, and some were subject to a change of ownership from state-owned to privately owned. This process becomes particularly interesting when seen in the light of Tania Li's (2007) work, where she shows how development projects are depoliticised by being rendered technical. Developing the Vietnamese countryside is similarly framed as mainly a matter of improving the infrastructure when in fact it involves a highly political issue, namely access to land and change of ownership rights, as communal land rights are being sold to private investors. Ninh Hiệp is a case in point: the increasing number of marketplaces and villagers turning to cloth and clothing trade in Ninh Hiệp—a visibly intensified phenomenon in the last 10 years—are the consequences of the marketisation process. The state's vision of modernity (*sự hiện đại*) and civility (*sự văn minh*) on the one hand and the trend towards new public–private relationships on the other are clearly reflected in the type of market recently constructed in Ninh Hiệp, namely privately invested multi-storey market buildings. The state's effort to regulate economic activities by supporting private market projects indicates the emergence of new public–private relations that are central to the current governing strategy of the Vietnamese state and are implicated within changing power structures. This suggests that in spite of the liberalisation of the economic sector through the introduction of the Open Door policy, the post-reform era is not marked by a general retreat of the state, but rather by new modes of governance. If the strong presence of the central state, direct interventions, and consistent socialist rhetoric and practices mark "old modes" of governance, "new modes" of governance are characterised by a seemingly distance of the central state as well as an ambivalent use of socialist and neoliberal ideologies. These new modes of government shall be examined closer in the following pages.

There is a consensus among scholars that neoliberalism is a contentious term, yet what it denotes is worth studying in its particular and contextualised manifestations. However, it should not be taken as an overarching and all-explaining trope. Drawing their inspiration from Foucault's notion of "governmentality", scholars in different parts of the world have recently examined neoliberalism as a mode of governance (Rose 1999; Ferguson and Gupta 2002; Ong 2006; Li 2007; Ong 2007; Ong and Zhang 2008; Ferguson 2010). Consequently, they pay particular attention to the state's role in creating a liberal, responsible, governable citizenry through techniques of self-governance. Taking a look at Vietnam and its northern neighbour, China, it becomes apparent that neoliberal calculation is to be found not only in liberal democracies, but also in late socialist regimes.

Thus, although a socialist-oriented market economy (or short: market socialism) is often seen as an oxymoron, it is not intrinsically contradictory—what are considered socialist or neoliberal logics and practices can coexist and even be mutually constitutive (Ong and Zhang 2008; Nonini 2008; Schwenkel and Leshkowich 2012). In this vein, neoliberal forms of self-management actually help sustain socialist rule. "Socialism from afar", as Aihwa Ong and Li Zhang (2008) dub this type of governance also discernible in China, is thus marked by a widening space between the socialist state and individually controlled everyday activities. Yet, even though the state operates from a distance, it is by no means less penetrating or less powerful. To give an example for neoliberal self-governance, we could take the notion of "civilisation" (*văn minh hóa*), an omnipresent idea in contemporary Vietnam that is not enforced upon, but rather promoted among the people to better oneself and advance the country. Civilisation, a concept whose origin lies in eighteenth century France and England,[1] is interpreted in its own way in the Vietnamese context: "The notion of being 'civilized' combines colonial ideas of cultural evolution and modernist aspirations for economic and scientific 'progress' with the ideal of a timeless spiritual past capable of providing an ethical-moral counter to the unruly forces of Western capitalism" (Pettus 2003, 83). The contexts, in which the notion of civilisation appears, will be presented in more detail at a later point.

In practice, "hybrid forms of governance" (Nonini 2008), even if not internally conflictive, are marked by ambivalence. Sometimes, they support global exchanges; at other times, they pursue a conservative, repressive cultural and political line (Nguyễn-Võ Thu-Hương 2008, 245). At the core of it is a fundamental problem with the concept of "freedom". According to official state rhetoric, there is freedom in regard to entrepreneurial and consumer choices in contemporary Vietnam. This rhetoric is strengthened by contrasting the present to the pre-*Đổi mới* period, a time marked by "a lack of choice in production and consumption of both material and cultural goods", and thus equated with a lack of freedom in retrospect (Nguyễn-Võ Thu-Hương 2008, 245). Yet, the most important aspect of this narrative is that the present is portrayed as a time of freedom when in reality the line between what is tolerated and what is not is sharply pronounced, and crossing it entails serious consequences. For Nguyễn-Võ Thu-Hương (2008, 246), this means that "Vietnam has two faces when it comes to freedom", expressed by the state employing distinct modes of governance to different segments of the population: one is encouraging middle-class subjects to be responsible for making choices (in regard to their health and well-being); the other is direct repression and coercion of lower-class subjects by the police.[2] What we see here is in fact the "normalization of the middle class" (Bélanger et al. 2012), a process that does not only inform consumption patterns by consolidating particular desires and tastes, but it also shapes notions of femininity and masculinity. In this sense, neoliberal governance does not target a small and exceptional part of the population, but is promoted as the new standard among a wide range of citizens. This leads to an adaption of Ong's (2006) argument when applied to contemporary Vietnam: rather than looking for the neoliberal logic in isolated, specialised economic zones, it is to be found in the urban centres.

An analogous paradox of this new mode of governance is that while the ability of well-educated individuals to climb the social ladder by working hard is celebrated, the actual possibilities are rather restricted. For the acquisition of licences and access to land, political connections are crucial. In fact, the privatisation of property has actually reproduced the class and social inequalities of the pre-revolutionary period in some ways, as these developments "have favored foreign investors and the upper echelons of Vietnamese society more than anyone else" (Harms 2012, 421). Drawing attention to simultaneous processes of the proliferation of new property rights and of the seizure and confiscation of land, Erik Harms notes that regarding the use of force, contemporary forms of land appropriation are not different from those carried out at various times in the history of Vietnam under different regimes, just that now investors collude with the state:

> Instead of blanket neoliberalism, power relations in Vietnam work like a bricolage of neoliberal precepts and classic top-down power; neoliberal celebrations of individual self-mastery combine with nationalist assertions of what's best for the country, creating a flexible and dynamic approach to power for those with the will and the means to assert their authority over others. (Harms 2012, 410)

Erik Harms and Nguyễn-Võ Thu-Hương both point out that ironies of freedom and privatisation are part of the everyday experiences of Vietnamese citizens and that rather than retreating, the state operates through various modes of governance. Similarly, the introduction of new technologies, such as automated teller machines (ATMs), and the availability of a wide range of consumer goods, which were promoted as heralds of modernity, mobility and freedom, has imposed new constraints in Vietnam. New banking technologies were not developed with the aim of financial inclusion, but so as to create "a system for orderly and legible economic exchanges" (Truitt 2012, 135). A decree issued by the government in 2007 demanded all state employees receive their salaries through the domestic banking system. Yet, rather than enhancing individual freedom, ATMs and banking services are experienced as bringing more restrictions for customers, as ATMs are often broken or out of cash and thus fail to deliver money, and banks do not take people's strategies of handling money into account. Elizabeth Vann's (2012, 2005) research revealed that famous, foreign-branded consumer goods, strongly desired by people belonging to the emerging middle class, were imported in the first years of market reforms, but as Vietnam became a major production site for consumer goods itself, shoppers lamented what they perceived as an increasingly domestic economy. Finally, although citizens are encouraged to consume, they are supposed to do so in accordance with state ideals, a process Ann Marie Leshkowich (2011, 2012) terms "rendering [consumption] moral". The rhetoric of morality in regard to consumption naturalises middle classness and in this way conceals the impact of structural inequalities on individual consumption practices. Thus, these apparently liberalising processes, furthered by the state, resulted in frustrating experiences for Vietnamese citizens who felt the limitations on the ability to act outside state and national boundaries (Vann 2012, 166).

Although the Vietnamese state and its representatives appear as powerful proponents of particular policies and forms of knowledge, one should be cautious to not overlook the influence of other actors, such as international organisations, ranging from the International Monetary Fund (IMF), World Trade Organization (WTO), World Health Organization (WHO), United Nations (UN) to grassroots nongovernmental organisations (NGOs) and transnational corporations (Schwenkel and Leshkowich 2012, 388). These non-state actors, promoting the expansion of foreign knowledge systems and capital investments, do not fit the typical top-down or bottom-up model of state–society relations, but cut across these "spatial imaginations of statehood" (Ferguson and Gupta 2002). Here is where the concept of "transnational governmentality", developed by Ferguson and Gupta (2002), is useful, because it draws attention to processes that construct vertically encompassing state power, and at the same time highlights the importance of mechanisms of governmentality that take place outside or alongside the nation state.

Altogether, the scholarship on Vietnam cited above holds the view that the reform era is not a time of declining state power and that deregulation and privatisation are avenues for state actors to secure their influence, rather than giving it away. One of the strongest advocates of this view is Martin Gainsborough (2010), who argues that instead of change, emphasis should be put on continuity and the reworking of existing power structures. Findings of one of his earlier studies indicate that companies in Ho Chi Minh City rely very much on the state for access to land and capital, licences and protection (Gainsborough 2003). Hence, this suggests that entrepreneurs need to have very intimate ties to the state to be successful, either by working as officials themselves or by having parents who belong to the political elite (Gainsborough 2010, 16). Tô Xuân Phúc (2012) follows a similar line of argument, based on his research on the practice of land right purchases in the countryside by *đại gia* (urban rich). People referred to as *đại gia* are wealthy urbanites who possess properties. They form a special segment within the greatly expanding middle class, not because of their disposable income, but because of their ability to acquire recreational property. According to Tô Xuân Phúc, the interest of *đại gia* in aesthetically pleasing locations to build weekend villas has resulted in substantial changes in the control of land in villages as the land rush has driven up the value of land in certain areas and led villagers to sell their land. In addition to offering relaxation in a beautiful environment, weekend villas also serve the purpose to perform a middle-class identity by celebrating a modern and "civilised" way of life. As an important matter of fact, among the *đại gia* are many government officials and their relatives as well as people otherwise intimately related to the state. These links "produce a strong belief that the *đại gia* derive their wealth from the state, but not through their official salaries, which could never support the construction of weekend villas and luxury goods", as Tô Xuân Phúc (2012, 152) notes. At the same time, they also contest the principle of egalitarianism and thus question the legitimacy of the state.

My study shares the view of the importance of the role of the state and the continuity of power relations and offers an example of seeming liberalisation and choice when in fact this process brings heavy constraints. While it is suggested that everybody can become a trader, it is in fact a matter of a combination of factors whether and in which way people can participate in the market as the level of access has been rising in the last couple of years. However, the study does not posit a determined power hierarchy, but acknowledges the existence of individual opportunities.

Privatisation of Markets

One core aspect of neoliberalism is the process of privatisation. For that purpose, I will elaborate on the notion of "private indirect government", originally developed in the African context by Béatrice Hibou (2004)[3] and inspired by Max Weber's notion of "discharge" and Michel Foucault's notion of "governmentality". "Private indirect government" was later applied to different contexts, for instance to investigate the privatisation of violence in Africa (Mbembe 2001), the equitisation of state companies in Vietnam (Gainsborough 2010) and the devolution of sovereignty in Burma (MacLean 2010). Examining privatisation in various domains, such as the privatisation of state enterprises, public services as well as regulatory and sovereign functions of the state, Hibou argues that practices of indirect government alter the very notions of public and private, licit and illicit. Yet privatisation should not be equated with a loss of state control; even if certain aspects of state power are reduced, the central state power is not in question but rather reasserts its power through these modes of governing. As Hibou (2004, 27) puts it: "Delegation of power never meant loss of power". In other words, the term "privatisation of the state" describes "two parallel processes—extended use of private intermediaries for an increasing number of functions previously devolving upon the state, and redeployment by the state" (Hibou 2004, 3).

Two points about her approach are crucial. One is the importance of historical trajectory. As the delegation of state power to private actors and the overlapping of state and elite strategies is not a new phenomenon as such, the particularities of each specific case must be elaborated carefully. In order to understand contemporary forms of privatisation, long-term processes of state formation in a particular context need to be taken into account, as state power is constantly negotiated. The other is that privatisation should not be seen as a deliberate strategy of governing, but as "the result of multiple, sometimes contradictory strategies, which reflect especially a lack of confidence in state institutions and primacy of allegiance over functional relations" (Hibou 2004, 40). Thus, it is not "the state" that acts in accordance with one coherent rationale, but numerous actors with various economic, political and social logics and interests.

While illustrating her argument with various case studies from countries across the African continent, she also stresses the applicability of the notion of private indirect government for other countries, for instance eastern European countries, Russia and especially China. Although regulatory and sovereign functions of the Chinese state are not transferred to private actors as in some African countries, decentralisation processes have had similar effects in regard to the transfer of responsibilities to local authorities. Thus, for China, Hibou (2004, 36–37) notes:

> Privatisation (…) cannot be interpreted as retreat by the state or by the political, but rather as the capacity of the political to find a place for the non-institutional, the unofficial, the non-central. (…) The de-concentration of power in favour of local authorities is not a process of pure loss; the central power and the public sphere remain decisive in the Chinese economy.

And further:

> Privatisation of the economy allows not so much control over the people as control over wealth, and especially possibilities of gaining wealth; it allows the renewal of bureaucratic power and moreover its conversion into economic power; it reflects investment by the government in the economy, and creates a fluid situation that has generated the economic miracle and new interests. (Hibou 2004, 37)

In contrast to China, in many African societies sovereign functions of the state are indeed transferred to private actors, as Achille Mbembe (2001) has noted. Being concerned with a particular form of private indirect government in Africa, namely the privatisation of coercion, he describes how deregulation and dismantling of the state lead to privatisation of violence, as private security companies take over sovereign functions of the state.

In Vietnam, the change from a planned to a socialist-oriented market economy entailed decentralisation of regulatory and sovereign functions of the state as well as privatisation of many state-owned companies and of formerly public services, such as health and education. Land, although decollectivised since Đổi mới, is still owned by the state, but land-use rights can be possessed, transferred and mortgaged (Kim 2007, 8). The concept of private indirect government was applied by Gainsborough (2010), who looked at the practice of equitisation of state firms in Vietnam. As he shows, the state often buys as much as 85% of the shares of a company and thus remains the main shareholder after equitisation. Hence, he suggests seeing privatisation, or equitisation, as a new form of indirect state interventionism.

Following Hibou and Gainsborough, I suggest the notion of private indirect government to understand the ongoing process of privatisation of public marketplaces and the planning and implementation of new market projects by way of shedding light on the collusion of private and state interests. Since the early 2000s, the development of traditional marketplaces is an important pillar of the modernising mission of the Vietnamese government, which for this reason has issued policies to regulate the construction, renovation and management of marketplaces all over Vietnam (Endres 2013, 357). That the marketisation process is in full swing in Ninh Hiệp is evident not only from the number of markets built in the last decade and the style of market buildings, but also regarding the form of management. The trend of private instead of public ownership of markets does not necessarily imply a lesser degree of involvement of state actors, but brings them in differently: while in public ownership the state is directly concerned with managing the market through the market management board and at the same time bears responsibility towards traders, in private ownership the market is managed by the investor—or another person in charge—and is primarily dependent upon the state for access to land and licences, and only in a second step upon the traders. Not only the indirect involvement of the state is paradigmatic for neoliberal governance, but also the focus on higher profit and better economic performance as well as the idea of modernity as defined through consumption.

Trading in Uncertainty

As traders, or entrepreneurs, are by definition risk-taking and uncertainty-bearing actors (Belshaw 1955: 147 cited in Barth 1963, 1), the kind of uncertainty that is particularly looked at in this book does not stem from the volatility of a market economy, but is to be seen in the light of a certain mode of governance. While the markets in Ninh Hiệp have greatly expanded and some traders were able to make immense profits generated through commerce, the rapidly changing environment has also created new uncertainties in the lives of the traders. For instance, in 2010, amid rumours of a possible privatisation of the old market, a few hundred traders went to the commune's People's Committee to express their disapproval of a change of management. Later, in 2014, the announcement of a new private market project sparked discontent in the village and once again led traders to protest in front of the commune's People's Committee. A change of formal structures, especially marketplace management, creates fear among Ninh Hiệp traders, because privately managed markets are expected to entail stricter regulation and higher fees and, above all, are suspected to be driven by demands of the market rather than by the demands of the people. There is great anxiety among traders that a multiplication of competitors due to the intensified marketisation process in Ninh Hiệp might endanger their businesses. What makes these developments even more problematic is the lack of transparency and communication. Not knowing whether and when the markets are going to change ownership and what will happen to them is not only stressful, but makes mid- and long-term business planning impossible. Thus, changing policies, unclear rules and vague norms allow for arbitrariness and the maintenance of fluidity between legal and illegal activities and are effective modes to deploy power in a discontinuous manner. In this sense, uncertainty is an effective mode to exert political power (Hibou 2004, Gainsborough 2010).

One must also bear in mind that certainty and uncertainty are not neutral or innocent categories and that its uncritical use can lead to misinterpretation and have harmful consequences:

> The notion of certainty is conventionally associated with order, integration, stability, regulation, and/or knowledge. As it's opposite, uncertainty stands for disorder, disintegration, instability and/or illegality; in a word, ignorance. From this commonsensical perspective, certainty has to be pursued, while uncertainty should be avoided and possibly eradicated. (Smart and Zerilli 2014, 234)

Connected to this is an interesting twist: as the Vietnamese state pursues the formalisation of the economic sector with the declared goal of bringing order and stability as well as to "beautify the city" (Lincoln 2008), it does so by employing measures that rise the level of uncertainty for those involved in the process. For instance, regarding the building of new markets in Ninh Hiệp, decisions were made behind closed doors and announced at short notice. Sometimes, regulations were implied rather harshly, yet at other times not at all, putting traders in a state of ambivalence. By the same token, however, uncertainty leaves room for manoeuvre for all actors. Incomplete implementation of regulations and inconsistent rhetoric means that there is space for negotiation and exception to the rule, offering windows of opportunity for individuals.

Another aspect of uncertainty and insecurity is its potential for human creativity (Eriksen et al. 2010) and its ability of being a productive force, for example in financial markets, where risk-taking is essential (Zaloom 2004). It is also argued that insecurity leads to social support (Benda-Beckmann and Benda-Beckmann 2000) and to "dependence [which] can be imagined as part of a positive and ongoing process of mutual sharing and reliance" (Schlecker 2013, p. 13). In this sense, uncertainty "can encourage an ethos of 'thick sociality'; that is, uncertainty and insecurity may prompt people to extend and deepen their social relations and engagements" (Cooper and Pratten 2015, 7).

In other words, situations of uncertainty encourage the seeking of relations of trust. Niklas Luhmann (1988, 97–98) even argued that trust "presupposes a situation of risk". Trust is closely linked to one's estimation of the actions of others. In this regard, economist Partha Dasgupta (1988, 51) has suggested understanding "trust" as referring to "expectations about the *actions* of other people that have a bearing on one's own choice of action when that action must be chosen before one can *monitor* the actions of those others". In order to be able to estimate the possibility for certain actions of others, knowing the other is crucial. As Dasgupta (1988, 50–51) pointed out, we do not trust others to do something because they say they will do it, but because "knowing what you know of his disposition, his available options and their consequences, his ability and so forth, you expect that he will *choose* to do it". While for Luhmann (1988, 96) familiarity is the main precondition for trust, Adler and Kwon (2002, 102) specify that "interpersonal trust is the result of familiarity, shared norms, and calculation, and it is buttressed by system trust".

Trust can be an incentive for and a result of cooperation—its crucial quality is that it becomes stronger the more it is used (Gambetta 1988). In this context, cooperation "is meant in the broad sense of agents, such as individuals, firms, and governments, agreeing on any set of rules—a 'contract'—which is then to be observed in the course of their interaction" (Binmore and Dasgupta 1986: 3, cited in Gambetta 1988, 213–214). Cooperation also includes the possibility to compete with each other. However, it is important to note that in order to compete in a non-destructive way, "one needs at some level to *trust* one's competitors to comply with certain rules" (Gambetta 1988, 215). Yet, the relation between trust and cooperation is not unequivocal: trust can, but must not necessarily, lead to cooperation. Relations of trust are ambiguous because they may also be used to achieve individual benefits instead of results that are in the interest of both or several parties.

As I will illustrate in Chap. 6, the banking and credit system in the village is essentially based on trust (*lòng tin*), as money is usually lent without a written contract. Although betraying somebody's trust, for example by not paying back a loan, may not have legal consequences, it will have social consequences, such as having a hard time getting a loan from anyone next time. The possibility to induce sanctions on people whose actions are not in accordance with an agreement is thus a critical factor. This is where the importance of Dasgupta's aforementioned statement, whereby the estimation of the actions of others is crucial, becomes apparent. Rather than communal altruism, it is the reputation of trustworthiness that counts. Although Dasgupta's vocabulary clearly stems from economic sciences, to think of reputation as a "capital asset" that has to be acquired gradually seems quite pertinent (Dasgupta 1988, 62). While trust plays a major role in interactions among traders and between traders and customers, another important aspect that will be discussed later on is citizens' trust in the government. Although, or maybe because, trust seems like a basic and ordinary feature of human life, methodologically it is a difficult concept. There are many reasons why people choose to rely on or collaborate with somebody, and trust is only one of them. For example, there are situations when one's trust in someone is low, but not trusting that person would leave one even worse off; or somebody's reputation concerning paying back loans is not good, but he happens to be my brother-in-law, so I feel compelled to lend him money regardless of his reputation or even my previous experiences.

Morals and Modernity

My endeavour to study a marketplace rests on the widely acknowledged assumption in anthropology that markets are much more than just sites for economic exchange. They are places where people meet, interact, create and cultivate meaningful relationships, and nurture their emotional well-being. In short, marketplaces are sites of rich social life. That this is particularly true for Vietnam is confirmed by the adage "Buôn có bạn bán có phường" (*Trading has friends, selling has a guild*). The social aspect brought to the fore highlights the fact that trading is not seen as an individual activity, but as deeply embedded in social relations. The second part of the adage points to the geographical concentration of a certain commodity being sold at one place, as was and to a certain degree still is the case in the Old Quarter in Hanoi.

Another important reason to focus on a marketplace is that they are a centrepiece of the Vietnamese state's attempt to modernise the country. Materially speaking, marketplaces are sites of commercial exchange and as such a crucial part of the economy. Yet, in the context of changing political economic relations in Vietnam, marketplaces also become sites of fierce contestation occurring between representatives of different levels of government, private investors and traders. Since the resumption of international business relations and the arrival of mass tourism, Vietnam is much concerned with its representation. Turning Vietnam into a modern country, as promulgated by the Vietnamese state since the 1990s, included the upgrading of marketplaces as one of its core tasks. One reason might be that markets are a crucial part of the built landscape in urban as well as in rural areas and therefore shape the "face" of a place. Another related reason may be that traders were not seen in a positive light even after Đổi mới, but were still labelled as "uncivilised", backward and immoral, much like during the high socialist period. In particular, they were portrayed as epitomising the downside of a capitalist economy: the triumph of money over education, neglect of cultural refinement and profit-seeking at all cost. By constructing new and renovating "traditional" markets, trade and traders should be tamed so as to fit modernity. This process, as we shall see in the following pages, was primarily driven by the state's vision of modernity as well as its decisions about the use of land, and private investors, who funded these projects. Thus, morality needs to be examined in the light of the political: "(…) they [morality and ethics] are not pure objects discernible in the social world but are most of the time intricately linked with other domains, in particular the political" (Fassin 2012, 15). I argue that the notion of morality is central to the lives of traders on three levels: (a) as a strategy for negotiating the boundaries of a moral community, (b) as a government tactic to project a legitimate image of itself and its policies and (c) serving as an existential function in the face of ambiguities triggered by the socialist and neoliberal economic orders. To address the inconsistent rhetoric and practices of the Vietnamese state, traders use the claim of the right to subsistence and perform moral identities, as I will show in Chap. 8.

In using the term "morality" rather than "ethics", I follow Monica Heintz (2009, 3–4) who argues that "ethics" refers to more codified and elaborated judgments whereas "morality" evokes the general discourse on what is good.[4] The word "moral" derives from the Latin word "mos" (*custom; way of comporting oneself*) and is defined within social interactions (Beidelman 1986, 2). Thus, morality as a crucial institution in society is not timeless and static, but is constantly negotiated and recreated between individuals and the social environment they live in. Rather than assuming individuals bluntly support moral principles, social interactions need to be examined in their complexity in order to shed light on how individuals "adapt, change their minds, get influenced, assert, transform and get transformed by others" (Heintz 2009, 11). As norm codification and moral justifications are often overemphasised in anthropological studies at the expense of the actual practice of individuals, Thomas Widlok (2009) suggests to investigate "morality in action", especially in situations of moral dilemma. The approach of methodological individualism, as proposed by Heintz, puts its focus on individuals and how they have "their own ways of defining their personal values, working through societal constraints, and adopt their own ways of translating beliefs and personal values into action" (Heintz 2009, 8). Through confrontation and harmonisation of values between individuals, a collective elaboration of values, or morals, evolves. This is a constant process, as individuals continuously negotiate, question or reaffirm existing morals. An important element for the study of morality is freedom of choice, as James Laidlaw (2002) and later Joel Robbins (2009) as well as Julia Cassaniti and Jacob Hickman (2014) among others have pointed out. The presupposition of a certain degree of freedom of choice about how to act in a given society is especially crucial if one argues from a methodological individualist position, as it understands the individual as an active force to produce and shape morals instead of being a passive recipient. Trying to bridge individual agency and social, political and economic structures, I am concerned with how actors are embedded in certain structures, and also how their actions shape and transform these structures.

Approaching Ninh Hiệp

Ninh Hiệp, located at the north-eastern edge of Hanoi, is known as a village with a rich history and a long-standing engagement with trade. The geographical location of Ninh Hiệp is important in two ways: first, it belongs to the Red River Delta, one of the two basins of Vietnam where economic life has been most bustling, from handicraft and trade to industrial production to the rendering of services in urban and suburban areas. Due to its overall successful economic performance, the Red River Delta has been propagated as a model for economic development to eradicate poverty in peripheral, mountainous provinces in northern Vietnam. For Ninh Hiệp, this means that it faced quite favourable conditions for its integration in wider economic relations. Second, Ninh Hiệp is situated near a major long-distance trading route connecting Hanoi and southern China, which turns its wholesale marketplace into a significant trading spot for herbal medicine, textiles and fabricated clothes. Traders supply neighbouring villages and towns as well as faraway places nationwide. Therefore, Ninh Hiệp can be considered an important commercial node that connects people and commodities at local, regional, national and international scales.

The clothing sold in Ninh Hiệp is diverse and can be categorised into countryside and urban style, yet this distinction is not necessarily clear-cut. The latter is destined to be sold in shops as well as in some markets in urban areas and ranges from skirts and dresses to blouses, shirts with imprints, coats and pants. A substantial part of these clothes target students and women who work in offices. Another part is geared towards young, trendy urbanites and their demand for clothes to accoutre themselves when going out. These clothes differ from the ones popular in rural areas in terms of style and price. The clothing to supply the rural populace is simpler and cheaper and is sold in marketplaces in the countryside as well as in peri-urban and urban areas. While some Ninh Hiệp traders wear what they sell, most of them do not wear the latest fashion but keep with a simple style, usually consisting of a pair of jeans and a T-shirt, or a *bộ đồ*.[5] (Fig. 1.1)

While the number of villagers working as traders has continuously grown since the early 1990s, it has multiplied in the 2000s, so much so that nowadays almost every household participates in commerce. Along with this trend, the commercial area in the village has greatly increased as new markets were built. At the time the research was conducted, there were four markets in Ninh Hiệp: a state-owned market (Nành market, or "old market"), two privately owned commercial centres (Sơn Long market and Phú Điền market respectively "new markets") as well as a shopping street ("Xóm 6" or "Fashion Street"), where residential

Fig. 1.1 Merchandise at a stall outside the old market

houses serve as shops. Due to the rapid spatial expansion of the market within only one decade, villagers refer to Ninh Hiệp as "the village in the market" (*làng trong chợ*).

Although many villagers are new to clothing trade, it was not hard to find families where two or even three generations are, or have been, traders. The family business is the most common type of economic organisation in Ninh Hiệp, usually consisting of the parents and their children, before they establish their own business upon getting married. In exceptional cases, siblings or in-laws establish a business together. Family businesses producing or selling on a bigger scale may hire workers, many of whom come from rather poor provinces, such as Nghệ An or Thanh Hóa. While some family businesses do not hire any workers at all, other businesses employ as many as ten or more workers. These workers support the family business in producing clothes and selling at the market, and either live with the family they are working for, or stay with other temporary workers.

In contrast to Ninh Hiệp's largely intermediary role and the resulting openness, the villagers' self-perception and discursive reproduction of a "traditional village" (*làng nghề truyền thống*) invokes a different image. Ninh Hiệp's status as an ancient craft and trading village was not challenged by its inhabitants, despite the fact that the bulk of the cloth and clothing sold in the last decades has not been made in the village but imported en masse from China and a few other countries and can therefore hardly be called "craft". This seemingly contradiction between traditional branding and incorporation into contemporary global processes is to be witnessed not only in Ninh Hiệp, but also in many other craft and trading villages in the Red River Delta. I could discern another dimension in this discrepancy when, upon my return from the field research, I bumped into a colleague who wore the exact same scarf that I had bought in a "traditional silk village" in the outskirts of Hanoi. She, however, bought hers in a market in Nigeria. I then remembered that I had also come across African traders in the big markets in Guangzhou, China, on my trip with Ninh Hiệp traders. Apparently, our scarves had embarked on long journeys from some Chinese workshop to the markets in Guangzhou, and then to marketplaces in Vietnam (in my case) or Nigeria (in her case) where they would be purchased by us. Thus, although there is a strong sense among Ninh Hiệp residents and inhabitants of other villages that their village is "traditional" or "ancient", their economic integration with regional and global processes stands in stark contrast to this rhetoric of antiquity and self-sufficiency.

This discourse, or "semi myth of village autonomy", was created as early as the 1920s during the French colonial period by nationalist and colonialist authors alike and was adopted and continuously reproduced by villagers (Woodside 1971 cited in Kleinen 1999, 7). As Martin Grossheim (1997, 86–90) has shown in his analysis of village conventions (*hương ước*), Vietnamese villages were in fact relatively autonomous in pre-colonial times. The famous Vietnamese adage "the law of the king yields to village custom" (*phép vua thua lệ làng*) and the proverbial bamboo hedge, which hid and protected the village, both embody this image (Endres 2000, 24–25). Yet, by no means were villages completely autonomous or closed entities (Grossheim 2003, 58).

Ninh Hiệp exemplifies the paradox of a village that possesses not only certain "traditional" features—e.g. long-established lineages and the practice of endogamy—but also a number of qualities that defy the idea of a corporate, static community. For instance, the fact that Ninh Hiệp merchants have interacted intensely with other traders from China and all parts of Vietnam for centuries suggests that it was everything but a closed community. According to Nguyễn Đức Nghinh (1993, 358–359), documents from the late seventeenth and early eighteenth century point to the influence of the mercantile economy on communes: "With the development of village markets during the previous centuries, the mercantile economy had deep effects on the organisation and activities of the commune, especially its lifestyle and the closed character of its economy". Following John Kleinen (1999), "traditional village" is a misleading term that should be rejected since it implies the absence of social change. Thus, despite the community spirit, a high degree of social cohesion and the identification of residents with their "traditional village", it would be inaccurate to portray Ninh Hiệp as being or having ever been a neatly bounded, static and corporate community.

Getting to the Markets

Arriving in Vietnam at the beginning of July 2012, I started taking language classes in Hanoi and went to Ninh Hiệp several times to get first impressions. In retrospect, these trips turned out to be very important because the markets did not look like this any time after. In the summer of 2012, the two new market buildings were completely empty except for three or four traders who had already opened a shop there. It was quite what I expected of a new market (completed in 2011, 1 year before my first visit)—it felt new, spacious, a cool breeze came through the empty aisles between the not yet opened shops. Having visited other newly renovated or rebuilt markets in Hanoi, some of which had been "upgraded" into shopping malls, for example Hàng Da market, I was not surprised to find a similar kind of lifeless, almost ghostly atmosphere. Yet, when I started the research upon completion of the language course in autumn 2012, the picture had already changed completely: the two previously uninhabited marketplaces were in full swing and seemed to be more crowded each day until the peak was reached shortly before Lunar New Year (*Tết Nguyên Đán*). One explanation could have been the "seasons of the market", meaning that the markets are increasingly crowded in the months before Lunar New Year, whereas the months after the Lunar New Year until the end of summer school holidays are said to be a slack period. However, the situation I encountered during my visits in summer 2012 did not repeat in spring and summer 2013. Even though the vendors at the new marketplaces complained that they have no customers, there still was some activity, and in comparison with 2012 almost all stalls on the ground floor were open. Therefore, what I have witnessed was the start-up and continuous development of a new market rather than a "failed" market project.

In October 2012, when I started to go to Ninh Hiệp on a regular basis, the market area seemed huge, inscrutable and really chaotic. Not only did I get lost in the midst of all these stalls and huddle of clothes, but I also found it extremely hard to remember the location of the stalls of the first vendors I met due to the overwhelming size of the marketplace with its well over 3000 vendors, let alone the customers who jammed the narrow aisles. Yet, soon after becoming better oriented with the market, I was even able to differentiate types of clothes, which, at the beginning, used to come across as the same.

Another feature of the marketplace that did not conform to my earlier expectations was the relative—but noticeable—calm and absence of tension in the atmosphere: traders in Ninh Hiệp showed little sign of overt and aggressive competition, both amongst themselves and in dealing with customers. Rarely, if ever, did I come across traders pestering passersby in an attempt to lure would-be customers into their stalls and shops. When I came by in the afternoon, traders usually played cards together, had a chat with a neighbour or even left their stall to visit other traders in the market. This does not mean that competition was inexistent, but it was a hint to me that it was perhaps expressed in subtle ways and that it was important at another level. What I wish to emphasise at this point is the friendly interaction with one another, which I did not observe to this degree when visiting markets in Hanoi.

Ninh Hiệp traders and their families form the core research subject and therefore receive the bulk of attention. In addition, I conducted conversations with customers who came to Ninh Hiệp for shopping as well as with various people living in Ninh Hiệp, among them transporters, local officials from the commune's People's Committee, the commune's cooperative as well as the local Women's Union, hamlet chiefs, coffee shop owners and the manager of a day nursery.

The scope of my work is not limited to the relationship between people and the state, but also expands on the dual role of actors who are representatives of the state and at the same time community members. In this sense, the local state and its position towards higher levels of government as well as towards inhabitants formed an important aspect of the research. Conversations with local officials and visits to the houses of hamlet chiefs in Ninh Hiệp revealed that they and their families are involved in the textile trade to a substantial degree. Thus, "the state" is a complex construct consisting of actors with varying interests, which may seem abstract and out of reach, yet at the same time permeates society and is part of the everyday life of people.

At the beginning of the research, I conducted a market survey that covered the old market, the two new markets and the stores in the shopping street in order to get an idea about the traders, their relationships with each other and with customers as well as about the goods traded. Conducting the survey enabled me to establish first contacts with traders and also guided the development of research guidelines for in-depth interviews. The traders who were welcoming I visited again. Gradually, I learned more about the market and their life as traders, especially when I spent extended stretches of time at one stall. Through this, I had the opportunity to follow conversations between vendors and customers and to learn how relationships with neighbouring traders were cultivated. The marketplace was considered a second home where all kind of activities beside selling could be done, ranging from eating, sleeping, chatting, reading the newspaper, playing cards, embroidering, preparing vegetables for dinner, to painting nails and braiding each other's hair, and generally observing what was going on. When staying at somebody's stall, I was usually given a pile of cloth to sit on, and shared stories and gossip. In turn I watched their stall when they had to go somewhere. Many of the traders with whom I established a close bond allowed me to conduct in-depth interviews. In contrast to informal conversations, the in-depth interviews took place at the traders' homes where a more private atmosphere could be enjoyed and where they felt more comfortable to talk than in the marketplace.

After having spent the first half of the research period almost exclusively at the marketplace, I began to carry out interviews with local authorities and villagers who did not—or not anymore—engage in trade. I was lucky that the vice-president of the commune introduced the nine hamlet chiefs (*trưởng thôn*) to me in order to help me getting access to the villagers. The chiefs, all of them middle-aged men, were not only willing to answer questions about their hamlet, their role in the hamlet and often also about their families and businesses, but also introduced me to elderly people in their respective neighbourhood of whom they thought would be willing to share their stories related to trading in the past. I also got to know another group of elderly men at a pagoda of one neighbourhood, where they meet every day after lunch. Depending on the day, there were around fifteen to twenty men playing cards in groups of four. This group of men was formed at school age and has been lasting for the following decades up to the present. Elderly women mostly stay at home, take care for small children, cook and do other housework. They could be met at home at times they were not busy. Most of these elderly people had great capacity for remembering and allowed me to conduct life-story interviews with them.

To be able to understand the role of Ninh Hiệp's markets in the larger trade chain, I followed the trade flow in both directions (producers and distributors/consumers). One trip brought me to Guangzhou, China, where the bulk of goods sold in Ninh Hiệp is bought. Having been invited by one of the traders to join the trip, this was a very intense and highly revealing experience. The other trip, with the intention to visit cloth markets in Vietnam which sell clothes from Ninh Hiệp, led to central and southern Vietnam (Đà Nẵng, Hội An and Ho Chi Minh City).

The fieldwork on which this book is based lasted 15 months, including 3 months of intensive language preparation, from July 2012 to September 2013. All data were collected in Vietnamese. For the survey and some of the interviews, I was supported by a research assistant.

Since the completion of the fieldwork, the marketisation process has continued at great speed. Sometimes, articles on Ninh Hiệp appear in Vietnamese online newspapers, yet, as all print and broadcast media of Vietnam—radio, television and newspapers—are state-owned, opinions expressed are considered to represent state entities. Especially the coverage of protests against decisions of the state should therefore be met with a careful stance. Comments, pictures and videos on social media, shared by protesters and sympathisers, form an alternative source of information that, however, also needs to be treated with care. I only use these sources of information to add to the data I conducted during the field research, which forms the core of this book.

Outline of Chapters

So far, I have elaborated on the key concepts for the study, drawing on different strands of scholarship. Having started with a short introduction to the concept of neoliberalism in anthropology, a discussion of recent anthropological studies in the field of governance in China and Vietnam has followed so as to delineate the particular political economy of market socialist systems. I have also introduced the concept of "private indirect government" in order to connect to a wider interdisciplinary debate about governance and economy, which focuses on the role of the state in privatisation processes. After having outlined the background of the state–market–society relation, I discussed three core concepts—uncertainty, trust and morality—that are important to examine the reorganisation of small-scale trade in the post-Đổi mới period in Ninh Hiệp. The underlying argument that connects these concepts is that the uncertainties produced in a particular political economic context are dealt with by establishing social networks, wherein trust is a crucial feature, and by creating a moral community.

While I have already provided a brief glance into the field site, Chapter Two goes into depth to describe Ninh Hiệp historically as well as in contemporary times. It depicts the commune's economic and administrative structure as well as the different markets in the village, their characteristics and the type of management. Elaborating on trade villages in the Red River Delta, the chapter sheds light on the role Ninh Hiệp played and continues to play in the textile trade in the region.

Chapter 3 gives a historical account of the organisation of trade in Ninh Hiệp in the last 50 years, particularly drawing on the notion of uncertainty. The chapter identifies a range of economic and political uncertainties and looks closely at strategies of traders to cope with them. I show that the turn to a market system did not necessarily lead to less restrictive governance, but that the formalisation of trade brought about another set of constraints. At the same time, I also argue that uncertainty can be a productive force because it encourages the creation and deepening of social relations and is thus conducive to social cohesion. Moreover, situations of legal uncertainty can provide chances that would not be realisable in a more certain context.

Chapter 4 analyses the Vietnamese family and the model of family businesses. While cooperatives were the main economic units during the high socialist period, the family was promoted as the core for economic organisation in the aftermath of Đổi mới, leading to a massive surge of family businesses in the early 1990s. Unlike other studies on family businesses in East and Southeast Asia that portray family businesses as either exploitative or overly harmonious, I aim to show a more complex picture by looking at different interests within and perspectives on family businesses in Ninh Hiệp while paying attention to generational relations.

Chapter 5 scrutinises the gendered effects of the new mode of governance. While the early phase of market liberalisation opened up opportunities especially for women to make a living as merchants, the subsequent process of formalisation of trade was driven almost exclusively by male politicians and investors and has resulted—at least in Ninh Hiệp—in the creation of spaces henceforth adopted by men. How this development impacted on the roles and expectations of women and men will be examined in this chapter. In the first part, the role of men—from "helper" to market vendor and sometimes co-mananger of the family business—and the shifting notion of masculinity is carefully analysed. The second part considers the role of women and reflects official as well as local ideologies of femininity.

Chapter 6 investigates the social organisation of trade and demonstrates the importance of social relations in business. Social relations do not only facilitate transactions between traders and their suppliers and customers, but also form the basis for the informal banking and credit system in the village. The notion of trust is crucial in this respect as there is no legal enforcement but only social sanctions in case of misconduct. Yet, some relations may turn out as a burden and constrain actions of traders. This chapter accounts for a variety of relations within and beyond the village and carefully analyses how they are used while at the same time examining the unequal ability among traders to establish relations.

Chapter 7 examines the spatial organisation of trade, ranging from bigger and smaller towns in various parts of Vietnam, to the countryside, and finally, to China. The latter is illustrated with a detailed ethnographic account of a business trip, which I was invited to join by some of the traders. Trust, and also distrust, is of crucial importance in the interactions at the Chinese markets. Yet, it is not the Chinese vendors that seemed to matter most to Ninh Hiệp traders, but the "translators", or more accurately shopping assistants, who served as intermediary between Chinese and Vietnamese traders. Therefore, this chapter illuminates the role of these assistants and thereby also clarifies the nature of trade relations between Vietnamese and Chinese traders.

Chapter 8 explores the notion of morality from three perspectives: one is to examine what traders in Ninh Hiệp perceive as moral by analysing moral discourses and look at how these moral rules are confirmed or contested by practices of using money. The moral rules following from these discourses and practices inform the actions of villagers and contribute to the formation of a village identity. The second perspective looks at morality as an important element of governing and how it legitimises efforts of the state to advance the marketisation process through the rhetoric of modernisation and civilisation. The third perspective focuses on traders' performances of a particular moral identity so as to counter the state's ambiguous actions.

The concluding part summarises the main points and discusses the current situation of the marketplaces in Ninh Hiệp as well as the relation between the case study and the current political economic context of Vietnam.

Notes

1. See Brett Bowden (2009) for more elaboration on the term and its origin.
2. To this, it should be added that repression is exercised not only along class lines, but also along political ones. Political dissents face repression as well, regardless of their socio-economic status.
3. The original work was published in 1999 in French, "La Privation des Etats".
4. The preference of the term "morality" or "ethics" also reminds of the two important sociologists Émile Durkheim ([1925] 1961) and Max Weber ([1930] 2001) and their respective way to deal with the topic.
5. *Bộ đồ* is a pair of colourful cotton clothes, popular among women throughout Vietnam to be worn in and around the house, and often, in marketplaces.

References

Adler, Paul S., and Seok-Woo Kwon. 2002. Social Capital: Prospects for a New Concept. *Academy of Management Review* 27 (1): 17–40.

Barth, Fredrik. 1963. Introduction. In *The Role of the Entrepreneur in Social Change in Northern Norway*, ed. Fredrik Barth, 1–18. Bergen: Universitetsforlaget.

Beidelman, Thomas O. 1986. *Moral Imagination in Kaguru Modes of Thought.* Bloomington: Indiana University Press.

Bélanger, Danièle, Lisa B. Drummond, and Van Nguyen-Marshall. 2012. Introduction: Who Are the Urban Middle Class in Vietnam? In *The Reinvention of Distinction: Modernity and the Middle Class in Urban*

Vietnam, ed. Van Nguyen-Marshall, Lisa B. Drummond, and Danièle Bélanger, 1–17. Dordrecht: Springer.

Benda-Beckmann, Franz, and Keebet Benda-Beckmann. 2000. *Coping with Insecurity: An 'Underall' Perspective on Social Security in the Third World.* Yogjakarta: Pustaka Pelajar.

Bowden, Brett. 2009. *The Empire of Civilization: The Evolution of an Imperial Idea*. Chicago: The University of Chicago Press.

Brenner, Neil, and Nik Theodore. 2002. Cities and the Geographies of "Actually Existing Neoliberalism". *Antipode* 34 (3): 349–379.

Cassaniti, Julia L., and Jacob R. Hickman. 2014. New Directions in the Anthropology of Morality. *Anthropological Theory* 14 (3): 251–262.

Cooper, Elizabeth, and David Pratten. 2015. Ethnographies of Uncertainty in Africa: An Introduction. In *Ethnographies of Uncertainty in Africa*, ed. Elizabeth Cooper and David Pratten, 1–16. Basingstoke: Palgrave Macmillan.

Dasgupta, Partha. 1988. Trust as a Commodity. In *Trust: Making and Breaking Cooperative Relations*, ed. Diego Gambetta, 49–72. New York: Blackwell.

Durkheim, Émile. [1925] 1961. *Moral Education: A Study in the Theory and Application of the Sociology of Education*. New York: Free Press.

Endres, Kirsten W. 2000. *Ritual, Fest Und Politik in Nordvietnam: Zwischen Ideologie Und Tradition*. Münster: LIT.

Endres, Kirsten W. 2013. Traders, Markets, and the State in Vietnam: Anthropological Perspectives. *Austrian Journal of South–East Asian Studies* 6 (2): 356–365.

Eriksen, Thomas H., Oscar Salemink, and Ellen Bal (eds.). 2010. *A World of Insecurity: Anthropological Perspectives on Human Security.* Anthropology, Culture and Society. London: Pluto Press.

Fassin, Didier. 2012. Introduction: Toward a Critical Moral Anthropology. In *A Companion to Moral Anthropology*, 20, ed. Didier Fassin, 1–17. Malden: Wiley-Blackwell.

Ferguson, James. 2010. The Uses of Neoliberalism. *Antipode* 41 (S1): 166–184.

Ferguson, James, and Akhil Gupta. 2002. Spatializing States: Toward an Ethnography of Neoliberal Governmentality. *American Ethnologist* 29 (4): 981–1002.

Gainsborough, Martin. 2003. *Changing Political Economy of Vietnam: The Case of Ho Chi Minh City*. London: RoutledgeCurzon.

Gainsborough, Martin. 2010. *Vietnam: Rethinking the State*. London: Zed Books.
Gambetta, Diego. 1988. Can We Trust Trust? In *Trust: Making and Breaking Cooperative Relations*, ed. Diego Gambetta, 213–237. New York: Blackwell.
Grossheim, Martin. 1997. *Nordvietnamesische Dorfgemeinschaften: Kontinuität und Wandel: Vom Beginn der Kolonialzeit bis zum Ende der Vietnamkriege*. Hamburg: Institut fur Asienkunde.
Harms, Erik. 2012. Neo-Geomancy and Real Estate Fever in Postreform Vietnam. *Positions* 20 (2): 405–434.
Heintz, Monica. 2009. Introduction. In *The Anthropology of Moralities*, ed. Monica Heintz, 1–19. New York: Berghahn Books.
Hibou, Béatrice. 2004. From Privatising the Economy to Privatising the State: An Analysis of the Continual Formation of the State. In *Privatising the State*, ed. Béatrice Hibou, 1–49. London: Hurst.
Kim, Annette M. 2007. North versus South: The Impact of Social Norms in the Market Pricing of Private Property Rights in Vietnam. *World Development* 35 (12): 2079–2095.
Kleinen, John. 1999. *Facing the Future, Reviving the Past: A Study of Social Change in a Northern Vietnamese Village*. Singapore: ISEAS.
Laidlaw, James. 2002. For an Anthropology of Ethics and Freedom. *The Journal of the Royal Anthropological Institute* 8 (2): 311–332.
Leshkowich, Ann Marie. 2011. Making Class and Gender: (Market) Socialist Enframing of Traders in Ho Chi Minh City. *American Anthropologist* 113 (2): 277–290.
Li, Tania. 2007. *The Will to Improve: Governmentality, Development, and the Practice of Politics*. Durham: Duke University Press.
Lincoln, Martha. 2008. Report from the Field: Street Vendors and the Informal Sector in Hanoi. *Dialectical Anthropology* 32 (3): 261–265. doi:10.1007/s10624-008-9062-9.
Luhmann, Niklas. 1988. Familiarity, Confidence, Trust: Problems and Alternatives. In *Trust: Making and Breaking Cooperative Relations*, ed. Diego Gambetta, 94–108. New York: Blackwell.
MacLean, Ken. 2010. The Rise of Private Indirect Government in Burma. In *Finding Dollars, Sense and Legitimacy in Burma, Washington DC: Woodrow Wilson Centre*, ed. Susan L. Levenstein, 40–52. Washington, D.C: Woodrow Wilson Internationa Center for Scholar, Asia Program.
Mbembe, Achille. 2001. *On the Postcolony*. Berkeley: University of California Press.

Nguyễn Đức Nghinh. 1993. Markets and Villages. The Rural Markets (chợ Làng) of North Vietnam. In *The Traditional Village in Vietnam*, 315–368. Hanoi: The Gioi Publishers.

Nguyễn-Võ Thu-Hương. 2008. *The Ironies of Freedom: Sex, Culture, and Neoliberal Governance in Vietnam*. Seattle: University of Washington Press.

Nonini, Donald M. 2008. Is China Becoming Neoliberal? *Critique of Anthropology* 28 (2): 145–176.

Ong, Aihwa. 2006. *Neoliberalism as Exception: Mutations in Citizenship and Sovereignty*. Durham: Duke University Press.

Ong, Aihwa. 2007. Neoliberalism as a Mobile Technology. *Transactions of the Institute of British Geographers* 32 (1): 3–8.

Ong, Aihwa, and Li Zhang. 2008. Introduction: Privatizing China: Powers of the Self, Socialism from Afar. In *Privatizing China: Socialism from Afar*, ed. Li Zhang, and Aihwa Ong, 1–19. Ithaca: Cornell University Press.

Pettus, Ashley. 2003. *Between Sacrifice and Desire: National Identity and the Governing of Femininity in Vietnam*. New York: Routledge.

Robbins, Joel. 2009. Morality, Value and Radical Cultural Change. In *The Anthropology of Moralities*, ed. Monica Heintz, 62–80. New York: Berghahn Books.

Rose, Nikolas. 1999. *Powers of Freedom: Reframing Political Thought*. Cambridge: Cambridge University Press.

Schlecker, Markus. 2013. Introduction. In *Ethnographies of Social Support*, ed. Markus Schlecker, and Friederike Fleischer, 1–15. New York: Palgrave Macmillan.

Schwenkel, Christina, and Ann Marie Leshkowich. 2012. Guest Editors' Introduction: How Is Neoliberalism Good to Think Vietnam? How Is Vietnam Good to Think Neoliberalism? *Positions* 20 (2): 379–401.

Smart, Alan, and Filippo M. Zerilli. 2014. Extralegality. In *A Companion to Urban Anthropology*, ed. Donald M. Nonini, 222–238. Chichester: Wiley-Blackwell.

Tô Xuân Phúc. 2012. When the Dại Gia (urban Rich) Go to the Countryside: Impacts of the Urban-Fuelled Rural Land Market in the Uplands. In *The Reinvention of Distinction : Modernity and the Middle Class in Urban Vietnam*, ed. Van Nguyen-Marshall, Lisa B. Drummond, and Danièle Bélanger, 143–56. Dordrecht: Springer.

Truitt, Allison. 2012. Banking on the Middle Class in Ho Chi Minh City. In *The Reinvention of Distinction: Modernity and the Middle Class in Urban*

Vietnam, ed. Van Nguyen-Marshall, Lisa B. Drummond, and Danièle Bélanger, 129–142. Dordrecht: Springer.

Vann, Elizabeth F. 2005. Domesticating Consumer Goods in the Global Economy: Examples from Vietnam and Russia. *Ethnos* 70 (4): 465–488.

Vann, Elizabeth F. 2012. Afterword: Consumption and Middle-Class Subjectivity in Vietnam. In *The Reinvention of Distinction: Modernity and the Middle Class in Urban Vietnam*, ed. Van Nguyen-Marshall, Lisa B. Drummond, and Danièle Bélanger, 157–170. Dordrecht: Springer.

Weber, Max. [1930]2001. *The Protestant Ethic and the Spirit of Capitalism*. London: Routledge.

Widlok, Thomas. 2009. Norm and Spontaneity: Elicitation with Moral Dilemma Scenarios. In *The Anthropology of Moralities*, ed. Monica Heintz, 20–45. New York: Berghahn Books.

Zaloom, Caitlin. 2004. The Productive Life of Risk. *Cultural Anthropology* 19 (3): 365–391.

2

The Village in the Market

As one approaches Ninh Hiệp after an 18-km ride on the main road from Hanoi to Bắc Ninh province, the side street to the village running along paddy fields underscores the rural character of the place. Long before reachin)g the village gate, clothing shops line both sides of the street. These shops are narrow on the side, but often reach far aback and sometimes are part of residential houses. In front of the shops, eye-catching clothes are displayed on steel racks and mannequins. Some traders sell outside the shops: either placing their merchandise on a small piece of cloth or of plastic on the ground or hanging them from a bar or rod welded horizontally into the exterior of the stall. There are clothes as far as the eye can see, predominantly for women but some also for men. This street leads straight to the old market in the centre of the village. The closer one gets, the more crowded and noisier it becomes, especially in the front and at the side of the old market, where vendors and customers on motorbikes, loaded with huge bags or bundles of clothes, jam the narrow streets.

Across the parking lot and food court in front of the old market are two new market buildings, where the commerce is less intensive than in the old market. In the street surrounding the old market in front of the

E. Horat, *Trading in Uncertainty*,
DOI 10.1007/978-3-319-55648-2_2

Nành pagoda is the village market held twice a day with vendors selling fresh vegetables, fruits, meat, fish, rice and noodles. Only the few vendors who sell kitchen items and votive paper for worshipping keep their stall open all day. Cloth traders usually visit the fresh market by motorbike on their way to bring the children to the day nursery in the morning or when taking them back in the late afternoon. The intra-village traffic is immense and adds not only to a constant relative high level of noise by motorbikes and transporters, but also to air pollution.

Yet, when getting away from the centre and walking through the village's narrow, labyrinthine streets, one will unavoidably come across remains of earlier times, such as old-style wooden houses from the beginning of the twentieth century, ancient archways with lithic animals as guardians, pagodas, small temples and shrines to worship deceased ancestors. In front of some of these houses are small gardens with trees and singing birds in cages, giving a feeling as if time had stood still. Their old houses are hidden behind modern multi-storey houses that are built very close to each other. In sunny weather, pavements and public places such as the ground in front of the pagoda and the communal house (*đình*) are used to dry medicinal plants. The particular odour stemming from drying medicinal plants and processing them is very strong and noticeable and is spread over the whole village on windy days.

Ninh Hiệp is situated in the north of Gia Lâm district at the edge of Hanoi province, adjacent to the communes Phù Đổng, Đình Xuyên and Yên Thường, and bordering Đình Bảng village as well as Phù Chẩn commune in Bắc Ninh province (Fig. 2.1). It is home to 23 historical sites, such as pagodas, temples and ancestral houses, of which 9 are certified as places of exchange of the ancient cultures of Kinh Bắc and Kinh Đô. With a population of 16,700 people in over 4000 households and an area of 488.86 ha in 2012, it is one of the most densely populated places in Vietnam. Of this area, 233.421 ha is agricultural land, 61.87 ha is residential land, 63.63 ha is industrial land, and the remaining 129.939 ha is non-agricultural land (UBND huyện Gia Lâm and UBND xã Ninh Hiệp 2013).

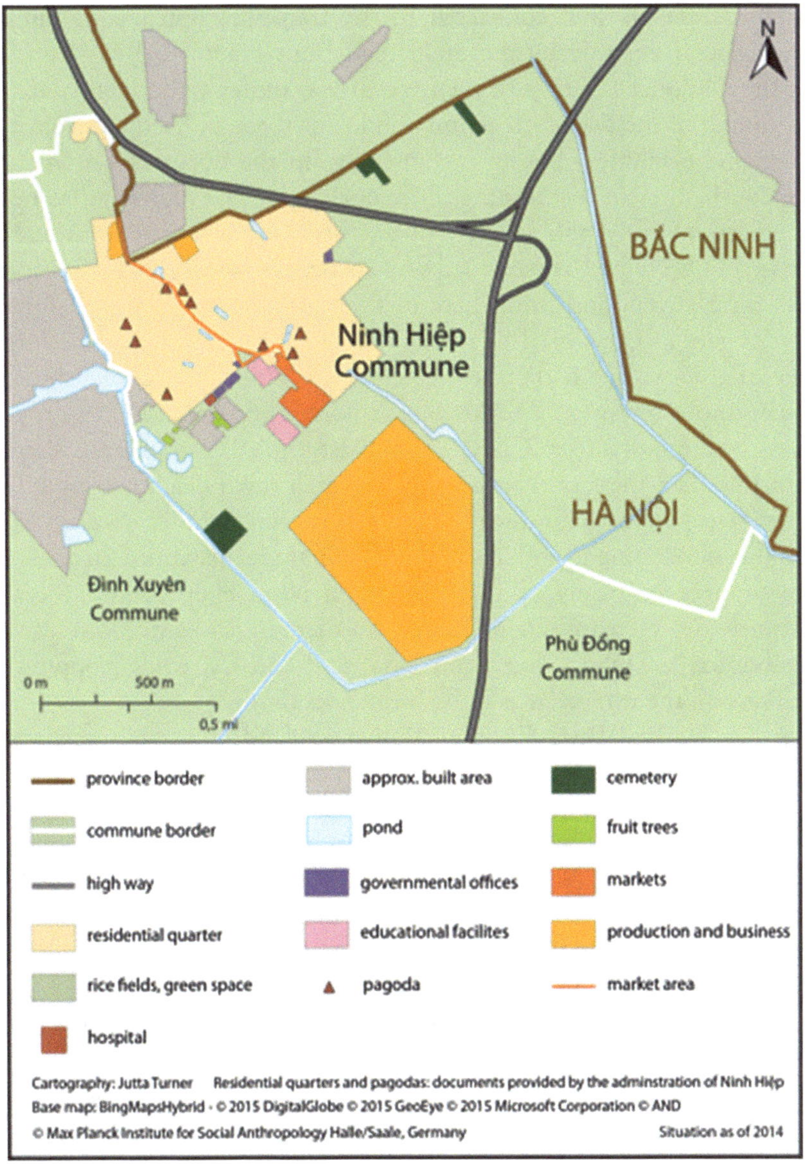

Fig. 2.1 Ninh Hiệp commune

Ninh Hiệp is well connected to the transport system and can be reached conveniently by the main road from Hanoi to Bắc Ninh, or by the National Route (QL A1), which was built by the French at the beginning of the twentieth century and runs through Vietnam from the Vietnamese–Chinese border in Lạng Sơn in the north to Cà Mau in the south, thereby connecting all major cities. The highway has been upgraded recently and underwent a crucial expansion right where it passes Ninh Hiệp. The new road was opened in January 2014 and leads to Thái Nguyên, and from there to the northern Vietnamese–Chinese border gate in Lào Cai. This means that Ninh Hiệp serves as the interface of the two main transport roads from China to Hanoi, which is of enormous importance for traders in Ninh Hiệp because they depend heavily on imports from China. In the past, the railroad played a significant role, and the fact that Yên Viên, a small town neighbouring Ninh Hiệp, was connected to the railroad system, was another crucial factor for the development and maintenance of trade networks throughout the country. Not only could traders from Ninh Hiệp commute easily between Yên Viên and Hanoi (and from there to the south), but also to the border in Đồng Đăng (Lạng Sơn) and Lào Cai while stopping at markets on the way, such as in Phú Thọ and Yên Bái.

As in the Red River Delta and other lowland areas, the population in Ninh Hiệp mainly consists of Kinh people, the ethnic majority in Vietnam. With the expansion of the market in the last 10 years, migrant workers from various places, some of them belonging to the Thái minority, came to Ninh Hiệp to make a living.[1] Of the approximately 80 to 100 lineages, which are to be found in Ninh Hiệp nowadays, 40 are said to have been there since "ancient times" (*ngày xưa*). Ninh Hiệp's immaterial cultural heritage is underlined by several famous scholars of earlier centuries, whose names are inscribed on steles in the Temple of Literature (Văn Miếu) in Hanoi. The most famous person, however, whose genealogical reference relates to the Nguyễn Đính lineage in Ninh Hiệp, is the Princess Lê Ngọc Hân (1770–1799), who was the daughter of Queen Nguyễn Thị Huyền and King Lê Hiển Tông and the wife of Nguyễn Huệ (who became Emperor Quang Trung in 1788 (Nguyễn Khắc Quỳnh 2004).

Craft and Trade Villages in the Red River Delta

The Red River Delta, which is seen as the cradle of traditional Vietnamese culture, especially the area nowadays known as Bắc Ninh province, is a region where craft villages appeared early in history for the purpose of producing luxury objects for the imperial capital as well as everyday items for the needs of a village society (Fanchette 2012, 260). These craft villages were tightly linked to the so-called District of 36 streets and guilds in Hanoi and other national and international markets as well as to areas where raw material came from. Another reason why many villages in the Red River Delta developed handicraft production and engaged in trade was that before the eighteenth century, the majority of the villagers either had no land for farming or the plots they owned were not large for sustaining themselves (Nguyễn Quang Ngọc 1993). Thus, although some villagers did farming and combined it with occasional trading, which could help them through difficult times, most people in trading villages relied on trade as their main profession. When commerce prospered and traders could accumulate capital, they did not work in their fields anymore, but still kept the land and hired labourers to work on it. With the trend towards specialisation, craft villages started to form economic clusters, in which each village concentrated on one step in the production and marketing chain of a product. Interestingly, this local production system persists in the Red River Delta to this very day, although it has undergone changes due to modernisation and urbanisation processes.

During the period of high socialism (starting in 1954 in the North and 1975 in the South), agriculture was strongly promoted, but craft and trade activities were still carried out to varying degrees in the villages in the Red River Delta (DiGregorio 2001; Fanchette 2012). Đổi mới brought about important changes in regard to the easing of micro-economic restrictions of entrepreneurial activities, so that in the first years after the introduction of the economic reforms, traditional craft and trade villages experienced strong growth (Spitzenpfeil 1999, 136–137). Even villages that had not produced crafts in the past joined the trend.

However, a few years after the euphoric take-off, many of these villages met severe challenges that would eventually lead to the stagnation of the local economy and sometimes force people to turn to other sources of income. The main problem for most of these villages was the competition with state-owned and larger private companies, which were in a better position to produce goods of higher quality and larger quantities due to their advanced technologies and mechanisation. At the same time, the demand for cheap—not to mention low quality—goods propelled imports from China, making it even harder for small village industries to compete. Because products from craft villages were not of a quality or market value comparable to other available products, many of these villages soon lacked a market for selling their goods. Furthermore, many craft villages encountered difficulties accessing capital needed for professionalising production (Spitzenpfeil 1999, 143–152). Another issue was reputation: because of the above mentioned disadvantages, some craft workshops attempted to compete with their rivals by resorting to using less and cheaper materials than what they would declare. Whenever these scandals resulted in public outcry, the reputation of the respective villages was compromised and in many cases led to a sharp decline in the number of placed orders.[2]

Having said that, a few villages in the area, such as the pottery village Bát Tràng, the wood carving village Đồng Kỵ as well as Ninh Hiệp, benefitted greatly from the changing circumstances. Bát Tràng was strongly supported and promoted by the state as an exemplar of economic growth through household production, whereas Đồng Kỵ found access to foreign markets and successfully signed contracts with partners in Asia and overseas. Ninh Hiệp, finally, adapted to the domestic demand for cheap clothing by specialising in imports from China and distributing them to wholesalers and retailers nationwide.

Touching upon Ninh Hiệp's history in the remainder of this chapter, I draw on a variety of sources of information. In addition to studies carried out by foreign researchers, most of whom are French, I rely mainly on books and documents produced by Vietnamese scholars as well as official reports of the socio-economic and cultural development of the commune. Three main authors are cited: Nguyễn Khắc Quỳnh, a local historian who wrote several books about Ninh Hiệp, mostly consisting of stories and poems; the district-level Communist Party with a book on the revolutionary history of Ninh Hiệp between 1930 and 2005; and an anonymous student and a staff member from the history faculty of the Hanoi National University of Education, whose work is fittingly titled *The History of Ninh Hiệp*. Although these sources have proven to be of great importance in depicting the past of the village, they do at times tend to be somewhat problematic. For instance, they sometimes contradict each other when it comes to dates or they provide no or only a few references for the arguments they put forth. All in all, when held to the standards of modern anthropology, one should retain a healthy level of scepticism with regards to their "impartiality" or "scholarly" value. However, they are the only available sources, and, when consulted with care, they have a great potential to provide valuable insight into the village history.

Introducing Ninh Hiệp

Local Economy

Ninh Hiệp's economy has been diverse from early on. In addition to agriculture as the main occupation, people in Ninh Hiệp lived from weaving and from processing and trading medicinal plants. In her study on Ninh Hiệp, the French historian Florence Yvon-Trán (2001) distinguished three main stages for the development of craft and commercial activities from the eleventh century to the nineteenth century: the emergence of craft activities during the Ly-Tran dynasty (1009–1400) and a "spontaneous" local market[3]; the expansion of the craft sector together with a growing volume of trade in the sixteenth and seventeenth centuries; and the intensification of commerce from the eighteenth century on. Traditionally, agriculture was the task of men while women weaved and engaged in petty trade, as an old saying in Ninh Hiệp confirms: "Nữ chức nam canh tùng sờ phú" (*Women weave, men farm, that's how wealth is made*) (Yvon-Trán 2001, 222). After the First World War, the production of leather items became a major economic activity for about one-fifth of the villagers (Lịch sử Ninh Hiệp, 26).

Because stitching leather was seen as a male craft, women started to take over some agricultural tasks beside weaving and trading. In the following, I will give a more detailed account of the rise and decline of the three main products—medicinal plants, cloth and leather—Ninh Hiệp has been known for.

The processing of and trade with medicinal plants are an important occupation of people in Ninh Hiệp. According to the legend, a woman called Lý Nhũ Thái Lão came from Thanh Hóa to Ninh Hiệp during the Ly dynasty (1010–1125). She gained her knowledge of medicinal plants through her father, and when he passed away, she followed his example to lead a simple life and cure sick people. She left her natal village and went northward, passing Hanoi, until Ninh Hiệp, where the villagers asked her to stay and teach them how to use medicinal plants. From then on, villagers travelled to various places to collect medicinal plants and brought them back to process and use them, and in the seventeenth and eighteenth century Ninh Hiệp became a centre to study about traditional medicine. Lý Nhũ Thái Lão is remembered until the present day and paid homage on the anniversary of her death, the eighteenth of the first lunar month. At the beginning of the 1990s, a small temple was reconstructed on the place of her former residence with money from donations (Yvon-Trán 2001, 220–222). Pierre Gourou (1936) noted that it is the standard pattern of craft villages to develop thanks to the initiative of a single person who invented a non-agricultural occupation and was imitated by other villagers. This person is usually worshipped as the village guardian deity (Endres 2000, 42–44).

Jennifer Sowerwine (1999), who investigated medicinal plants' trade before and after Đổi mới between the highland and the lowland, refers to Ninh Hiệp as a legendary centre of medicinal plants since ancient times. According to her, in the past medicinal plants could be gathered in the forests surrounding Ninh Hiệp, whereas nowadays herbs for northern medicines (*thuốc Bắc*) are imported from China, and herbs for southern medicines (*thuốc Nam*) are purchased from traders in northern Vietnamese provinces, such as Lào Cai, Thanh Hóa, Yên Bái, among others (Sowerwine 1999, 136). One of the main produce for which Ninh Hiệp is famous for is lotus, which is processed until today and widely distributed in various forms, either to cure diseases or as a gift on special occasions, such as for weddings.

Women in Ninh Hiệp have been famous for "small cloth" (*vải nhỏ*) or "Nành cloth", as is remembered by elderly people reciting the following poem: "Vải Nành tơ Báng thì mua, Tam Sơn, Nội Duệ có cho chẳng màng" (*Buy cloth from Nành and silk thread from Báng, don't take the one from Tam Sơn and Nội Duệ*) (Lịch sử Ninh Hiệp, 22; Nguyễn Khắc Quỳnh 2004, 190). Small cloths were made from a special kind of cotton yarn of high quality and were known to be thin and smooth (Dương Duy Bằng 2002, 556). The inscription on one of the walls of the temple to honour Lý Nhũ Thái Lão indicates that she did not only pass her knowledge of medicinal plants to the villagers, but also taught them weaving. Silk and cotton production expanded from the eleventh century, and weaving was a common activity in rural Vietnamese households according to observations of Chen Fu, an ambassador of Dai-Viet, at the end of the thirteenth century (Yvon-Trán 2001, 222). Two reasons have certainly contributed to weaving becoming popular in Ninh Hiệp: first, cotton could be planted after the harvest of rice when most fields were not used, so it did not interfere with other agricultural tasks. Furthermore, cotton production and weaving did not pose technical obstacles. While women in Ninh Hiệp were skilled weavers, they were not professional in sericulture. Elderly women remember that only a few people had knowledge of it, while the majority of people bought silk thread in surrounding areas. In contrast to cotton, the growing of mulberries and the weaving of silk is complex and needs meticulous care. In addition, while cotton was produced for domestic use, silk was a luxury product and as such controlled by the state and was not allowed to be worn by common people as it was the clothing of the court (Yvon-Trán 2001, 223–224).

Besides the early knowledge of villagers of the textile craft and Ninh Hiệp's favourable geographical position in terms of access to the transport system, a major reason for the development of the textile craft and trade in Ninh Hiệp was its intense economic exchange with the neighbouring commune Tiên Sơn, which holds one of the biggest wholesale markets in northern Vietnam, called Giàu market (Lịch sử Ninh Hiệp, 22). According to villagers, the weaving loom was a standard accessory in each house until the beginning of the 1970s, but had not been used much since the 1930s or 1940s due to a shortage of raw materials towards the end of the colonial period (Đảng bộ huyện Gia Lâm [Gia Lâm district Party] and Ban chấp hành đảng bộ xã Ninh Hiệp [Party Executive Committee of Ninh Hiệp] 2007; Dương Duy Bằng 2002, 558). From then on, weaving experienced a rapid decline and was given up eventually. Trade with cloth, on the contrary, was carried out continuously and even experienced a "Golden Age" during these years (Abrami 2002).

In addition to textiles and medicine, Ninh Hiệp was famous for leather. It is said that the leather craft was brought from France by a villager from Ninh Hiệp, called Thạch Văn Ngũ, who served the French army during the First World War. Upon coming back to Ninh Hiệp, he started to produce leather items such as bags, suitcases, belts, saddles, shoes and sandals and opened the first leather shop in Hà Trung Street in Hanoi. As the demand for leather products rose from the 1920s onwards, he taught the trade to fellow villagers and encouraged them to open stores (Nguyễn Khắc Quỳnh 1996, 7). While most villagers opened shops to sell leather products in Hanoi, some went as far as Saigon (nowadays Ho Chi Minh City) to make a living from producing and selling leather items. Once in Saigon, villagers from Ninh Hiệp joined forces and founded an association with the aim to support each other and help newcomers *("Phù Ninh tương tế hội")* (Nguyễn Khắc Quỳnh 2004, 324). When the war between China and Japan broke out in 1937 as a precursor of the Second World War, the leather craft in Ninh Hiệp experienced a peak as the Japanese needed leather products to equip their army and contracted with leather workshops in Ninh Hiệp. Later, during the First Indochina War from 1946 to 1954, some villagers joined the resistance, while others stayed in their workshops to supply the military with products made from leather. In 1960, a craft cooperative (*hợp tác xã thủ công*) with over 300 members was established to equip the army in North Vietnam with leather items during the Second Indochina War. When the war ended in 1975, the demand for leather items sank drastically and the production thereof was only maintained on a small scale until the leather cooperative was finally dissolved in 1994 (Dương Duy Bằng 2002, 570).

The development of these three different crafts reaffirms not only the resourcefulness of Ninh Hiệp villagers and their ability to supply products that are sought after, but also their early and thorough integration into regional and superregional networks. Nowadays, like other craft and trading villages in the Red River Delta, Ninh Hiệp's economic sector is composed of agriculture and a mix of different non-agricultural businesses (Tô Duy Hợp 1995, 287). In 2012, the local economy was dominated by handicraft and small industry (59.6%), followed by trade and services (38.7%), and agriculture to a minor degree (1.7%) (UBND huyện Gia Lâm and UBND xã Ninh Hiệp 2013). Due to the strong and sustained economic growth since the year 2000 and especially from 2008 to 2013,[4] Ninh Hiệp became one of the wealthiest communes in northern Vietnam (UBND huyện Gia Lâm 2008). There are no reliable numbers on how many households are involved in the cloth trade,[5] but from all the people I got to know there were not more than a handful of families who completely stayed away from it. While these statistics and observations speak a clear language regarding the economic insignificance of agriculture, villager's self-representation was more complex: according to my findings, and also in line with the account of Dương Duy Bằng (2002, 574), agriculture was often said to be the main occupation, while non-agricultural production and trade were considered as side occupations in households that usually rely on two to three different economic activities. Nevertheless, almost no household solely lives from agriculture, and those who do cultivate their fields usually hire workers for this purpose. Mr. Xuân, a hamlet chief, confirmed this point: "Nowadays, households which rely one hundred per cent on agriculture are very rare, because if they don't sell one thing they sell something else. Nobody would go home and do nothing when farm work is done. Generally speaking, this does not exist". Since agriculture is a seasonal occupation, those not involved in trade work as temporary labourers in small industries nearby.

I often encountered the seemingly paradox relation between agriculture and trade in conversations with villagers and therefore addressed the issue in interviews with hamlet chiefs, for example with Mr. Tịnh who said: "One hundred per cent of the households engage in trade [in this hamlet], there is nobody who does not work as a trader, but agriculture is still said to be the main occupation". It follows that villagers spend most of their time for and draw the main income from their so-called side occupation, as Mr. Cường assured: "The main occupation brings a minor income, and the side occupation, which is trade, brings the main income. Agriculture does not allow people to build houses like this with three, four or five floors. If one can live from agriculture, this is good already".

Even if Ninh Hiệp has more agricultural land than other communes in Gia Lâm district, it is one of the most densely populated communes in Vietnam and the amount of land per person is decreasing and becoming fragmented. Besides elderly people who have always done farm work, there are only a few villagers who keep doing agriculture wholeheartedly. Yet owning a piece of land to plant rice and growing some fruits and vegetables, and sometimes raising a small number of chicken or pigs, is important to people in Ninh Hiệp, as Mr. Quảng explained: "The income from farming is not significant. The purpose is not profit but a stable source of food". In addition, land serves as a security net to fall back on. Economic strategies and the degree to which households rely on agriculture or are involved in trade differ between the hamlets. Hamlet Seven, where leather items were produced in the past, has the highest number of people working in agriculture (60% of the households) nowadays, while hamlet Six, which is almost fully covered by the market, has the lowest.

The fact that Ninh Hiệp people stress agriculture as the main occupation has several historical and contemporary practical and moral components. First and foremost, in the past as well as nowadays, agriculture, especially rice production, is of immediate importance for subsistence. Second, even though most people do not cultivate their rice fields themselves, it is preferred to hire labour to work in the fields than to buy rice at the local market. This is not only in order to be less dependent on others, but also because the quality of one's own rice is usually seen as superior. An even more important reason is to keep land as property, in the hope that the state will allow to change its land use.[6] Third, during pre-colonial, colonial and post-colonial times until very recently, trade was the least prestigious occupation and was placed at the bottom of the social order, while agriculture was considered as honest and productive work and was therefore more valued (Labbé 2014, 29). Taking a closer look at the Vietnamese expression of "side occupation" (*nghề phụ*), the suffix *phụ* means not only "help" and "secondary to", but also "minor", and thus captures the subordinate position of trade within the household economy (Labbé 2014, 29). Fourth, and maybe most significant, is the self-perception of Ninh Hiệp people who conceive of themselves as a peasant community in the countryside, traditionally relying on agriculture. This issue will be discussed in more depth in Chap. 8.

Administrative Structure

The smallest administrative unit in Vietnam is the village (*thôn, làng, phường*) or commune (*xã*), consisting of hamlets (*xóm*) and lanes (*ngõ*). Ninh Hiệp is a special case in this regard as it lacks the category of *thôn*. Only the categories of *xóm* and *xã* are officially used in Ninh Hiệp. The difference between a village and a commune is not always clear, but most scholars use the term *làng* when referring to the life space of a rural population, while the term *xã* corresponds to the political space (Labbé 2014, 25).[7] In this book, I will refer to Ninh Hiệp as a village except for when I am explicitly writing about its political structure as a commune.

Nowadays, Ninh Hiệp consists of nine hamlets, each of which has particular traits and specialises in one or two crafts, which often correspond to its traditional structure. Each hamlet has a house of culture (*nhà văn hóa*), where regular meetings of the hamlet chief (*trường thôn*) and the inhabitants of the hamlet are held. Hamlet chiefs are elected directly by household representatives. Once elected, they have to attend regular meetings at the commune, where general commune and particular hamlet issues are discussed. Serving as intermediaries between the people and the local state, they are in charge of representing the interests of the people of their hamlet as well as informing them about new policies and decisions made in the meetings. Moreover, they should help resolving conflicts in their hamlet, which arise most often around the issue of land inheritance. In these cases, the head of the patrilineage (*trường họ*) also plays a significant role.

The current hamlet chiefs in Ninh Hiệp are all male and in their 50s or early 60s, except for one who is only 47 years old and just took over the position in 2012. Some of them were new to the position at the time I conducted research, while others have been doing it for nearly 20 years. Visiting each of them at their home, their different living conditions struck me. While some lived in small, rather old houses, others had big, multi-storey houses, equipped with modern television flat screens, massive ancestral altars and additional rooms full of Chinese and European antiques. All of them participated in cloth trade through their families, and most of them produced clothes at home. One even had a workshop on the second floor of his house, where his son and his daughter-in-law employed 10 workers.

When looking at the map of the commune (Fig. 2.2), one will recognise that the hamlets close to the old market were also involved to a higher degree in trading cloth (hamlets Four and Five), while the ones further away relied more on agriculture (hamlets One and Two, Six and Seven),

Fig. 2.2 Ninh Hiệp commune by hamlets

produced leather items (hamlets Three and Four, Six and Seven) and processed and sold medicinal plants (hamlets Eight and Nine). The hamlet that has undergone the most radical change is hamlet Six. From being a rather poor and mostly agricultural hamlet, it turned into the richest hamlet with the highest land price since the expansion of the market that now covers almost the whole area of the hamlet. In the past, before the expansion of the marketplace, hamlet Eight used to be the wealthiest hamlet thanks to the steady demand of medicinal plants. In my daily conversations with villagers, hamlet Eight was often depicted as a closed subcommunity of people who used to marry only within the hamlet, had a certain way of speaking and did generally not interact much with people from other hamlets in the past. However, in recent years, since cloth and ready-made clothes experienced a much higher demand than medicinal plants and have therefore become more profitable, socio-economic differences between hamlet Eight and the rest of the community became less prominent. Also, the participation of some households from hamlet Eight in cloth trade was conducive for the opening up and integration of the hamlet into the wider community life.

The Markets

The Nành market, named after the village's *chữ Nôm* name Kẻ Nành,[8] is the oldest market in Ninh Hiệp. Determining the exact time of the establishment of the Nành market is difficult, but according to the local legend it goes back as early as the period of the Emperor Lý Thái Tông (1028–1054) (Lịch sử Ninh Hiệp, 27). Starting off as a place where people came to exchange goods for everyday consumption, the market grew bigger continuously and not only offered vegetables, rice, meat, fish and shrimps, but also thread, cloth and even buffaloes and cows. As the village specialised, products such as traditional Vietnamese and Chinese medicinal plants as well as silk and cotton cloths were traded, too. Two steles from the eighteenth century, which give an account of the market's enlargement and of its change of location, hint at the Nành market's importance in the region and suggest that it was very significant to the life of the local population (Nguyễn Khắc Quỳnh 2004, 319).

In the second half of the twentieth century, from the socialist revolution to Đổi mới—when private trade was not permitted—the market was somewhat reduced as villagers sold cloth clandestinely in the streets instead of at the market. It was only a few years after Đổi mới that traders started to sell cloth at Nành market again. First, the market expanded around the Nành pagoda in the years from 1985 to 1990, and in 1995 the Nguyệt Trì pond was filled to get additional space for stalls. Finally, the establishment of a permanent market building in 2001 gave cloth trade a boost and marked the starting point for Ninh Hiệp to become the main provider of cloth and ready-made clothing in northern Vietnam and other parts of the country. With the expansion of the market area, fresh products and textiles were segregated physically from one another even more than before: the large covered market building became solely used for selling cloth and ready-made clothing, while fresh products are now sold on the small square in front of the Nành pagoda. When talking about the Nành market nowadays, one refers to the cloth and clothing market, not the fresh market.

In the village, the Nành market is called "Old Market" (*chợ cũ*) (Fig. 2.3), because of the traditional look of the market building and because it is the continuation of the first market in the village. it currently accommodates 1125 stalls, each of which is filled with rolls of fabric or heaps of ready-made clothes and is not bigger than 3 square meters. Sometimes clothes are hung up or lie on a wooden board for display. When the market closes in the evening, the goods are left at the stall, only covered with a piece of cloth. The old market is a one-storey building and comprises of two parts, which at first sight seem to seamlessly merge into each other. When taking a closer look, however, one will recognise that the roof of one part is higher and thus makes the hall more spacious, while the other part feels stuffy and gets unbearably hot in summer because the roof is considerably lower. Furthermore, the aisles that crisscross the first part run straight and parallel to each other whereas the aisles in the second part are more chaotic and look as if they have evolved spontaneously rather than having been planned on a drawing board. The reason is that the stalls in the second part already existed long before the market building was constructed. This older part of the market even houses a temple and a few private homes where people live and sell cloth. The more spacious part of the old market was built in October 2001 and eventually put into use 1 year later. Subsequently, the original parts of the old market were partly renovated in September 2003 and in December 2009 (HTX xã Ninh Hiệp 2012).

Before the old market was constructed, those villagers who wanted to have a stall were asked to support the building of the market financially.[9] The stalls were then assigned to the traders by lot. As the stalls at the main aisle were a bit more expansive then the others, some people swapped their assigned stall for another. Thus, even if the assignment of the stalls was in principle a matter of luck, villagers with money could buy themselves into a better location if they found somebody to accept the deal. At that time, it may not have been foreseeable how much the land price would rise in the coming years and hence how valuable these stalls along the main aisle would become. What is certain, though, is that the location in the market laid the foundation for most traders' careers in the coming years.

Fig. 2.3 Nành market ("Old Market")

As only those villagers who had supported the building of the market were entitled to have a stall, the old market is perceived of as "in the hands of Ninh Hiệp people". The few people from outside the village who came later as traders are therefore not stallholders, but usually subtenants. Stalls can be rented for 5 years; afterwards the contract has to be renewed. The old market was first managed by the local communal administration and since 2007 by the commune's cooperative (*hợp tác xã*), which created a market management board for this purpose. The market management board collects fees to cover expenses for services (security, water, electricity, sanitation, cleaning) and is in charge of keeping the market in good condition. The rental fee for a stall depends on its location. When renting it directly from the cooperative, the prices range from 3 to 4 million VND (142–189 USD at the time of the research) per year for a stall inside the market to around 10 million VND (473 USD) per year for a bigger shop at the side of the market.

When paying a close look at the sellers in different areas of the old market, an interesting picture emerges: generally, the stalls far away from the main aisle are operated by middle-aged and elderly traders selling rather cheap merchandise, such as pieces of cloth, simple clothing for elderly people, leftover clothing from the previous season and the like. Many of these vendors are the ones who originally got the stall through the aforementioned allotment or through a deal in those early days. As these stalls are not in great demand due to their bad location, stallholders cannot make much profit, if at all, from renting these stalls to other traders. Therefore, if a vendor retreats from business, these stalls usually go back to the cooperative, which then rents them out to other traders. The situation for the stalls directly at or very close to the main aisle is completely different: as these stalls are extremely crowded with customers at almost any time of the day, they are much sought-after selling spaces and, therefore, stallholders can cash in on renting them out directly to fellow traders. When transferring stall use rights among one another, traders charge several hundred million VND per year for a stall inside the market and up to a billion VND (almost 50,000 USD) per year for a stall facing the main aisle. As a consequence, many of the original stallholders do not work as vendors anymore, but rent out their stall. Most of the traders along the main aisle are young, as selling in such a crowded place is physically demanding. Moreover, because it is very competitive, one needs to be ahead of others in terms of setting trends and therefore frequently travel to China to import new merchandise, or design clothes oneself.

Opposite of the old market, across the parking lot which is lined with numerous food and tea stalls, are the two new privately owned, multi-storey commercial centres "Sơn Long" and "Phú Điền", both established in 2011 (Fig 2.4). Until autumn of 2013, only the shops on the ground floor of both markets were open, whereas the shops on the second and third floor were partly rented out and were used as storage rooms. Although there are some market activities, they are not as busy as the old market. With their tiled floor, moving stairs and slight elevation above the ground they differ significantly from the old market.

These two markets are not only more spacious, but also cooler and cleaner. The shops here are bigger than the ones in the old market and have enough room to invite customers in. Instead of the merchandise lying in a pile, clothes are displayed on mannequins or hung on hangers to attract potential customers, and many of these shops are carefully decorated with wallpapers. As these stalls have iron shutters, they can be locked at night. The aisles between the stalls are large enough

Fig. 2.4 Sơn Long and Phú Điền commercial centre ("New Markets")

for transport carts to deliver the merchandise directly to the stalls. Many traders in Ninh Hiệp agree that the new markets seem modern; some say that they are beautiful and convenient; however, most traders fault the new markets for lacking the usual hustle and bustle of customers. Clothes sold here tend to be slightly more expensive than at the old market. Traders can acquire stall use rights for a maximum of 50 years—the maximum time for lease of land in Vietnam—for 1.5–3.5 billion VND (70,000 USD–165,000 USD), again depending on the location of the shop. Alternatively, shops can be rented year to year with an annual cost of around 150–500 million VND (7000 USD–23,000 USD).

While most vendors at the old market are middle-aged women, the average age of vendors at the two new markets is much lower, and a remarkable number of them are men. Many of these vendors are the children of traders with a stall at the old market and do not have much experience as traders yet. Elder, more experienced vendors usually prefer to keep their stall at the old market, because they are afraid of losing their regular customers if they move to another stall. Younger traders, who have not yet an established clientele, like the new markets, because the shops are more spacious, comfortable and can be decorated. With their wooden floors, colourful wallpapers and additional decorative objects such as mirrors and lamps, these shops resemble fancy fashion boutiques in Hanoi. Another difference between the old and the new markets lies in the merchandise: at the old market, cloth, home-produced clothing and low-quality Chinese-made clothes for men and women of all ages are sold, much of which end up at markets in the countryside all over Vietnam. In contrast, at the new markets fashionable and a bit more expensive clothes from China are sold, except for a few shops selling home-produced clothes or clothing from Ho Chi Minh City. The old and the new markets differ not only in appearance and the goods sold, but also in the form of management. Public markets, such as the old market, are subject to negotiations between the people and the state when interests diverge. Private management of a market, in contrast, is organised top-down without the involvement of the people. Furthermore, becoming a stallholder in the new market is a matter of money, as everybody who has the financial means, be it a person from Ninh Hiệp or outside, can purchase a stall.

In addition to the old and the two new markets, a fourth market is held on both sides of the street diverging from the main road between Hanoi and Bắc Ninh and leading to the commune and straight to the market halls. The first part of the market looks improvised with piles of cloth lying messily on a wooden board, only canopied by a piece of plastic which is spanned between wooden poles. This part existed even before the old market was constructed in 2001, but allegedly due to an issue over taxation traders at this market had to move to the old market, with only a few traders staying behind and still using the selling space. The remaining part of the market, however, consists of residential houses, which line the street and use the ground floor as a selling space. Villagers call this market simply "Xóm 6" because it is on the land of hamlet Six. Before the rapid growth of the marketplace, this street was a street like any other in the commune, lined with houses, which often had small shops or drugstores located on the ground floor. Due to the popularity of Ninh Hiệp's marketplace in the region, a rising number of local villagers seized the opportunity to launch new businesses, which in turn necessitated a physical expansion of the market space. The residents of Xóm 6 were lucky because they could just turn the ground floor into a shop and sell textiles and ready-made clothes at home. The rising land price makes the renting out of a few square meters a very lucrative business for residents, in addition to the profit they make as traders. The ground floor of houses is often divided into two to three narrow shops, so that the house owner can sell in one shop and rent out the remaining space, including the front and side of houses. Shop rental prices are much higher in this area than everywhere else in the commune, and because competition is also much harsher, conflicts between traders are more likely to happen. Shop tenants in Xóm 6, most of whom are young or middle-aged women with selling experience, therefore have to be ahead of others in terms of fashion trends—that is why it is also called "Fashion Street"—and need to increase sales to be able to pay the very high and still rising rental fee.

Finally, there are two other markets: one is *chợ Baza* (Bazaar market), built in 2006; the other is just next to it, constructed in 2013. They are actually not built on the land of Ninh Hiệp, but of the neighbouring village, which belongs to Bắc Ninh province. Because of their geographical proximity and due to the fact that most vendors are people from Ninh Hiệp, these two markets are briefly mentioned here, but were not part of my research. In any case, at the time of my research the stalls in *Baza* market were abandoned, except for the ones in the first row, directly along the main street. Consequently, the market was considered a failed market among villagers. One reason may be that the market is located too far away from the other markets and is thus not convenient for customers to reach. Another explanation relates to the rumour that there are ghosts, resulting in villagers not being eager to rent a stall there.

Notes

1. Since they are not registered as residents, they do not appear in official statistics and their number is therefore hard to estimate.
2. For a coverage of the topic in local online media, see Vietnamnet (2015).
3. What she calls a "spontaneous" local market is basically the exchange of goods of daily consumption and some of the crafts the villagers produced on a very small scale.
4. The average annual economic growth rate for the years 2008–2013 was between 15 and 16% (UBND huyện Gia Lâm and UBND xã Ninh Hiệp 2013).
5. In order to get a licence, traders have to register at the Finance and Planning Department of Gia Lâm district; unfortunately, the only list I could obtain is incomplete and inaccurate.
6. For more elaboration on this reasoning, see Nguyễn Phương Lê (2011, 98).
7. A more extensive discussion can be found in Papin (1997, 33–34) and Nguyễn Tuấn Anh (2010).
8. *Chữ Nôm* was the Vietnamese language based on Chinese characters before the usage of the Latin script. *Kẻ* means "ancient" as well as "land where exchange is done" (Lịch sử Ninh Hiệp, 8).
9. It is common practice in Vietnam that public markets are funded partly by the state and partly by traders who are guaranteed a stall in return. In the case of the old market, the state paid 1.7 billion Vietnamese Đồng

(VND) (around 116,000 USD in January 2001) while the people in Ninh Hiệp contributed the remaining 2.3 billion VND (157,000 USD).

References

Abrami, Regina M. 2002. Self-Making, Class Struggle and Labor Autarky: The Political Origins of Private Entrepreneurship in Vietnam and China. Ph.D. thesis, University of California, Berkeley.

Đảng bộ huyện Gia Lâm (Gia Lam district Party), and Ban chấp hành đảng bộ xã Ninh Hiệp (Party Executive Committee of Ninh Hiep). 2007. *Lịch Sử Cách Mạng. Đảng Bộ và Nhân Dân Ninh Hiệp* [History of Revolution. Party and People in Ninh Hiep]. Hanoi: Nhà xuất bản văn hóa dân tộc.

DiGregorio, Michael R. 2001. Iron Works: Excavating Alternative Futures in a Northern Vietnamese Craft Village. Ph.D. Thesis, University of California.

Dương Duy Bằng. 2002. Tiểu Thủ Công Nghiệp ở Ninh Hiệp (lịch Sử và Hiện Tại) [Handicraft in Ninh Hiep (in the Past and Present)]. In *Le Village En Questions (Làng ở Vùng Châu Thổ Sông Hồng: Vấn đề Còn Bỏ Ngỏ)*, ed. Philippe Papin and Olivier Tessier. Hanoi: Bibliothèque vietnamienne EFEO, nhà xuất bản Lao Động—Xã Hội.

Endres, Kirsten W. 2000. *Ritual, Fest Und Politik in Nordvietnam: Zwischen Ideologie Und Tradition*. Münster: LIT.

Fanchette, Sylvie. 2012. The Craft Villages of the Red River Delta (Vietnam): Periodization, Specialization, Specializations. In *Local Agri-Food Systems in a Global World: Market, Social and Environmental Challenges*, ed. Filippo Arfini, Maria C. Mancini, and Michele Donati, 259–278. Newcastle: Cambridge Scholars.

Gourou, Pierre. 1936. Les Paysans Du Delta Tonkinois. Etude de Géographie Humaine. Ph.D. thesis, ed. D'art et d'histoire, Paris.

HTX xã Ninh Hiệp. 2012. Tình Hình Hoạt động Công Tác Quản Lý Kinh Doanh Khai Thác Chợ Nành Xã Ninh Hiệp [The Situation of Management Activities of Business Operators at Nành Market in Ninh Hiệp]. 10/BC-HTX.

Labbé, Danielle. 2014. *Land Politics and Livelihoods on the Margins of Hanoi, 1920–2010*. Vancouver: UBC Press.

Nguyễn Khắc Quỳnh. 1996. *Phù Ninh. Quê Hương Công Chúa Ngọc Hân* [Phu Ninh. Hometown of Princess Ngoc Han].

Nguyễn Khắc Quỳnh. 2004. *Chuyện Cũ Làng Nành* [Old Stories of Nành Village]. Hanoi: Nhà xuất bảnvăn hóa dân tộc.

Nguyễn Phương Lê. 2011. The Redivision of Labour in a Red River Delta Village in a Globalized Economy. In *Labour in Vietnam*, ed. Anita Chan, 91–118. Singapore: ISEAS.

Nguyễn Quang Ngọc. 1993. Về Một Số Làng Buôn ở đồng Bằng Bắc Bộ Thế Kỷ XVII-XIX [Commercial Villages in Northern Vietnam in the 18th-19th Centuries]. Hanoi: Hội sử học Việt Nam.

Nguyễn Tuấn Anh. 2010. Kinship as Social Capital: Economic, Social and Cultural Dimensions of Changing Kinship Relations in a Northern Vietnamese Village. Ph.D. thesis, VU University Amsterdam, Amsterdam.

Papin, Philippe. 1997. Des "Villages Dans La Ville" Aux "Villages Urbains"—L'espace et Les Formes Du Pouvoir a Hanoi de 1805 a 1940. Paris: Paris 7.

Sowerwine, Jennifer. 1999. Economic Liberalization, Gender and Traditional Botanical Medicine in Northern Vietnam. In *Women's Rights to House and Land: China, Laos, Vietnam*, ed. Irene Tinker, and Gale Summerfield, 131–142. Boulder: Lynne Rienner.

Spitzenpfeil, Annette. 1999. Craft Villages in Vietnam's Economic Transformation Process. In *Vietnamese Villages in Transition*, ed. Bernhard Dahm, V.J.H. Houben, Martin Grossheim, Kirsten W. Endres, and Annette Spitzenpfeil, 121–154. Passau: Department of Southeast Asian Studies, Passau University.

Tô Duy Hợp. 1995. Some Characteristics of the Changing Social Structure in Rural Vietnam under "Doi Moi". *Sojourn: Journal of Social Issues in Southeast Asia* 10 (2): 280–300.

UBND huyện Gia Lâm. 2008. *Gia Lâm—Văn Hóa và Phát Triển* [Gia Lâm—Culture and Development]. Hanoi: Nhà Xuất Bản Văn Hóa Thông Tin and Công Ty Văn Hoá Trí Tuệ Việt.

UBND huyện Gia Lâm, and UBND xã Ninh Hiệp. 2013. Báo Cáo Thành Tích [Performance Report].

Vietnamnet. 2015. Craft Villages. *Vietnamnet*. http://english.vietnamnet.vn/fms/tags/craft%20village/index.html.

Yvon-Trán, Florence. 2001. Artisanat et Commerce Villageois Dans Le Việt-Nam Prémoderne, Du XIe Au XIXe Siècle (Le Cas de L'ancienne Agglomération Villageoise de Phù Ninh [Région de Kinh Bằc]). Bulletin de l'Ecole Française d'Extrême-Orient 88 (1): 217– 247.

3

Trading in Uncertainty

"Trade in the past was not easy—it was forbidden after all", said Mrs. Huế, a 76-year-old former trader, as she stirred the porridge she was cooking in her dim kitchen. "We were in constant fear of being caught!" That this was not the case anymore became clear in the course of our conversation, as she praised today's situation as one of freedom, where people could pursue any economic activity they wanted. Compared to what her generation had experienced before Đổi mới, traders could now sell at the market without having to worry, she explained to me. On the way from her house to the old market, I recalled the stories she had told me, until I reached the tiny stall of Mrs. Dung in one of the almost hidden aisles in the back of the market. Mrs. Dung, a woman with a mild face but strong voice, was in her early sixties and mother of five children, all of whom sell at the market. Before I could ask her how things were going, she started to tell me the most recent rumour concerning the attempt to privatise the old market, and that it was more necessary than ever to stand up to protect the market. This rumour in different versions was part of many conversations and did thus not come as a surprise. In fact, the possibility of a change of market ownership, accompanied by a feeling of deep uncertainty about how things

E. Horat, *Trading in Uncertainty*,
DOI 10.1007/978-3-319-55648-2_3

would unfold in the near future, was so present at that time that it may be considered the number one topic among many traders. Thus, rather than freedom, contemporary traders were experiencing the limits of a seemingly liberal economy, and a powerful, albeit distant, state.

While in the accounts of trade in the pre-reform era the terms *nguy hiểm* (dangerous) and *sợ* (fear) were often used, in the post-reform period *không chắc chắn* (uncertain) was the most common adjective for describing trade in conversations and interviews. This separation is not strict, however, as supply and demand in the past may also have been uncertain for traders, and fear of being cheated by suppliers is likely to exist today. Yet, overall, the traders' experiences with commerce before and after Đổi mới were different—not restriction versus freedom, but clear versus vague regulations, and a close versus a distant state.

The aim of this chapter is to draw attention to the productive side of uncertainty, especially in terms of social support and the deepening of ties of solidarity. In the following, I will examine the textile and clothing trade in the village during the last 50 years with a focus on the perceived fears and uncertainties of traders, and their ways of coping with them. I will roughly divide the time into three stages: the period of strict economic planning in the 1960s and 1970s; the transition period (1980s), during which the introduction of the Open Door Policy was a formative event; and the post-reform period, marked by economic liberalisation (1990s–present). The restructuring of the economic system from a planned to a socialist-oriented market economy in the second half of the 1980s brought about fundamental formal changes, which had immediate and dramatic effects, as Ronnås and Ramamurthy (2001, 2) pointed out. However, as I will show in this chapter, for traders in Ninh Hiệp it was experienced as a gradual rather than disruptive transformation.

Fifty Years of Trade

Planned Economy Period (1960s and 1970s)

Throughout the period between independence and the introduction of the Open Door Policies, which includes the Second Indochina War (1954–1975) and the subsidy period (*thời kỳ bao cấp*, 1976–1986),

North Vietnam pursued a planned economy. Production, distribution and consumption were centrally planned and tightly controlled; private small-scale trade was illegal. The central state monopoly of foreign trade allowed for exercising control not only over production and exports, but also over imports necessary for industrialisation and modernisation. Only state-owned companies and cooperatives were allowed to operate in the trading sector. Citizens were given coupons, which permitted them to purchase a limited quantity of certain commodities to cover basic day-to-day needs (Beresford and Phong 2000; Abrami 2002). According to one informant, during the subsidy period peasants were only allowed to buy four metres of fabric per year while city dwellers were not allowed to go beyond five metres. Upon using up one's coupon for a certain fabric, one had to buy fabric in an underground black market if more was needed. As several analysts have shown, villagers in northern Vietnam during the 1960s–1980s did not always act in accordance with what authorities expected or stipulated. Ninh Hiệp was no exception in this regard, as villagers have continuously engaged in trade. During the subsidy period, trade was a side occupation and involved only small amounts of certain goods, not comparable to the volume of trade after Đổi mới. Moreover, before Đổi mới, villagers clandestinely sold in the streets or at home as opposed to selling openly in permanent market stalls as it is currently the case.

Nevertheless, Regina Abrami (2002, 383) called the 1970s a "Golden Age" for Ninh Hiệp, as villagers there were comparatively better off than people from other places. In her thesis, she described in detail how small traders in Ninh Hiệp used inter-communal, informal economic networks to interact with producers and customers. These networks were built during wartime when men from Ninh Hiệp were sent as soldiers to places all over Vietnam. Furthermore, traders worked together with local cooperatives in order to get protection. These local cooperatives had contracts with state companies to supply the goods they required. A noteworthy case was the deal between the Vietnamese army and the leather cooperative in Ninh Hiệp, not only just because it was an order that paid off as long as the war lasted, but also because a shortage of skins that were needed for gun-holsters made travels to upland areas necessary. Thus, members of the leather cooperative were given travel papers to go on "business trips" legally to obtain skins from faraway areas. This was an important chance for them to foster upland–lowland commercial linkages (Abrami 2002, 376–377). At the time, small traders dealt with everything that was demanded. Beside textiles and traditional medicine, which they were specialised in, they also dealt in monosodium glutamate (MSG), sugar, meat and other things.

Abrami (2002, 385–386) depicted the strategy of Ninh Hiệp textile traders in detail: first, they "borrowed" medicinal plants from fellow villagers in order to exchange them for textile coupons from farmers in surrounding areas. With these coupons, they went to the Intershop in Giảng Võ Street in Hanoi to obtain cloths.[1] Afterwards, they sold the imported high-quality cloths illegally in the village market or directly out of their homes. Finally, they paid back the "loan" they initially took out with the medicinal plants, either in textiles or in textile coupons. The main advantages of Ninh Hiệp traders were their extensive networks as well as their information and experience about what and where to buy and to whom to sell. Furthermore, a decisive factor was the support villagers received from the local police and militia. Local authorities did not enforce extreme measures adopted by the central and district governments, such as raiding homes without warrants. Quite the contrary: local officials routinely warned villagers in advance of raids (Abrami 2002, 378).

Prevalent in the narratives of former traders was their willingness to take risks, even though this entailed stress and a high level of anxiety, as was the case with what Mrs. Yên told me. She was 60 years old in 2012 and one of those villagers who had been trading all their lives. She has a small stall in the old market, where she sells plain-coloured white, brown and black fabric of medium quality, which she buys from other traders in the village. Mrs. Yên buys their leftover stock at a reduced price. Her stall is difficult to find and comes across as one of the oldest stalls in the market, only consisting of a wooden board with piles of fabric. She herself sits on another pile of fabric. The stall is separated into two halves by a wooden pole. In the other half, an elderly, blind woman sells a similar type of cloth. They have known each other for a long time and are on friendly terms. When recounting old life stories,

Mrs. Yên would explain in great detail how it was like to be a trader during the subsidy period and the stress that accompanied the constant fear of being caught by the police:

> We were nine children in my family, all of whom engaged in trade in addition to farming for the cooperative. When leaving home to go together to faraway places to exchange goods, we didn't know if we would be able to sell something, and whether we could come back safely or would be inspected and lose our wares.

Another recurring theme was the hardship due to the lack of food. The experience of not having enough food to eat—not even of the staple rice—figured dominantly in Mrs. Yên's memories of this period:

> I remember that the generation of my mother used to weave cloth from silk thread they had bought in neighbouring villages. Later, when thread became a scarce good, weaving was given up and villagers started to produce and sell clothes. During the subsidy period, we were given coupons to purchase four metres of fabric a year. However, we could not buy fabric in the countryside but were forced to sell the coupons in town. Some people sold coupons, others bought them to purchase more fabric to produce clothes and sell them. In this way, we could make a little bit of money. Another way to obtain fabric was to buy it from people who travelled to former Soviet and Eastern European countries as labourers or students and brought it back when returning to Vietnam. Even with the little extra income we made from illegal trading, my family went to bed hungry. It was endlessly hard (*khổ vô cùng*) and dangerous.

Not only Mrs. Yên, but also all traders of her age I talked to remembered this time as extremely hard and dangerous. Not a single person spoke about the past without emphasising that food was always in short supply and people were suffering from hunger. Thus, although Abrami (2002) referred to the 1970s as a time of relative prosperity in Ninh Hiệp, from the village perspective it was not a time of abundance at all.

According to traders from the village, they would go as far as the provinces bordering China (e.g., Lào Cai, Cao Bằng and Lạng Sơn) to buy a few metres of fabric and wrap it around the body to bring it back undetected. If passing through undetected was a challenge, passing through undetected and alive was another. As some pointed out to me, some traders died trying to make the journey for having wrapped the cloths too tightly around their body. While on the way back from the border region to the village, the traders were at risk of being stopped any moment by the police and being subject to random inspections. Understandably, this was the source of fear and anxiety for the traders who did not wish to lose their belongings and goods. Hence, when leaving the community to go to other places in order to exchange goods, the fear of being caught by the police was a constant companion. Mrs. Thâu, an 81-year-old former trader, narrated:

> My life in the past was very hard. I went to markets such as the one in Phú Thọ, only bringing one bag. I wrapped 20 metres of cloth around my body—I was thin at that time—and put some metres of cloth in the bag I was carrying. I went by train. Bicycles were owned primarily by the few well-off, and unlike nowadays there were no motorbikes back then. I would take the train to Yên Viên [neighbouring village of Ninh Hiệp], but if I had stayed on the train until reaching the station I would have been caught and would have lost everything. So I had to jump off just as the train began to decelerate before completely stopping at the station. The bag had to be thrown off the train, and I had to jump off after it immediately in order to avoid apprehension and lose the goods. Once I put one foot out of the wagon, I had to jump off, otherwise the force of the wind would throw me off the train and possibly kill me.

Goods, especially textiles, were sold at home or in the streets around the marketplace. Traders only carried a few pieces of cloth in a basket at a time so as to be able to run away if the police showed up. Unlike today's vendors, who can sell hundreds of metres of fabric at permanent stalls, in the past traders engaged in a type of small-scale street hawking (*buôn thúng bán mẹt*). As Mrs. Quế, a 76-year-old former trader, recounts:

> The market did become busier after the years 1973 and 1974, but it was still not as crowded as it is now. Traders used to sell cloth in small quantities. We could not sell as freely as we do now. We'd sit in the street, each vendor with her own small basket, ready to make a run for it if the police reared its head. But we were rarely caught when in our own community, because [the higher authorities] had to inform the commune administration about the raids in advance and they would in turn keep us in the loop and thus allow us to take our goods and hide in the houses.

The last part of this statement is telling because it explains why Ninh Hiệp could engage in trade even during the subsidy period when most other villages had to rely on agriculture and could only produce and trade secretly and outside the cooperative due to fear of severe punishments. Just as Mrs. Quế and other former traders pointed out, the local authorities in Ninh Hiệp were supportive of private trade activities.

In her study of four handicraft villages in northern and southern Vietnam, Spitzenpfeil (1999, 143) also argued that the support of the local administration for entrepreneurial activities in the pre-reform period was a decisive factor for the later success of villages, because it allowed people to build and maintain networks and to generate capital for investments in the future. She found that the most successful businesses were those that managed to clandestinely develop their entrepreneurial freedom in the pre-reform period. Hence, while in some villages local authorities were very strict in forcing people to invest all their time and effort into agricultural production for the cooperative, they exhibited more lax policies in other villages, allowing people to produce crafts and engage in trade as side businesses.[2]

Danielle Labbé (2014) reported similar findings when studying a peri-urban village in the surroundings of Hanoi. She argued that the engagement of villagers in the so-called outside economy[3] (also called "fence-breaking") expanded beyond survival-oriented activities and reached unprecedented levels in the 1970s. Her analysis challenges static accounts of village life under the planned economy in showing the influence of private practices on urbanisation processes long before the formal launch of the Open Door Policy. Similar to Abrami's (2002) observation in Ninh Hiệp, Labbé notes that in Hòa Mục,

> Next to their official occupations as agricultural cooperators, factory workers, or civil servants, locals became informal wholesalers and market vendors (…) The case of Hòa Mục contributes to this research [of the existence and significance of the outside economy] by revealing how quasi-private control over residential land (a legacy of the partial land reform) and the lax policing of this resource by local bureaucrats enabled the reproduction of market-oriented activities under the plan. (Labbé 2014, 160)

These stories demonstrate how illegal trading activities were common, but also risky. Even though traders did not know whether they would be controlled or not, they were conscious of the risks involved and were fully aware of the possible outcomes. On the one hand, Ninh Hiệp prospered precisely because villagers were willing to take risks by engaging in illegal activities; on the other hand, they pursued strategies to reduce risks, for example by cooperating with the local authorities that protected them. The inter-community networks of producers and customers created and maintained by traders during this period were crucial for the later development of Ninh Hiệp. Hence, private trade during the subsidy period was a hard, risky, but also lucrative activity for those involved.

Transition Period (1980s): From Plan to Market

As mentioned in the previous section, when shortages of goods for domestic consumption became acute towards the end of the 1970s, fence-breaking became a more popular way to alleviate adversity. Yet at the same time, these illegal economic activities aggravated the shortages within the planned sector of the economy (Beresford and Phong 2000, 35). Starting from the Sixth Plenum of the Central Committee in August 1979, the planning system was gradually loosened in the subsequent years due to a change in thinking at the highest levels of leadership. Several key policy measures concerning foreign trade, agriculture, state-owned industry and the pricing system were put in place in the years 1980 and 1981: As a first step, Government Decree no. 40-CP was issued in February 1980. It allowed certain localities to engage directly in trade with foreign partners in order to find new markets, thereby openly challenging the monopoly of central planning. In January 1981, the Party Secretariat promulgated Order no. CT-100, aimed at spreading the contract system in agriculture throughout Vietnam, and also Government Decree no. 25-CP, which permitted industrial enterprises to expand production beyond the output previously stated by the central state. In addition, major price reforms were announced in the same year, and in 1984, an even more progressive resolution on foreign trade followed (Beresford and Phong 2000, 39–48).

As these early reforms called for a limitation of the foreign trade monopoly and thereby restricted central planning and undermined the fixed price system, they did not find favour with conservative politicians. The fear of straying too far from the accepted tenets of socialism meant that other sectors, such as small-scale trade, were controlled tighter in the first years of the 1980s. These years of zigzag policies were marked by a deep uncertainty about the trajectory of state policy and produced a stop-and-go approach that led to the controversial actions of trade liberalisation and restriction (Beresford and Phong 2000, 57).

The central government's effort to eradicate illegal trade at the beginning of the 1980s did not reach its target in Ninh Hiệp. Rather, it strengthened the trend that had emerged in the previous years. Local officials, being part of the informal trading system, continued to cover private traders (Abrami 2002, 389). Abrami called these relations "synergies": while the intervention of commune and cooperative officials in private sector trade brought merchants legitimacy and protection, local officials could reap profits to raise their meagre salaries (Abrami 2002, 402). The persistence of illegal economic activities was conducive to Ninh Hiệp in general and to families with traders in particular, for it compensated the shortages resulting from the planned economy. It is noteworthy that more than just a few villagers were involved in trade. In fact, it was a fairly common activity, even amongst families who worked for the state. According to Abrami, the wives and daughters of local officials in particular were recognised as successful traders. As Ninh Hiệp is held together by kinship ties, villagers had no interest in denouncing their own kin and family members. Therefore, the central state's direction to control illegal trade on the local level was far from a success story.

This lack of success is reflected in a reported encounter between the Party Secretary in Ninh Hiệp and district officials in the early 1980s. Upon hearing about the new campaign to tighten the control of illegal trade, the secretary apparently shouted at district officials: "Do you expect me to arrest my wife?" (Abrami 2002, 382). Clearly, conflict of interests between the local and the central state continued throughout the years. In the case of Ninh Hiệp, disapproval of regulations and their implementation was strong among local level governments:

> In Ninh Hiệp, for example, the campaign to eliminate illegal traders in the early 1980s compelled agricultural cooperative officials to make arrangements with a number of communes elsewhere to allow informal traders to deposit their purchases in their storehouses rather than worry about transporting their goods back to Ninh Hiệp. This, in turn, encouraged the supply and marketing cooperative to look to the military for business partnerships, including transport. No police officer would check a military truck. As such, they were the ideal vehicles to move goods in and out of Hanoi. In such an environment, it was not difficult for local governments to persuade independent traders to collaborate with them. (Abrami 2002, 393)

But, as Beresford and Phong (2000, 19) have argued, this did not always work to the detriment of the central policy directions. Rather, it appeared to be a symbiotic relationship, characterised by mutual opportunities and constraints. While local authorities had the capacity to act independently to some degree, their activities were also restricted by their superiors; and, by the same token, the Vietnamese state apparatus could not override local interests completely.

> The pressures and realities of transformation from below and the perceived requirements for economic reform from above have interacted to produce a series of compromises which have affected a gradual and rather successful transition from plan to market over the last two decades. Looked at in a dynamic context, it is this symbiosis of central, local authority and private activities that have both produced the reform process in Vietnam's economy and continue to influence its development today. (Beresford and Phong 2000, 19)

The efforts to change the economic system in the early years of the 1980s culminated in the launch of the Open Door Policy in 1986. Some of the most important changes were the de-collectivisation of land and the legalisation of the private sector and of foreign trade. The first step to legalise private trade was to establish a system of two-way trade (*buôn bán hai chiều*).

The first time I ever heard of the "two-way trade" system was at a café I frequented during my fieldwork. The place, located near the old market, was run by Mr. Thâm, a local villager in his mid-50s. Mr. Thâm would often regale old stories, especially about the war, the revolutionary period and the organisation of trade at that time. He would point out the importance of the system for the people of Ninh Hiệp. Shortage, uncertainty and fear had left strong imprints in his memories. As he once told me,

> Before the introduction of the Open Door policy when trade was banned, it was not clear whom to trust and whom to have business relationships with. The danger of being caught and losing the wares was a pervasive reality. And if one was caught, who could one turn to for help? Traders were considered as traffickers, marketeers, and in violation of the law.

In two-way trade, which lasted from 1988 to about 1992, traders from Ninh Hiệp served as intermediaries between producers and state enterprises. According to Mr. Thâm, it was easy for traders in Ninh Hiệp to connect producers and buyers because of their experience in long-distance trade and their trade networks spread across Vietnam. During the subsidy period, cooperatives were in charge of this task. At that time, private traders unofficially worked with the cooperatives to bypass the risks involved in the "free", black market. Hence, two-way trade was the formalisation of this collaboration between cooperatives and private traders, and between state companies and cooperatives.[4]

Labbé (2014, 160) argued in a similar vein when she stated that "the first years of the Đổi mới reforms (1980–90) mainly institutionalised endogenous practices deemed illicit under the plan", thus creating "a favourable environment (including legal sanction) for local populations to expand and adapt earlier patterns" rather than to generate new practices.

In *The History of Revolution* (*Lịch Sử Cách Mạng*), published by the Communist Party of Gia Lâm district (2007), two-way trade was mentioned very briefly as having been encouraged by the Communist Party of Ninh Hiệp, following the guidance of the central government, and having led to a rapid development of family businesses in the community from 1986 to 1990. Although the state withdrew from managing peasant households as early as 1979 (Spitzenpfeil 1999, 121), it was in the context of Đổi mới that family businesses were strongly and explicitly encouraged, and became the most popular form of economic organisation in Ninh Hiệp and elsewhere. The family in general became the core institution in society after Đổi mới, effectively taking over the responsibility of looking after its members from the state (Wisensale 1999, 608).[5]

The first years of Đổi mới—from the decision to change the economic system to the implementation of the reforms—were rewarding for people in Ninh Hiệp. Many took over the role as brokers to connect producers and buyers and were thus able to adapt to the rules of the socialist-oriented market economy. In this way, traders could earn and save money for later investments. The easing of what had been a tense relationship with China after Vietnam's invasion of Cambodia and the 1979 China–Vietnam border war led to an agreement on the re-establishment of "small volume trade" in 1989 (Beresford and Phong 2000, 130), another important step conducive to Ninh Hiệp traders. In addition, a decree to allow foreign trade was passed in 1990 (Beresford and Phong 2000, 50–51). It aimed at legalising private trade and was the official signal to develop trade businesses. Even though private trade was now officially sanctioned, in practice traders still had to struggle in the first years of Đổi mới as it was a gradual transition.

Mr. Thâm, the local café owner, remembers very well that traders continued to face the risk of arrest until about the year 1992. Abrami (2002, 393) also mentions that in the late 1980s–early 1990s period, traders would still have to exercise vigilance and caution when crossing toll gates and engaging in "unofficial taxes" (i.e. bribery). This has to do with the severe fiscal crisis during those years when local budgets underwent contractions and local authorities attempted to absorb "contributions" from smugglers in order to collect extra-budgetary revenues (Beresford and Phong 2000, 17).

In summary, the years of the launch and implementation of the Open Door Policy had a profound impact on the lives of traders, but rather than bringing about immediate change, it was a gradual transition that involved the legalisation of activities Ninh Hiệp people had been carrying out for years, and, in some cases, even decades. In practice, however, traders were still running similar risks when openly making deals.

As Mr. Thâm remarked, even after the opening of the economy, the situation for traders was not clear for a long while. Regulations were written in a vague language and sometimes contradicted each other, and the police continued to exercise significant control over traders. While they were gradually granted more freedoms, they still could not count on legal protection. The Law on Commerce, which stated the rights of entrepreneurs and called for the establishment of a Court for Business, was launched as late as the year 1997 (Vietnam 1997). However, according to conversations with traders in Ninh Hiệp, it was (and still is) not common to bring cases to court. Despite the unstable business climate, the said years were crucial for the financial gains that would later on pave the way for further investments and initiating new business ventures in the following years and decades.

Post-Reform Period (1990s and 2000s)

Cloth traders from Ninh Hiệp did not only sell in their own native village, but many of them commuted to Hanoi to operate a stall at the Đồng Xuân market, one of the oldest and biggest covered markets in Vietnam built by the French at the end of the nineteenth century. When a fire destroyed large parts of the Đồng Xuân market in 1994, most traders went back to Ninh Hiệp and continued to sell cloth on a small scale until the first permanent market was built in the village in 2002. The villagers consider this to be the starting point of the strong development of the textile and clothing trade.

The marketplace has also expanded spatially, now covering large parts of the village. In recent years, the first market building—the so-called old market—was enlarged and renovated. The street leading to the market turned into a major shopping area as well, and two completely new market buildings were established. Compared to the time before Đổi mới, traders in Ninh Hiệp can nowadays do business freely without the fear of being chased. Despite the transformations in the politico–economic context, trade is still an uncertain business. However, the sources of contemporary uncertainties are quite different today and are intimately linked to the new techniques of governance. The post-reform period is marked by three main features, each of which relates to a specific kind of uncertainty:

Firstly, the village economy was reintegrated into international markets. Even though trade by definition implies a connection of economies through local, regional and international commercial relations and Ninh Hiệp villagers are known for being experienced long-distance traders, the previous economic system never depended on foreign markets to the extent that the current system does. On the one hand, the level of interdependence of economies on a global scale has dramatically risen in the last decades. In Vietnam, the economic opening and the country's move away from its former socialist partners to the much more volatile world market have increased exposure to price fluctuations, which has in turn led to a subsequent increase in uncertainty. On the other hand, the legalisation of foreign trade and the resumption of commercial relations with China have given Vietnam's powerful neighbour to the north a special place in the country's economic outlook. Almost everything sold in Ninh Hiệp is imported from China, be it fabric or clothing, with only a few exceptions.[6] Chinese fabric is used even in village-based production of clothing. The dependence of Ninh Hiệp on China is accompanied with various uncertainties: for instance, an extremely one-sided balance of trade, which means that one side is exclusively a consumer and the other exclusively a producer; the excessive reliance on one business partner; and most importantly, the trade restrictions resulting from the tense political relationship between the two countries.[7]

Secondly, the expansion of the market has led to enhanced competition and economic inequality. In the short-run, the restoration of the old market and the continuous enlargement of the trading area saw the successful attraction of new customers. However, in later years the supply-to-demand ratio has been perceived as being unbalanced. Of crucial importance for the understanding of competition in the village is the change in the organisation of trade: while initially each trader only had one stall in the old market, the establishment of additional markets created new opportunities for buying or renting more stalls and encouraged family members to increasingly sell at the market. Some families were able to invest more money than others in purchasing stalls, and some families had already established trade relationships with various parts of Vietnam while others had not. As a result, their businesses developed to varying degrees and along different trajectories. Soon, socio-economic differences between families in the community became more pronounced. Furthermore, the production of clothes at home was intensified during the years of strong economic growth. Hence, along with the shift from individual to family businesses, trade went from being a side occupation to a main occupation for most households in Ninh Hiệp. This high reliance on one economic activity increased the vulnerability of households in the face of fluctuations. In addition, skyrocketing land value in the marketplace area translated into a markedly higher risk for traders to run into debt when failing to generate the turnover needed for paying the stall rent.

Thirdly, the state's intensification of the marketisation process in the early 2000s led to the establishment of new markets and to the renovation and modernisation of existing markets across Vietnam (Endres 2014b).[8] The legalisation of trade as stipulated in the Đổi mới reforms did not mean deregulation, but rather a form of regulation resulting from shifting power relations. This process has promoted new public–private relations, as it has allowed private investors to enter the stage. "Accumulation by dispossession" is one of the core pillars of neoliberalism according to David Harvey (2005, 160–161), typically involving the privatisation of common goods to make them accessible for a privileged few. Even though Vietnam is officially referred to as a socialist-oriented market economy, in practice it adheres to neoliberal logics and capitalist forms of globalisation (Schwenkel and Leshkowich 2012). The sale of land-use rights and the privatisation of previously common goods are part of a far-reaching process of private capital accumulation, made possible by the liberalisation of economic activities through the Đổi mới reforms. In contrast to neoclassical economic presumptions, these developments have in fact increased corruption and other forms of illegality and informality in Vietnam, for example tax evasion and smuggling (Beresford and Phong 2000; Endres 2014a). These developments have greatly contributed to the feeling of uncertainty among traders, for how the evolution of the marketplace corresponds to a large part to state decisions, which are not always transparent for traders.

Exemplary of this trend was an attempt to privatise the old market in 2010. Upon hearing of this, stallholders at the old market closed their stalls for several days in order to protest against the planned privatisation in front of Ninh Hiệp's People's Committee. The protest was held successfully. Participants argued that the old market could not be sold without their consent since they had provided two-thirds of the capital needed to build it. Consequently, privatisation efforts in the old market were temporarily abandoned. At the same time, however, land-use rights of a plot of land opposite the old market were sold to investors, who in turn built two new multi-storey private market halls.[9] The mere thought of the privatisation plans in 2010 provokes unease amongst traders, partly due to fears it might happen again. They fear that in case of a change in ownership of the old market, stall rental fees will rise significantly. Moreover, any upgrade to the market and its renovation would mean a halt to their businesses and a subsequent loss of customers.

Thus, uncertainties in the post-reform period are generated mainly by the integration of the village economy into broader political and economic systems and by the growing marketisation trend in the village along with fiercer competition and privatisation. Traders perceive these uncertainties as a threat to their livelihoods because they have only limited alternative strategies to make a living comparable to the current one. Furthermore, they deal in large amounts and risk becoming trapped in debt if they cannot conduct business as they expect. These uncertainties are reinforced by the poorly developed legal system and the authorities' exploitation of uncertainty as a ploy to exert authority and control. What the latter entails will be described in more detail in the next section.

Governing Uncertainty

Paying attention to shifting power relations, indicated by a weakening of the local state vis-à-vis the town-level government and private investors, is crucial when identifying the different types and magnitudes of uncertainties, as well as the challenges of the status quo. The role of the local authorities carries great significance: Although the decision to implement major changes in the marketplace is made at the higher levels of the government, it is the local authorities that are tasked with the actual implementation of those decisions. Interactions between Ninh Hiệp traders and representatives of the state include varying degrees of uncertainty. Some of the encounters with state officials may be inconvenient but predictable, such as the registration of a business to apply for a trade licence and the payment of taxes. Others are less predictable, such as the inspection of traders for counterfeit and smuggled goods. These inspections are carried out a few times a month in the street leading to the village by the staff of the Market Management Department of Hanoi (*Chi cục quản lý thị trường Hà Nội*) in collaboration with policemen of the Economic Police Department of Gia Lâm (*Cảnh sát kinh tế huyện Gia Lâm*). Moreover, every now and then, a group of special police forces (*Cảnh sát cơ động*) come to "tidy up" the streets in the village.[10] This corresponds to Hibou's statement about the state showing its presence in fits and starts, but in a vigorous manner. Finally, situations that create a high level of uncertainty for traders are for instance changing as well as unclearly formulated regulations and decrees. During my fieldwork, this state of uncertainty produced by changing regulations was often mentioned in conversations with traders in Ninh Hiệp. Keeping up with constantly changing regulations written in a way that leaves space for interpretations was difficult for them, they said. Especially, regulations concerning the relationship with China (e.g. entry visas to China, import tax for goods entering Vietnam) have been reformulated and tightened several times and thus heavily impacted traders and their businesses.

The concept of private indirect government is helpful in understanding the ongoing process of the selling of land-use rights to private investors to establish new marketplaces. These privately funded and managed markets are not to be thought of as entities outside of the state's reach, but in fact have to conform to the state's requirements and in many ways embody the state's vision of modernisation as stipulated in the master plans of 2007 and 2015 for market development (see Bộ Công Thương [Ministry of Industry and Trade] 2007; Bộ Công Thương [Ministry of Industry and Trade] 2015). Unlike other scholars who applied the concept of private indirect government, I am not primarily concerned with private investors, in this case the market owners, but with the role of local cadres and, most of all, the traders and their stance on the collusion of public and private actors.

Representatives of the local state inhabit a particularly interesting, but also ambiguous, double role as commune members and state servants. Marketplace renovations, enacted by higher levels of government, stress local officials' intermediary position and thereby highlight the difficulty to reconcile multiple interests and expectations. One example of the transformation of marketplaces and the management of markets is the study on ethnic markets in a province bordering China by Christine Bonnin and Sarah Turner (2014). In the last few years, the trend to upgrade public markets and to establish privately owned markets has increased in Vietnam and often affected traders negatively as it has given rise to insecurity and uncertainty. The authors point to the problem of the relation between different levels of the government, especially the exclusion of local officials from planning meetings and the lack of communication between local actors and district and provincial authorities. The case of the ethnic minority market that Bonnin and Turner investigated is quite typical for market development across Vietnam, whether in upland or lowland, rural or urban areas. According to the authors, the provincial People's Committee created plans for the renovation of marketplaces according to the national framework with the advice of the Department of Industry and Commerce, which were then disseminated to the district's People's Committee which then repeated the same procedure at the commune level. Subsequently, local officials involved in the management of the marketplace had to make plans for renovating the market in accordance with the guidelines from above, which again had to be approved by officials from the province and the district before implementation. According to Bonnin and Turner, local officials were not kept informed by higher levels of the state and only had a vague idea about the future of the marketplace. This led to hostilities and tensions on the side of traders because they felt insecure and left out of the planning process when local officials—the only accessible arm of the state—could not provide them information.

The dynamics described above bear a close resemblance to the situation in Ninh Hiệp, as my conversation with Mr. Thắng, a leading figure in the market management board of the old market, would reveal. Although it is his responsibility to allocate stalls to traders and keep track of stallholders, he made clear that his position does not allow him to make decisions regarding the management of the market itself. This decision fell within the competence of the People's Committee of Hanoi, which decided in the early 2000s that the People's Committee of Ninh Hiệp should directly manage the market. However, when the demand for selling space rose dramatically within a few years and managing the market became more time consuming, the communal cooperative was assigned to create a market management board to head the operations. Despite the limited scope of Mr. Thắng's position and power, Ninh Hiệp people expect him to defend their interests and trust him to preserve the market as public property. It is only because of the people's trust that he can manage the market, he said. "If people don't trust you, you can't do anything. Only if you win the heart of the people (*lòng dân*), you can do". Thus, many traders pin their hopes on the cooperative and the local state to withstand pressure from above.

During our conversation, Mr. Thắng emphasised the importance of his intermediary role. Traders at the old market need him to confirm that they are indeed stallholders whenever they wish to take out a loan from the bank. In case a trader cannot pay back the money in due time, the bank will inform Mr. Thắng and tell him to close down the stall. This, however, had not happened yet, as Mr. Thắng assured me.

But his role is not without friction. Mr. Thắng is evidently caught in a conflict of interests between higher levels of government and the people of Ninh Hiệp. The interests of these two sides collide as the traders at the old market insist that the cooperative should continue to manage the market, while authorities at the town and district level push for the renovation of the old market and—as became apparent in the 2010 incident—favour privatisation.

A prominent aspect of Mr. Thắng's role was a lack of transparency. Recently, he was involved in the administrative aspects of a plan for the renovation of the old market. For a long time he did not hear back from the district's People's Committee to whom the plan was submitted and was thus left in the dark about what was going to happen. He, just like the rest of the community, did not know how the future of the market would look like. To my surprise, however, this uncertainty did not trouble Mr. Thắng the least bit. He was not at all enthusiastic about the prospect of changes in the management since he enjoyed doing the job. Additionally, there was very little incentive for him to switch jobs since his wife and many of his relatives were traders at the marketplace. In the same conversation, he expressed the tense relation between the community and higher levels of the state, and particularly his own complicated position as a community member and state employee. When talking about the higher-level authorities and investors involved in the development of the old market, he emphasised that they (*người ta*) were not from Ninh Hiệp but had money and power to decide the fate of the market. He, however, was from Ninh Hiệp. And although he himself had developed a plan to upgrade the market as he was told to do by his superiors, he sees the old market as the people's property and should not be taken away from them.

When asking Mr. Thắng how he maintains good relations with the traders so as to establish trust, he answered that openness (*công khai*) and transparent planning (*quy hoạch minh bạch*) were the two most important factors. And yet although Mr. Thắng presents himself as a "man of the people", his and other local authorities' popularity in the commune is far from unchallenged. Their reputation suffered immensely when the approval of yet another private market project became public in January 2014. As soon as the news spread in the commune, traders at the old market shut down their stalls and went to the People's Committee of Ninh Hiệp to demand details of the plan. Much to their outrage, they learned that the planned project called for the relocation of the old market's parking lot and the moving of the secondary school from the centre to the periphery of the village. Their frustration escalated even further when the president of the commune could not provide more details or even a rough time frame for the project. According to an article in an online Vietnamese newspaper, what evoked discontent among villagers and in the wider public were "irregularities" in the way local authorities appointed contractors to demolish the parking lot and the school before having the official documents in their hands (Châu Anh 2014).

On the one hand, this case illustrates the extent to which local officials often feel under pressure from higher levels of government as well as from their community because they are supposed to provide information which they either do not possess or is not as detailed as locals demand. On the other hand, it also shows that for traders in Ninh Hiệp, this way of being governed from a distance and not being given accurate information about the near future adds to the already uncertain situation they find themselves due to the rising competition and other business-related risks. As I mentioned earlier, while personal relations with local officials were crucial for traders in the past, the significance of these connections has markedly diminished in the post-reform era due to the limited role of local officials in the planning and decision-making processes of market projects. Higher levels of government are out of reach for all but a few powerful individuals, who are able to successfully build relations and propose projects in line with the state's vision of modern markets. Their relevance, however, is defined by the state's higher goals and ideals.

Talking of "the people" or "traders" in a general way does not do justice to the different interests of individual actors. For some traders, especially the younger ones, the marketisation may not have been bad after all, as it has provided them with an opportunity to obtain a stall. Furthermore, traders with enough money benefitted from marketisation by acquiring more than one stall so as to operate at different locations in the market, or to rent them out to other vendors. In the following section, I examine traders' strategies to cope with uncertainties, while paying particular attention to the dynamics that govern how a particular group of traders, who were active in recent protests, interact with government authorities.

Debunking the Socialist Rhetoric

When facing uncertainties rooted in the state's ambiguous actions and decisions, traders either try to get around or confront state policies and practices with moral claims. Getting around official policies manifests itself in different forms: operating a stall without a business license, evading taxes, not declaring imported goods when bringing them into Vietnam, and using public places as selling spaces. At times, these practices acquire an unmistakable visibility, as with the claiming of public space for private purposes. Other times, traders would talk about their less visible acts of opposition to state power. As some traders would tell me, if one wanted to make a profit, one had to find ways of evading taxes, because otherwise all profit would go to the state. Furthermore, the import of Chinese clothing and counterfeited Western brands through informal channels is substantial for their businesses. Thus, uncertainty can also offer scope for action, especially in combination with informal, illegal, and not-yet-(il)legal practices (Nordstrom 2000; Smart and Zerilli 2014).

The populace may rely on moral claims to exert pressure on the state and use policies and legislations as a boomerang to hold the state accountable to its own rules (Labbé 2014, 172–173). The potency of moral claims and their relevance to policy decisions was abundantly evident in the previously discussed privatisation attempt in 2010 in Ninh Hiệp, whereby the traders were able to impede a project by making their voices and moral arguments heard. In Ninh Hiệp, resisting decisions of the state is most visible in the form of protests against new market projects. When analysing current developments—protests and moral claims—I specifically look at a group of traders at the old market, whose solidarity with each other is based on the common pursuit of ensuring that the old market remains a public property. Most of these traders are middle-aged women, who contributed financially to the establishment of the market in 2001, and many of them were already engaged in trade prior to Đổi mới. Another experience they share is that they have benefitted not as much from the market boom as others, especially because the stalls that were allotted to them were located in the least desirable parts of the market. Thus, while considering themselves as the "original traders" and remembering the obstacles related to trade in the pre-Đổi mới period, they see their businesses threatened in the wake of the state's push for market transformation. What the traders at the old market pointed out most strongly was their appreciation of freedom and their dislike of being managed by a private company.

One of these traders is Mrs. Dung, who I mentioned at the beginning of this chapter. The market is, as she emphasised, all the villagers have, the main source of income. Therefore, it is important to protect it from being sold. She said:

> There are four, five investors who want to buy the [old] market, but we won't let this happen. We protest and let our voices be heard. This is a market, it belongs to everybody, not to one person with a lot of money. We don't want to depend on anybody. The market is our bread and butter (*miếng cơm manh áo*, lit.: rice and shirt). When somebody has finished school, has no job, they can sell at the market. We don't want a company to step in. They say they want to build a second and a third floor, and that we could stay in the ground floor. But reconstruction costs a lot of money. Once they have built more floors, they will raise our stall rent fee, too.

Mrs. Dung continued that the traders at the old market would like to partially renovate the building, but they wanted to use their own money to do so. In particular, they want to lift up the roof so that the market is cooler and the air less stuffy. What she suggests is that each trader contributes money for the renovation according to the size and location of one's stall, so that those with a big stall facing the main aisle pay more than those with a small stall in the back of the market. This would be a fair solution, she said, and, most importantly, would assure them to keep control over the market.

Although the privatisation attempt in 2010 was impeded as a result of the traders' protests, the town and district level state took steps to further the marketisation process in the village. Subsequently, the traders who wanted to keep the market a public property joined forces for collective action. They organised protests in front of the local government as well as sometimes the district's or even town-level People's Committee to voice their outrage towards the state's policies, especially since the approval of the third private market in January 2014. This project drew a particularly strong reaction from villagers because it laid claim to the land on which the secondary school and the parking lot of the old market stood. According to villagers, approving this project would have a negative impact on education by placing private over public interests and would at the same time lead to the eventual closing down of the old market. They worried that if customers could not park their motorbike next to the market but are forced to park it more than one kilometre away, they would stop coming to the old market and instead go to a market with a parking lot.

When on 18 December 2015 special police forces went into Ninh Hiệp to enforce the appropriation of the land that had been designated for the construction of the new trade centre, they were met with fierce resistance from some hundred traders who demonstrated in the street by holding up Vietnamese flags. In the days that followed, children did not go to school but accompanied their parents at the protests before the People's Committee of the commune. In addition to that, traders occupied the parking lot of the old market day and night. By establishing a fully decorated ancestral altar with a big picture of Hồ Chí Minh and portraits of martyrs, they appealed to the government and the Communist Party, arguing that appropriating public land to pursue private interests was not in accordance with socialist ideas of equality. Next to the altar, they put a coffin so as to demonstrate their readiness to sacrifice their lives in order to protect the old market. Furthermore, some traders wrote letters to government officials to urge them to retreat from expropriating the communal land. After several days of protests by traders and their children, the demolition of the parking lot was put off while the plan for the new trade centre underwent a fresh round of scrutiny (Dũng Nguyễn 2015). The Deputy Prime Minister of Vietnam decided that the chairman of the People's Committee of Hanoi should thoroughly inspect the complaints and claims raised by Ninh Hiệp traders. Measures should then be taken to settle the case in accordance with Vietnamese law and report the decision to the Prime Minister before 31 December 2015 (An Lê 2015).

As the case illustrates, the traders exerted pressure on the state by arguing that the approval of this market project was tantamount to the state's violation of its own principles in numerous ways. Not only should land not be expropriated from the poor and be given to the rich, but, as the Party's ideology of social justice suggests, public goods—the old market and the school—should not be destroyed for the benefit of one or a few individuals. As education has been a cornerstone of many state campaigns for decades, sacrificing the school, of all things, for another private market was in stark contrast of official rhetoric. On top of that, the school had been renovated only 3 years before the plan. Tearing it down now would highlight just how short-sighted state planners had been. Finally, the traders claimed that this project would seriously threaten their livelihood, as the market was all they had to generate an income.

To support their claims and demand social justice in the spirit of Hồ Chí Minh, Ninh Hiệp traders usually brandish national symbols, such as the Vietnamese flag and wear T-shirts of the same colour and pattern (red with a yellow star). During a protest in April 2014 in Hanoi, they wore red shirts with yellow lettering "I love my homeland Vietnam" (*Tôi yêu tổ quốc Việt Nam*) on the front side under the star and "Request the three levels of government to give back the land to the people of Ninh Hiệp, Gia Lâm district, Hanoi city" (*Yêu cầu 3 cấp chính quyền trả lại đất cho nhân dân Ninh Hiệp, huyện Gia Lâm, thành phố Hà Nội*) on the back. In addition, they had red headbands on which the following was written: "Party! Rescue the people of Ninh Hiệp" (*Đảng ơi! Cứu nhân dân Ninh Hiệp*). This way of articulating demands linked to the government while at the same time openly approving of the state and the Communist Party is typical for protests in Vietnam, as Ben Kerkvliet (2014) noted. He observed that most protests in Vietnam are similar to each other—not only in form, but also in content. A major reason for protests is land confiscation and low compensation, and the ensuing feeling of injustice. To a certain extent, these protests resemble the model drawn by the rightful resistance approach, where citizens use the state's law and rhetoric to raise awareness of their rights in a peaceful way (see O'Brien and Li 2006). Yet, Kerkvliet argues that in many cases the rights protesters assert go beyond those officially acknowledged, and thus exceed the theory of rightful resistance. Often, citizens do not ask for compensation just enough to survive, as James Scott's (1976) moral economy approach would have it, but demand to negotiate directly with investors to reach a price equivalent to the land's real value (Kerkvliet 2014). The protests in Ninh Hiệp are strikingly similar to Kerkvliet's observation: although villagers invoke the right to make a living, their claims go beyond the mere subsistence level. They do not only assert that land should not be confiscated against their will, but they also perceive it as unjust to be paid a low compensation, if at all, while the investors enrich themselves.

Uncertainty has been a constant companion of traders in Ninh Hiệp. Yet, not only have the sources of uncertainty changed according to the political–economic context, but shifting power relations have had a substantial impact on how uncertainties were perceived and dealt with. While the support of local cadres was fundamental in the pre-Đổi mới and transition period for traders to be able to engage successfully in trade, the new modes of governance in the post-reform era have shifted power relations and thereby put traders in Ninh Hiệp in a much more vulnerable situation.

Mrs. Dung and many other traders perceive the post-Đổi mới period as one of ambivalence. The coupling of the socialist rhetoric of an equal and democratic society with neoliberal practices of privatisation and the expropriation of communal land leads to a paradox situation where the promulgated freedom of being a trader is restricted through laws that aim to "upgrade" marketplaces and "civilise" trade, thereby making markets a much less inclusive space. Traders find themselves trapped between an unpredictable state, privatisation processes and a vague legal framework. Nevertheless, they are not at the complete mercy of an all-powerful state, but actively seek ways to organise their business. As the most recent privatisation attempt vividly demonstrates, publicly voiced moral claims exert strong pressure on the state and in doing so may challenge decrees, even if they have already been authorised by higher levels of government. I attempted to shed light on the productive side of uncertainty and to stress the adaptability of traders when dealing with difficult situations. The productive side of uncertainty is by no means restricted to economic success, but also includes the creation of support networks within the community and more generally the reproduction of the community by the maintenance of relations of mutual dependence and trust.

However, a word of caution is warranted here. Although the productive side of uncertainty offers a helpful perspective, we must avoid the pitfalls of overlooking the ever present realities embedded in a precarious socio-economic context. While accounts of traders' success in dealing with uncertainty might be uplifting, one must never lose sight of the material realities associated with occupying the lower end of a power hierarchy, which can have profoundly detrimental consequences on how one deals with uncertainty in day-to-day life.

The question of how businesses are organised in the realm of the family leads us to the next chapter. Family businesses are not only the locus of intimacy and trust, but also of potential conflict. Rather than static and isolated entities, they should be seen as dynamic formations connected with each other and embedded in a particular context.

Notes

1. For more information on the functioning of Intershops, see Melanie Beresford and Đặng Phong (2000, Chap. 6).
2. The question of whether Ninh Hiệp produced enough to meet the plan, respectively, what happened if they did not reach the target is neither tackled in the literature nor do I have empirical data to give an accurate answer.
3. The term "outside economy" (*kinh tế ngoại*) denotes household-based economic practices, which were not carried out for the cooperative but to contribute to the income of one's family.
4. I did not find much official or secondary data about this particular system except for a short note in Abrami's (2002, 389) dissertation, where she mentions two-way trade as "marketized form of exchange between

and among state and cooperatives". Therefore, I rely mainly on conversations and interviews I conducted.

5. According to Chaps. 4, 5 and 6, 1986 Marriage and Family Law (Vietnam 1986).
6. Alternative markets that were sometimes mentioned besides Vietnam are South Korea, Japan, Thailand, Malaysia, Indonesia and the Philippines.
7. The tense relationship between Vietnam and China relates to the South China Sea issue, a territorial dispute involving six countries. Although this is not a new issue at all, it bears high potential for conflict as it is still unresolved. After two battles—the Battle of the Paracel Islands in 1974 and the Johnson South Reef Skirmish in 1988—and dozens of confrontations between Vietnamese and Chinese forces since then (Hayton 2014, 23), the conflict flared up again in May 2014 when China deployed an oil-rig off the Paracel Islands, leading to a 6-month-long diplomatic crisis between the two countries and multiple anti-China protests in Vietnamese cities (Panda 2015; Hayton 2015).
8. See Decree no. 02/2003/ND-CP of January 14, 2003 on Development and Management of Marketplaces (Vietnam 2003a).
9. According to the Law on Land from 2003, land-use rights can be obtained for a period of 50 years (Vietnam 2003b).
10. By "tidy up", I mean the maintenance of orderly public space, which is enforced—sometimes violently—by special police forces in Hanoi and adjacent areas. This happens in Ninh Hiệp one to two times a year for several days. Traders know about this shortly in advance and can prepare their stall accordingly. Still, it is a strong interference into their businesses and leads to a major loss for traders because they cannot sell for days and "die" on their goods (*chết hàng*).

References

Abrami, Regina M. 2002. Self-Making, Class Struggle and Labor Autarky: The Political Origins of Private Entrepreneurship in Vietnam and China. Ph.D. thesis, University of California, Berkeley.

An Lê. 2015. Phó Thủ Tướng Yêu Cầu Giải Quyết Dứt điểm vụ Việc ở Ninh Hiệp [The Deputy Prime Minister Requires a Final Decision on the Matter in Ninh Hiệp]. *Đời Sống Pháp Luật [Legal Life]*, December 25. http://

www.doisongphapluat.com/tin-tuc/tin-trong-nuoc/ptt-yeu-cau-giai-quyet-dut-diem-vu-viec-o-ninh-hiep-a125901.html.

Beresford, Melanie, and Đặng Phong. 2000. *Economic Transition in Vietnam: Trade and Aid in the Demise of a Centrally Planned Economy*. Cheltenham: Elgar.

Bộ Công Thương [Ministry of Industry and Trade]. 2007. *Phê Duyệt Quy Hoạch Tổng Thể Phát Triển Mạng Lưới Chợ Trên Phạm vi Toàn Quốc đến Năm 2010 và định Hướng đến Năm 2020 [Approving the Master Plan to Develop the Market Network on a National Scale until 2010 and Orientations towards 2020]. Số 12/2007/QĐ-BCT*. http://vanban.chinhphu.vn/portal/page/portal/chinhphu/hethongvanban?class_id=1&mode=detail&document_id=52836.

Bộ Công Thương [Ministry of Industry and Trade]. 2015. *Phê Duyệt Quy Hoạch Tổng Thể Phát Triển Mạng Lưới Chợ Toàn Quốc đến Năm 2025, Tầm Nhìn đến Năm 2035 [Approving the Master Plan to Develop the Market Network on a National Scale until 2025, Visions until 2035]. Số 6481/QĐ-BCT*. http://thuvienphapluat.vn/van-ban/Thuong-mai/Quyet-dinh-6481-QD-BCT-2015-Quy-hoach-tong-the-phat-trien-mang-luoi-cho-toan-quoc-den-2025-280779.aspx.

Bonnin, Christine, and Sarah Turner. 2014. Remaking Markets in the Mountains: Integration, Trader Agency and Resistance in Upland Northern Vietnam. *The Journal of Peasant Studies* 41 (3): 321–342.

Châu Anh. 2014. Chợ Vải Nổi Tiếng Ninh Hiệp đang Bị "bức Tử"? [Is the Famous Cloth Market in Ninh Hiệp Forced to Commit Suicide?], March 18. http://bizlive.vn/du-an/cho-vai-noi-tieng-ninh-hiep-dang-bi-buc-tu-120997.html.

Đảng bộ huyện Gia Lâm [Gia Lam district Party], and Ban chấp hành đảng bộ xã Ninh Hiệp [Party Executive Committee of Ninh Hiep]. 2007. *Lịch Sử Cách Mạng. Đảng Bộ và Nhân Dân Ninh Hiệp [History of Revolution. Party and People in Ninh Hiep]*. Hanoi: Nhà xuất bản văn hóa dân tộc.

Dũng Nguyễn. 2015. Tạm Dừng Dự án Trung Tâm Thương Mại ở Ninh Hiệp [Pause the Project for the Commercial Centre in Ninh Hiệp]. *Tiền Phong [Pioneers]*, December 30. http://www.tienphong.vn/xa-hoi/tam-dung-du-an-trung-tam-thuong-mai-o-ninh-hiep-953167.tpo.

Endres, Kirsten W. 2014a. Making Law: Small-Scale Trade and Corrupt Exceptions at the Vietnam-China Border. *American Anthropologist* 116 (3): 611–625.

Endres, Kirsten W. 2014b. Downgraded by Upgrading: Small-Scale Traders, Urban Transformation and Spatial Reconfiguration in Post-Reform Vietnam. *Cambridge Anthropology* 32 (2): 97–111.

Harvey, David. 2005. *A Brief History of Neoliberalism*. Oxford: Oxford University Press.

Hayton, Bill. 2014. *The South China Sea: The Struggle for Power in Asia*. New Haven: Yale University Press.

Hayton, Bill. 2015. A New Confidence-Building Process for the South China Sea? *The Diplomat*, November 26. http://thediplomat.com/2015/11/a-new-confidence-building-process-for-the-south-china-sea/.

Kerkvliet, Benedict J. 2014. Protests over Land in Vietnam: Rightful Resistance and More. *Journal of Vietnamese Studies* 9 (3): 19–54. doi:10.1525/vs.2014.9.3.19.

Labbé, Danielle. 2014. *Land Politics and Livelihoods on the Margins of Hanoi, 1920–2010*. Vancouver: UBC Press.

Nordstrom, Carolyn. 2000. Shadows and Sovereigns. *Theory, Culture & Society* 17 (4): 35–54.

O'Brien, Kevin J., and Lianjiang Li. 2006. *Rightful Resistance in Rural China*. Cambridge: Cambridge University Press.

Panda, Ankit. 2015. 1 Year Later: Reflections on China's Oil Rig "Sovereignty-Making" in the South China Sea. *The Diplomat*, December 5. http://thediplomat.com/2015/05/1-year-later-reflections-on-chinas-oil-rig-sovereignty-making-in-the-south-china-sea/.

Ronnås, Per, and Bhargavi Ramamurthy. 2001. *Entrepreneurship in Vietnam: Transformation and Dynamics*. Copenhagen: NIAS Press.

Schwenkel, Christina, and Ann Marie Leshkowich. 2012. Guest Editors' Introduction: How Is Neoliberalism Good to Think Vietnam? How Is Vietnam Good to Think Neoliberalism? *Positions* 20 (2): 379–401.

Scott, James C. 1976. *The Moral Economy of the Peasant: Rebellion and Subsistence in Southeast Asia*. New Haven: Yale University Press.

Smart, Alan, and Filippo M. Zerilli. 2014. Extralegality. In *A Companion to Urban Anthropology*, ed. Donald M. Nonini, 222–238. Chichester: Wiley-Blackwell.

Spitzenpfeil, Annette. 1999. Craft Villages in Vietnam's Economic Transformation Process. In *Vietnamese Villages in Transition*, ed. Bernhard Dahm, V. J. H. Houben, Martin Grossheim, Kirsten W. Endres, and Annette Spitzenpfeil, 121–154. Passau: Department of Southeast Asian Studies, Passau University.

Vietnam. 1986. Marriage and Family Law. http://www.refworld.org/docid/3ae6b54dc.html.
Vietnam. 1997. *Commercial Code. 58 L-CTN*. http://vietnamembassy-usa.org/news/2002/10/commercial-code-10-may-1997.
Vietnam. 2003a. *Development and Management of Marketplaces. 02/2003/ND-CP*. http://www.moj.gov.vn/vbpq/en/Lists/Vn%20bn%20php%20lut/View_Detail.aspx?ItemID=8898.
Vietnam. 2003b. *Law on Land. No. 13-2003-QH11*. http://moj.gov.vn/vbpq/en/Lists/Vn%20bn%20php%20lut/View_Detail.aspx?ItemID=8269.
Wisensale, Steven K. 1999. Marriage and Family Law in a Changing Vietnam. *Journal of Family Issues* 20 (5): 602–616.

4

Building Families, Building Businesses

Family businesses in East and Southeast Asia have attracted attention in various disciplines in the social sciences over the last decades, often in combination with the question of economic growth. Especially in the contexts of China, Hong Kong and Taiwan, there were lively discussions about whether the family and particular family values and organisation structures were an obstacle to, or rather the engine for, economic growth (Whyte 1996; Creed 2000; Yeung 2000). The debate about cultural values and economic performance was inspired by Max Weber's seminal work on the Protestant ethic, based on the assumption that a Protestant ethic was compatible with an "attitude which seeks profit rationally and systematically" (Weber [1930] 2001, 27). Confucian values, however, were considered as contradictory to individual capitalist accumulation. While studies that saw Chinese families as obstacles for economic growth stressed nepotism and paternalism, other studies emphasised the success of Chinese family firms and their collectivism, loyalty and mutual care (Redding 1990).

However, in anthropology, the debate was branded as Orientalist in attempting to essentialise "Chinese culture" and keep it in an ever-traditional state. Susan Greenhalgh (1994) was a prominent critic of

E. Horat, *Trading in Uncertainty*,
DOI 10.1007/978-3-319-55648-2_4

the Orientalist view and instead called for a critical examination of Chinese family businesses with a focus on internal power structures.[1] She argued that the ideology of Confucian culture and economic development, henceforth called the "Confucian thesis", concealed systematic gender and generation inequalities, on which the economic success was actually built. In her article, she depicts Taiwanese family firms through the lens of patriarchal familism and points to "steep inequalities of gender and generation" within the family firm. However, understanding power structures simply as domination and oppression exerted by a male family patriarch over his subordinates—wife, children and workers if any—does not capture the complexity and multidimensionality of how power in family businesses actually works. Such studies tend to comprehend power structures as stable, clear and one-dimensional. I aim to challenge this view with my research in trying to grasp subtle, and at times ambiguous, dynamics and processes within families. I argue that family businesses in Ninh Hiệp do not function like capitalist enterprises, but are multipurpose entities. Following Leshkowich (2014, 78), family businesses are not to be taken as naturally given but must be understood in the specific context in which they emerge. Yet, in contrast to Leshkowich (2014, 96), I argue that in Ninh Hiệp family businesses are not necessarily seen as a last resort, but often as the best possible solution to deal with a rapidly changing environment. Rather than maximisation of economic profit, the rationale underlying family businesses is to satisfy diverse needs while using the available resources. These needs are not only of an economic nature, but are also socially and emotionally significant. Besides being a unit of production and consumption, the household is also a locus for practical and emotional care, even if family members may at times be at odds with one another regarding their priorities and interests for themselves and for the family. In this sense, the family reproduces society through recreating and at times challenging social norms and systems of value.

In order to understand family businesses, it is indispensable to also examine the Vietnamese family, as there is no clear boundary between business and family—a fact that can be seen in several aspects. For instance, getting married and establishing a business usually coincide. Furthermore, the house is not only used as residential space for family members, but also as a working space; equally, the market stall is used not only for selling, but also for various other activities, such as playing cards and chatting with friends, preparing vegetables for dinner, reading and embroidering. Most families do not clearly distinguish between household and business budgets, but spend money for household consumption and business ventures alike. Thus, family and business are spatially, temporally, financially and emotionally inextricable. In this chapter, I will shed light on two dimensions: one focuses on the family as the subject of national politics, while the other stresses internal processes and structures within families, respectively family businesses.

The Vietnamese Family in the Second Half of the Twentieth Century

The family is a central economic and social institution in Vietnam and is often regarded as a focus of social change (Haines 2006, 197). Importantly, the family is also a highly politicised unit, as a closer look at the history reveals. In Confucian doctrines, the family was represented as a microcosm of society and the fundamental basis of the national macrocosm (Gammeltoft 1999). Later, during revolutionary times, the family was considered the "cell of society", according to Hồ Chí Minh's famous dictum: "If society is good, the family will be good; if the family is good, society will be good" (Gammeltoft 1999, 75). Since Đổi mới and subsequent modernisation and urbanisation processes, the family became even more indispensable as the state reduced public services and transferred its responsibility partly to the family.

In order to understand the Vietnamese state's preoccupation with the family, laws and regulations directed at the institution of the family need to be looked at closely. In the following sections, I will recount the major policy developments that shape the family in the course of more than 50 years. According to Vũ Mạnh Lợi (1991), the Constitution of the New Democratic and Republic State of 1946 already contained directives towards the family, especially targeting the abolition of the practice of arranged marriage, which was seen as detrimental to gender equality by the Socialist state. Subsequent decrees, for example Decree 97, passed in May 1950, further supported free-choice marriages by recognising the right to choose a spouse (Jayakody and Vũ Tuấn Huy 2008, 210). The Marriage and Family Law of 1959 was another crucial document that shaped the family in North Vietnam, as well as after the reunification in 1975 of the entire country. This law encouraged equal rights for men and women, the prohibition of bride- and groom-wealth and large wedding feasts, and discouraged so-called superstitious beliefs and practices, such as fortune telling and horoscope reading (Jayakody and Vũ Tuấn Huy 2008, 215). Moreover, it rendered polygamy illegal and declared monogamy as the official form of Vietnamese marriage and codified basic rights of women and children against oppression and abuse in the home (Wisensale 2000, 80). More generally, the law aimed at modernising the country by eliminating all sorts of inequality as well as practices that were seen as opposed to social and economic progress, especially religious practices (Malarney 1996; Kleinen 1999; Endres 2001; Taylor 2007). During this time, commonly referred to as the revolutionary era, the state-defined purpose of the family was to contribute to build an equal society, to defend the country and to raise children as useful citizens of society (Vũ Mạnh Lợi 1991). Land was collectivised, and cooperatives were the main units of production. Although households were allowed to use 5% of the land for consumption (Abrami 2002, 2), some households engaged in extra economic activities, especially petty trade, to make ends meet.

It was only in the context of Đổi mới that household-based production was officially propagated. According to Danièle Bélanger and Magali Barbieri (2009, 21), the role of the family to support and benefit from the reform process was crucial:

> In Vietnam, the family was initially the strongest institution with the position, the means, and the motivation to take advantage of the new economic opportunities created by the reforms. A series of policy measures specifically intended to accelerate the household's ability to reinvest its productive role, making the family instrumental in the implementation of the reforms, further reinforced this phenomenon.

However, the family gained not only more freedom to choose how to sustain itself, but was also reminded of the duties and mutual obligations among family members to care for each other, according to the renewed Law on Marriage and the Family of 1986 and the 1994 Decree on Marriage and the Family, amended in 2000 (Vũ Mạnh Lợi 2000; Wisensale 2000). These laws can be seen as a direct response to the thorough socio-economic changes underway since the mid-1980s, dealing with the major concerns of the state in the face of the opening and exposure of the country to foreign influences. The main issues these laws tackled were rights and responsibilities in conjugal and intergenerational relations, in particular mutual assistance in the parent–children and grandparent–grandchildren relation, out-of-wedlock births, adoptions and divorce, as well as marriages between Vietnamese and foreigners and adoptions of Vietnamese children by foreigners (Wisensale 1999). Thus, while households were strongly encouraged to perform as independent economic units, they were constrained in other aspects and were especially cautioned to not adapt to Western family models and values. One example, according to Rukmalie Jayakody and Vũ Tuấn Huy (2008, 219), was the concern over cohabitation, as stated in the 2000 Family and Marriage Law: "To protect [the] marriage and family system, males and females who live together without marriage are not recognized by law".

After having offered an insight into the state's ambition to shape the family through laws and regulations, I will now discuss its impact on a few key issues, starting with the findings of Jayakody and Vũ Tuấn Huy (2008). Their data on family change are based on a comparative study of "The War Cohort" (married between 1963 and 1971), "The Reunification Cohort" (married between 1977 and 1985) and "The Renovation Cohort" (married between 1992 and 2000). The strong discouragement of arranged marriages and the promotion of free-choice marriages seem to have yielded the intended result, with more people reported that they chose their spouses with parental approval or independently in later cohorts. Concerning wedding practices, the state seems to have had the most control over the war cohort, since the elaborateness of weddings that the state tried to minimise has markedly risen in later cohorts, in terms of the food served, the gifts received and the bride wealth paid. Moreover, later cohorts also increasingly sought for advice from fortune tellers. Regarding post-marital co-residence, the state's endorsement for couples to decide freely where to reside after marriage and not be drawn into customary practices did not bring the planned effect, as the number of couples living with the husband's parents has risen in later cohorts, while matrilateral co-residence and independent habitation have declined.

The authors stress two main findings: first, they conclude that there is a trend towards less state control over time; second, they note that although the Vietnamese family has changed profoundly in the last decades, the direction of change was not consistent. While the second finding, indicating that some features of the contemporary family seem to imply a change away from pre-socialist patterns, whereas others seem to point to a return, or revival of them, is supported by most scholars (e.g. Bélanger and Barbieri 2009; Werner 2009, among others), the first finding is challenged by some (Gammeltoft 1999; Werner 2009). It is argued that when looking at other areas, especially gender and family planning, the state apparently did not withdraw its grip on the family in the aftermath of Đổi mới, but continuously revised and detailed legal stipulations regarding the family. This argument is in accordance with neoliberal governance insofar as the state is not less influential in shaping the family than in the past, but applies other techniques. This idea will be further elaborated in the next chapter. Here suffice to illustrate this point briefly with the example of the family planning policy—stipulating that each couple is only allowed to have one or two children—which was propagated through the "happy family" (*gia đình hạnh phúc*) campaign. According to this campaign, two conditions were decisive for a happy family: sufficient finances, mainly achieved through hard work and family planning, and harmonious family relations. That the state's impact on the family proved to be remarkably thorough and long-lasting was demonstrated by Gammeltoft (1999), whose study on a rural village in the Red River Delta illustrated how villagers adopted the idea of the happy family as the ultimate aim of hard daily work. However, the campaign's ideal was not uncritically applied everywhere in Vietnam. In Ninh Hiệp, for instance, hard work and harmonious relations between family members are valued, but the goals of family planning are clearly undermined, as a look at Ninh Hiệp's relatively high birth rate for third child births shows.[2] Villagers often emphasise that a family should have at least three children, but four or five were good, too. Thus, the state's "two-children-happy-family" ideal is not only not internalised in Ninh Hiệp, but even actively resisted.

Jayne Werner (2009), who has conducted research on gender and the state in a village in close proximity to Hanoi, points out that "the successful Đổi Mới family was defined as a market-oriented, efficient unit ready to join the global age" (Werner 2009, 59) and that "the new vision of the family was linked to both the production and reproductive goals of the state" (Werner 2009, 71). Shortly after Đổi mới, most households in this village have switched to trade, with the result that most women became the main breadwinner of the family yet not with the same recognition as men. She shows convincingly how gendered discourses of the household and the construction of womanhood are used as tools for governance by the Vietnamese state, and that the state eventually undermined the goals of gender equality that it formally advocated in some areas of social policy, for instance in education, access to the labour market and to high social positions, as well as an equally shared responsibility to participate in social work (Werner 2009, 61).

Lương Văn Hy (1989) makes a similar point in regard to kinship practices and gender equality. He notes that although women have made significant achievements in the public domains in the twentieth century and the importance of patrilineage has generally declined, the structural parameters of Vietnamese kinship have remained remarkably resilient. He emphasises that the complexity of the kinship system is not paid due justice if it is seen as having changed from male-oriented (patrilinear) to non-male-oriented (bilateral). Thus, rather than greater gender equality as promoted by official regulations cited above, in reality the continuity of both patrilinear and bilateral elements in kinship results in an ambiguous position of women vis-à-vis men.

Thus, the family did not lose significance in the context of globalisation and modernisation processes, but plays a key economic, social and political role in contemporary Vietnam. As I have tried to show in this part, the family is at the very heart of social transformation, adapting to and actively shaping processes of change. It is crucial to remember that the transformation in Vietnam in the mid-1980s, often seen as being induced by the Đổi mới policies, is to be understood as the result of preceding processes, which did not leave much choice for the state other than to legalise and accept a de facto situation (Abrami 2002; Bélanger and Barbieri 2009, 4). Therefore, even though the Vietnamese state tried—at times more, at times less successfully—to shape the institution of the family, I agree with Bélanger and Barbieri's (2009, 5) analysis that Vietnamese families have been active forces of change and resilience and thus should be seen as "complex and connected entities that reflect actively and strategically". In terms of gender, especially regarding the position of women in society, the agenda the Vietnamese state pursued had ambiguous effects—while gender equality and the disconnection of women with the domestic sphere were propagated since the beginning of the Socialist era, the expectation of women to meet family obligations is still prevalent today, as we shall see in Chap. 5.

In the following section, I will outline the Vietnamese kinship system, first in general terms, then with a focus on Ninh Hiệp, especially highlighting the ambivalence between idealised patrilineal rules and contesting practices.

Kinship System and Contesting Practices

Many scholars working on Vietnam understand the Vietnamese kinship system as being patrilineal. There is much evidence for this assumption, for instance the existence of patrilineages, the distinction between the paternal, or "inside" (*nội*) and maternal, or "outside" (*ngoại*) sides of the family and its implications, household and residential arrangements, and continuing preference for sons among large parts of the Vietnamese society. Yet, kinship structures are more complex and not homogenous, especially when considering the important economic role of women and their "rights to inherit, accrue, independently manage, and dispose of property" (Haines 2006, 32). As Haines explains, from early on a combination of factors has influenced Vietnamese society at large and the kinship system in particular. Therefore, "one might well find within [the kinship system] elements that, having different sources, are neither homogenous nor simple reflections of any unitary underlying structure" (Haines 2006, 5).

Whitmore (1984) warns of overemphasising similarities between Chinese and Vietnamese social organisations and proposes instead to consider Southeast Asia as a more suitable region for comparison. Thus, even though Vietnam is often considered a patrilineal society, according to Haines the kinship system reflects both patrilineal and bilateral, or even matrilineal, elements among particular social groups at different times (see also Hy Văn Lương 1989). Applying this "mix of influences" approach, as Haines calls it, has three main advantages: first, instead of looking for a static "patrilineal system", emphasis is given to multiple, often ambiguous, elements of kinship, gender and familial roles. Second, the approach does justice to the diversity of influences at different places and times throughout Vietnamese history. In his work, Haines particularly mentions the Cham influence and its strong matrilineal impact in Hội An in Central Vietnam in the seventeenth and eighteenth centuries, as it developed into a major commercial town thanks to the strong trading role of women.[3] The important economic function of women in Vietnamese households has been maintained to the present day, as I will show below. Third, the approach helps to avoid conceiving Vietnamese kinship as a monolithic structure and instead urges observers to look at the complex set of kinship structures and interactions (Haines 2006, 6–8). For the analysis of family businesses in Ninh Hiệp, this approach is very valuable because it accounts for the complexities and ambiguities in the structures of the businesses and the practices of its members. Placing emphasis on actual kinship practices instead of the kinship system helps avoid a static view as it focuses on the flexible and dynamic nature of kinship and the role of actors to actively shape it.

There are quite a few patrilineal practices that are important and meaningful for the people in Ninh Hiệp: first of all, the attendance of anniversaries and the worshipping of ancestors among one's patrilineage continue to be of utmost importance. In addition to an often massive and richly decorated ancestor altar inside the house, some villagers built a lineage hall (*nhà thờ họ*) to show their respect and devotion.

Conversations with villagers further revealed that in case of conflicts, advice from the head of the patrilineage (*trư ởng họ*) is seen as more significant and binding than attempts of the hamlet representative (*trưởng thôn*) to resolve a dispute. In terms of co-residence, it is expected of the eldest son and his wife to stay in the house of his parents after marriage and to take care of them. In turn, the eldest son will inherit the house and the land the house is built on. However, if there is more than one son, the residential land is usually split and divided among the sons so that each of them can build a house on his parcel. Finally, a preference for sons is often expressed.

Yet, when taking a closer look at these patrilineal practices, they turn out to be not that strict and coherent, and sometimes even contradictory to the rule. To start with the last point mentioned, although there is a preference for sons, it is by no means to be understood as a general preference for sons. In line with what was suggested by Haughton and Haughton (1999, 115) for other parts of Vietnam, most people in Ninh Hiệp wish to have at least one son, ideally as the first child, but value daughters and sons equally. Having a son is important for the continuation of the patrilineage, but beyond that sons and daughters are interchangeable for most tasks in the family. There is no education gap between women and men in contemporary generations, and even though parents sometimes consider a higher education more important for sons than for daughters, it does not have a significant impact on reality. Interestingly, in families with one daughter and one son, it can even happen that daughters are encouraged to pursue higher education because the son is supposed to stay back and care for the parents. In general, families that value education and have the means to afford higher education in Hanoi or abroad usually do not distinguish between sons and daughters but support all children equally.

In regard to co-residence, the rule of the eldest son staying with his parents is usually applied. Nevertheless, there are situations that require negotiations and adaptions of the living arrangement. For example, if the eldest son has pursued further education and as a result has moved away from the village to work somewhere else; if the personal relationship between the eldest son, his wife and his parents is contentious; or if, in exceptional cases, one of the other children has no other option than to stay at the parent's house. It is important to note that living arrangements are flexible and can change several times, depending on the life trajectories of the family members. One remarkable feature repeatedly mentioned by villagers is that, in contrast to the general rule in Vietnam of the wife following the husband, Ninh Hiệp women who get married to men from outside the village often stay in Ninh Hiệp and demand their husbands to settle down in the village. However, due to a lack of statistical data, I am not able to give an accurate account of the ratio of non-village men moving in as a result of marriage compared to the proportion of village women moving out so as to follow their husbands. The number of women who marry men from outside is generally quite low, and the only one I knew moved to Hanoi to live with her husband.

Finally, in terms of inheritance, daughters also get their share.[4] Yet, what is perhaps just as important as inheritance is the financial allowance (dowry or pre-mortem payments) daughters receive from their parents when they get married. Instead of land, they get a considerable amount of money to build a house and to establish their own businesses. How much they get depends on the conditions of the family, but it should be enough to ensure her and her husband the start of an independent life. If the husband's family is in a financially more favourable position than the wife's family, his family may support the building of a house or contribute seed money to the business. In conversations with traders, they often explained that the purpose of their business and their hard work was their children's future, which would—hopefully—be outside the market, but if in the market, they should at least have a stall to start their own business. Therefore, in order to acquire one or several stalls at a good location, parents save money for years.

When it comes to business, the matrilateral bond is often more important than the patrilineal. When growing up, daughters contribute to the business of their parents, and when getting married, most of them establish their own business instead of being incorporated into the business of their parents-in-law. Fundamental trade-related knowledge and experience is transmitted from mother to daughter from early on, and even after a daughter has established a new business, mother and daughter often help each other. Thus, while the link between mother and daughter, and also among siblings, is often very strong, the relationship between mothers-in-law and daughters-in-law can be, but is not necessarily, very well developed. This seems to be the case in other parts of Vietnam as well, at least in Ho Chi Minh City, where Leshkowich (2014, 85–88) has made similar observations during her research in Bến Thành market.

Family Businesses in Ninh Hiệp

As the literature on family businesses suggests, the family business is not to be conceived as a separate entity from the family and usually embodies the same structures. While in patrilineal East Asian societies—Taiwan (Greenhalgh 1994), Korea (Leppänen 2007; Park 2011, 2012) and Japan (Hamabata 1990; Bestor 2004)—men are the head of the family and likewise the manager of family businesses, in bilateral Southeast Asian societies, for instance Indonesia (Alexander 1998; Brenner 1998), family businesses are usually run by women. The Vietnamese case is particularly interesting, because the kinship system and gender roles are complex and at times ambiguous, a fact that is reflected in family businesses in Ninh Hiệp. On a blog, the rather special labour division in Ninh Hiệp families was recently stressed, saying that wives were the pillar of the household economy and allegedly contribute 90% of the household income (N.N. 2015). This situation thus contradicts the proverb "Của chồng công vợ" (*property of husband, labour of wife*), the meaning of which is that husbands accumulate and own property, whereas wives make important contributions to support them. The author of the article suggests inverting the phrase to "Của vợ công chồng" when describing families in Ninh Hiệp. In the following sections, I will examine the idea of reversed gender roles more closely. In order to provide a short insight into families and how they organise their businesses, I will first introduce the family of Mr. Thâm, whom I briefly mentioned in the previous chapter.

Mr. Thâm, a man in his mid-fifties and with a boyish smile, was one of the first people I met in the village. His coffee shop, situated at the corner just outside of the market, is popular amongst male traders, taxi and motorbike drivers and customers alike and is crowded at almost any given time of the day so long as the market is open. It is a simple outdoor café with plastic tables and small chairs, offering ice-tea, coffee, fresh sugar cane juice, soft drinks and snacks. Mr. Thâm would often wear simple shorts and a T-shirt, and on his head a green pith helmet of the sort worn by Vietnamese soldiers, as a relic of the time when he served in the army. In the second half of the 1970s, he was sent to Cambodia, and after coming back to Ninh Hiệp in the early 1980s, he worked as a farmer until he opened the café 5 years ago. He employs two girls from another province and his sister-in-law, who runs the café when he goes home for lunch, or when he has to attend weddings, funerals or important events of his patrilineage. His wife, Mrs. Hồng, had already been a trader before the launch of the Đổi mới policies. His café and Mrs. Hồng's shop are on the same street, just about ten metres apart from one another, which means their paths cross several times during the day. Every now and then, they will stop to have a short chat, or make arrangements if need be.

Their first child Huy, born in 1983, lives with his wife Hoa and their newborn baby in their house. Although Mrs. Hồng and Hoa both sell clothing at the market, they have separate businesses. Yet, as they live under one roof, they pool part of their earnings for household-related expenses. Huy constantly commutes between home and the market in order to support Hoa, either with selling and transporting goods, or with cooking and taking care of the baby. In the morning, he goes to the market with Hoa to help her set up her stall, while his mother looks after the baby. When Hoa's stall is ready, he immediately returns home to care for the baby, making it possible for his mother to open the shop. He usually stays at home until noon to prepare lunch. He then brings a lunch box to Hoa at the market and afterwards goes back to his parents' house to eat with them. In the afternoon, he also looks after the baby, unless his wife needs his help with something. In this case, he brings the baby to his grandparents or to his mother's oldest sister, who has already retired from business. If his mother and Hoa come back early in the evening, they will cook dinner, otherwise it is Huy's turn again.

Ngọc, their second child and first daughter, was born in 1984. She lives with her husband, who runs an electronics store, and their school-aged children in a modest house. When they got married, neither his parents, who were farmers, nor her parents could provide the start-up money necessary for her to establish her own business. Instead, Ngọc's mother asked her to participate in her women's clothing business. For a mother and daughter to be business partners is not common in Ninh Hiệp, as children—except for the eldest son—normally move out when they get married, start their own business and handle their finances independently. Yet for Ngọc and her mother, this seemed to be a perfect arrangement, because their husbands are heavily invested in their own work and cannot support them. As Ngọc and her mother both have additional responsibilities related to their households, they are glad to be able to divide labour flexibly between each other. Ngọc frequently travels to China to import clothing for their business, while Mrs. Hồng stays back in Ninh Hiệp to attend to the shop. When both of them are in the village, they often work at the shop in shifts. Both women had the option of developing their own businesses separately. However, the result would inevitably have been two much smaller scale independent businesses generating far less profit while requiring even greater labour. Mrs. Hồng is more than content that she now has more time not only to dedicate to her grandchildren, but also to visit the pagoda more often than she used to when she was younger and managed the business singlehandedly. When Mrs. Hồng runs the shop, Ngọc uses the time to do the household chores, drops off and picks up her children from their school, and frequently visits her parents-in-law. Also, running a single business together has another advantage: Ngọc grew up helping her mother and is thus familiar with the way her mother conducts business. Last but not least, the "joint venture" is an opportunity for both to stay in close contact and to maintain and further foster the emotional bond between them.

Sometimes, when both Mrs. Hồng and Ngọc are busy, the second daughter, Hằng, helps out in the shop. Born in 1991, she was just about to finish her agricultural studies when I first met her. Upon asking about her future plans, I realised that although she did not yet have a clear-cut vision of her future professional pursuits, she was quite explicit about not wanting to end up selling in the market, because she found it tedious and boring.

In July 2013, months after my initial encounter with the family, with an unmistakable twinkle in her eyes, an excited Mrs. Hồng conveyed the message that Hằng was going to get married. Hằng's future husband was Mrs. Hồng's best friends' son, as she eagerly told me, a classmate of Hằng, whose family also lived in Ninh Hiệp. His family was also involved in trade long before Đổi mới, and, according to Mrs. Hồng's account, seemed to be quite well off. Right after graduation and just a couple of weeks before the wedding, his parents arranged a stall for them at the old market so that he and Hằng could establish their own business upon getting married. She was not excited about becoming a trader, but gave into the plan eventually, as it seemed reasonable in the given situation. Since he was the eldest son, Hằng moved to be with him and his parents. Although both of them had acquired university education, they were accustomed to helping out in the family business from an early age and thus knew the essentials about the clothing trade and could start their own business right away. The financial support offered by his parents allowed them to buy merchandise and to pay for the stall rent fee. Since Mr. Thâm and Mrs. Hồng were in a financially less fortunate position and had to support not only Huy and his wife, but also Ngọc's and Mrs. Hồng's business activities, they were glad about the help of Hằng's in-laws. However, Mr. Thâm and Mrs. Hồng followed the wedding custom still practiced in Ninh Hiệp, whereby the bride's parents buy the bed and all its accessories—that is, a mattress, a blanket, pillows and bedclothes.

The above case is demonstrative of a number of pertinent aspects of family businesses in Ninh Hiệp. As mentioned previously, the matrilateral bond is usually more pronounced in business than the patrilineal. Although most businesses are restricted to the nuclear family, the bond between mother and daughter is often very strong, even after daughters have established their own businesses. Most traders said their mother was the first and most important person to turn to for business-related problems. Furthermore, parents support all of their children—not necessarily equally, but according to their capacity and the specific situation. Women are the managers of family businesses and spend most of the day at the marketplace, while men often commute several times a day between home and the market in order to carry out different types of work.

Finally, the family business does not only serve an economic purpose, but also fosters familial bonds. The greatest advantage of the family business model is the satisfaction of diverse needs of family members, and the flexible accomplishment of a range of tasks. This is made possible by the fact that family members most often continue to live in close proximity and maintain cross-cutting ties between their families and businesses. However, the predominance of the family business model also puts pressure on young people who aspire to another job not related to trade. The different needs of family members are not always compatible with each other as we shall see in the coming sections.

Formation and Labour Division

Family businesses in Ninh Hiệp are usually limited to the nuclear family, though sometimes they include a few hired workers. It is only in rare cases that relatives are part of one's family business, and if so, are normally just temporary. Likewise, the involvement of married children in the parent's business is not prevalent, except for bigger businesses with a workshop for production. In this case, the eldest son and his wife, who usually live together with the parents, may join and eventually take over the business.

Traders have to register their business at the district's People's Committee in Gia Lâm according to the type of work they do, for instance home production, small-scale trade, or a combination of both. A family business basically consists of a married couple, usually with the wife being the manager. The establishment of a business normally coincides with marriage and the building of a family, except for some villagers who switched from another occupation to trade in the later part of their life. That the business is a family venture is already indicated by the name, which is almost always a combination of the first names of the wife and husband, for example "Xuân Hinh" or "Hiền Thủy".

Thus, while the wife manages the business, the husband's contribution is seen as "assistance" (*phụ*). What this implies in reality varies greatly from business to business. In most businesses, the husband carries out production and transport-related tasks, such as cutting fabric, sewing, bringing fabric or clothes from home to the market or to customers, helping the wife set up her stall in the morning and taking the goods back home or to the storage room in the evening. If the couple hires workers to produce clothing at home, the husband may supervise the production process. Most women traders work as vendors at the marketplace and maintain relationships with customers, design patterns and manage the budget. Although both men and women may go to other markets to buy fabric and clothing, it is often women who give instructions and make buying decisions. While some men support their wives full time in the business, others have an additional job and assist only part time. Some men were said to do part of the household chores at times, for example cooking and looking after children. However, this highly varies from family to family.

Children tend to help in the family business, usually from the age of fifteen or sixteen, until they get married and start their own business, often as early as from 18 to 22. Helping in the business is not only done out of necessity, but also to learn the practical work of a trader and the functioning of the market. Children sell at the market stall of their parents, either independently or side by side with their parents. They receive pocket money for everyday expenses, for example for snacks or to meet friends in a tea shop, and every now and then their parents buy them more expensive things, such as mobile phones, computers and computer games, and increasingly sponsor travels to popular destinations within Vietnam.

Generational Relations and Business Succession

Some studies on family businesses suggest that business succession is immensely important, for example Theodore Bestor's (2004) study of the world's biggest wholesale fish market in Tokyo, named Tsukiji. Describing vividly how family firms are divided into branches and handed down to consanguine, affinal and fictive kinship members, he mentions that family firms are sometimes traceable for seventeen generations. He especially stresses the master–apprentice relation as a path to succession, which denotes the practice of giving sons of friends and cousins the opportunity to become an apprentice and, in some cases, help them with establishing their own business, become a business partner or eventually take over a branch of one's business (Bestor 2004, 241–244).

Sylvia Yanagisako (2000, 2002), who has investigated silk businesses in Como in northern Italy, provides another example. The firms she examined are established, expanded and continuously invested in for the purpose of passing them from father to son. As Yanagisako (2000, 55) notes:

> Fathering a family and fathering a business are mutually interdependent projects of creation in the cosmology of kinship and business, family and capitalism, which are conveyed in firms' origin stories. To head a family is to provide for it, including providing the productive means of the independence of the family and the means to reproduce that independence in the next generation.

Two points are especially noteworthy in this case: one is the reinforcement of an idealised notion of gender, here masculinity, through an appropriate economic activity. The other is the aspect of class and the reproduction of power through patrilineal business succession from one generation to the next. Thus, the "patriarchal desire (…) for filial succession and family corporate continuity" that Yanagisako (2000, 62) stresses throughout the paper brings together the reproduction of masculinity and class, in this case the upper bourgeois fraction of Como's industrial-capitalist class (Yanagisako 2000, 55).

The case in Ninh Hiệp, however, is quite different. Neither are family businesses headed by men, nor do they enjoy outstanding recognition and prestige in the Vietnamese society. Also, most of them are not passed on from one generation to another. In Ninh Hiệp, the time span that constitutes a generation is short, since early marriages and childbearing are commonplace. At the time their children get married, the parents are still too young to retire from business. Expanding the existing business by including one's children is also not a desired option in most cases. From the outset, the reason to build a family business is not to pass it on to the next generation, but to earn and save money in order to provide for a better future of one's children. Most parents do not consider continuing the trade business as a suitable option for their children to move socially upwards. I suggest seeing this in the light of the ambiguous social standing of traders in contemporary Vietnam: on the one hand, small-scale petty traders have long been despised and occupied the lowest rank of the social ladder. On the other hand, the category of entrepreneurs, which emerged after and mostly consists of (self-made) businessmen in urban areas, is perceived as belonging to a newly constituted middle class. Family businesses in Ninh Hiệp are somewhere in between, neither to be put on a level with small-scale petty traders, nor with private capitalist entrepreneurs.[5] Moreover, in the light of the rapid socio-economic changes contemporary Vietnam is undergoing, trade businesses are not perceived as a stable, reliable means to build a future on. And, as a last point, being a trader is very hard work and involves constant worrying, and thus parents hope for a physically and mentally less stressful occupation for their children.

In reality, however, most children stay back in the village after completing secondary or high school and become traders. Some stated openly that they did not anticipate ending up in the marketplace, like Lan, who is only sixteen years old and one of the youngest vendors at the market. She said that she always wanted to become a teacher, but when she did not pass the exam to enter high school, there were not many other options than becoming a trader.

Even many young people with a university degree return to Ninh Hiệp to sell at the market. This is mainly due to two reasons: one is the difficulty of entering the formal employment sector and the lack of well-paid jobs for graduates in Hanoi and surrounding places. Several informants holding a bachelor's degree told me that after having had an interview for a job in a state-owned company, they decided to go back to sell at the market due to the low salary offered by the company. The other reason for returning to the village is the convenience of combining family and business as well as the independence that comes with establishing a trade business in the village.

As Bélanger and Pendakis (2009, 280) note, education is not only a key for one's individual career, but also a means to enhance the prestige of one's family:

> For young women, succeeding in education is a way to demonstrate to one's parents her worth and increase her own family's status in the village. Educational achievements symbolically represent the best way for young women to "pay back" their parents for their care and love; failing to meet parents' expectations and hopes is a source of shame and discouragement.

In Ninh Hiệp, the level of education not only contributes to one's family status, but also brings with it the expectation of an appropriate form of employment. Those who study successfully but fail to find a proper job and return to the marketplace are ridiculed and seen as having failed by those who never attempted to achieve a high education. As a successful career brings prestige to the family, children, who are considered as having failed, are not only being looked down upon by their peers, but also affect the status of the family negatively. Yet, that becoming a trader is not necessarily a last resort, but a strategy actively decided for will be illustrated by the following stories of Ngân, a woman trader first at the old, then at the new market, and Hiến, a male trader at the new market.

I met Ngân on one of my first visits to Ninh Hiệp when I was walking through the narrow aisles between the stalls in the old market, trying to help the daughter of my host family to find a pair of jeans for her father. Coming to Ngân and her mother's stall and asking about the prices of the jeans they had on display, Ngân smiled at me and said: "You can talk in English with me!" I winced at her accent, and it took a moment to overcome my surprise of meeting somebody at the market who could speak more than just the standard "hello, how are you". Upon asking her about her English language skills, she responded that after having graduated in tourism from Hanoi University, she successfully applied for an internship abroad, where she subsequently worked for 6 months. After coming back to Vietnam, she kept applying to various national and international companies in the hope of finding a position abroad again, yet without success.

During the time I conducted my research in Ninh Hiệp, Ngân and I met frequently. She eagerly explained to me the details about the market, and sometimes, when her mother was not around, she would let me help her arrange the merchandise. It was not difficult to see that she had a lot of practice dealing with customers. When we talked, she often recalled her time abroad and told me about her life there, especially praising the many activities she did in her leisure time and the freedom she experienced.

After she had worked full time at the market in the autumn and winter of 2012, Ngân did not appear at her mother's stall after the Lunar New Year's break. When I asked her mother where Ngân was, she said, with a tone of satisfaction in her voice: "Ngân works now". I understood that this meant that Ngân had found employment outside the marketplace, but still did not know what kind of work it was. Her mother continued: "Ngân works for a travel agency in Hanoi. At the moment, she is in Halong Bay with a group of tourists". From then on, I saw Ngân only at the weekends, when she was off and came to the market to help her mother in her free time. Whenever I asked her mother about her, she would say that Ngân was currently in Thailand or some place in Vietnam with a group of tourists to show around, emphasising how busy she was.

While her mother seemed pleased about Ngân working in an office in Hanoi with frequent trips to other places, Ngân revealed that she found the job exhausting and boring, and after getting in trouble with her boss, she quit and came back to the village. She did complain not only about the long hours she had to work, but also about the bad pay, which was significantly lower than what she had earned as a trader. To be clear, Ngân did not particularly like selling at the market and did not see her future confined to three square metres of a market stall, but dreamed about going abroad and lead what she called "a modern life". Yet, as these dreams have not become a reality, and the prospect of a professional career in Vietnam seemed rather dim, she went back to sell at her mother's market stall without complaining much.

There were two main issues at stake that bothered Ngân's parents. One was that despite her good education, language skills and international working experience, she could not find a stable, well-paid job.

Though becoming a trader is common among Ninh Hiệp people of her generation, the fact that Ngân's educational background is very much above average, made her return to the marketplace seem inadequate. The second issue, which caused them even more of a headache, was the fact that Ngân was not yet married. Being a woman of 25 years of age and not married was a rarity in the village. It was clear from the conversations with Ngân's mother that there was not a single more important thing on earth for her other than that Ngân would find a husband and start a family as soon as possible. Her entire life seemed to depend upon this very essential fact.

Consequently, as an unmarried daughter, Ngân still worked for her parent's business instead of establishing her own one. Even though there was enough work to share among the family members, her parents were unhappy that she did not do what they thought was best for her. Ngân, however, felt very much under pressure from her parents' expectations, but did not give in to finding another job or a husband.

When the tensions between Ngân and her parents got worse in the following months, she decided to open a café right next to the new markets with money from her parents. By opening a café, she hoped to have at least a little bit of distance from her bemoaning parents, and also more independence. This was not exactly how her parents wanted to see her, and also not what she had hoped for herself, but it was an acceptable short-term solution to decrease the tensions in the family and not further damage the status of her family.

Ngân's case shows that while her parents conceive the marketplace as a viable avenue for themselves to earn a living with which to support their children's education, they hope for a more adequate occupation for their daughter. Ngân, however, has her reasons for returning to the village. It also demonstrates clearly that neither the father as the head of the household nor her mother as the manager of the family business, but Ngân herself makes the decision of where to work. Yet, her decision indicates a combination of her own interests as well as thoughts about her parents' considerations, especially regarding the family status. Thus, family businesses are the outcome of a bundle of needs of several actors, and figure as a locus of intimacy as well as potential conflict.

Another villager who chose to become a trader in spite of having a well-paid job was Hiến, a male trader of 31 years of age, who sells sportswear at the new market. Although customers take a look at his merchandise every now and then, the vending is not too stressful most of the time. When there are no customers and no new merchandise arriving, he usually sits in front of the shop on a chair, reads the newspaper or chats with stall neighbours. In the afternoon, he often helps Ngân's mother, whose stall is just opposite his shop, to prepare vegetables for dinner. When male traders pass by his stall to visit him, he quickly boils water in an electric kettle to offer a cup of green tea—the traditional Vietnamese custom when guests pay a visit to somebody's home.

When I met Hiến during my research, it was his second year as a trader. In the past, he had studied engineering at the Hanoi University of Science and Technology (*Trường Đại học Bách Khoa Hà Nội)* and then worked for several years at different construction sites, some of them in Hanoi, others all over Vietnam. For him, returning to his home village (*quê hương*) and becoming a trader was not at all a strategy of last resort, but a deliberate decision in order to combine what he considered most important, not only for himself, but for his family, as he emphasised. As an engineer, he had a good social standing and a decent income, but he could not spend much time with his wife and three children because the work required him to stay at construction sites, often far away from home. As a trader, however, he can be with his family every day and support his wife, not only financially like before, but by sharing labour in the business and at home. Moreover, he can frequently visit his parents, his wife's parents and other close relatives and attend ritual events. Because most of his friends did not move away from the village, he now has the opportunity to meet them more easily than before and sometimes even joins them for a football game. Finally, he stated that being a trader means freedom (*tư do*) and allows him to be his own boss, in the sense of working for and according to the rhythm of his family and carry out diverse family- and business-related tasks in a flexible manner. His current work as a trader is demanding and his days are long as he and his wife have a small workshop at home where they cut and sew clothing in the evening. Moreover, his income as a trader is only about two-thirds of his previous pay as an engineer. Yet, his business is successful, and altogether, Hiến is happy about the situation and thinks that the diverse needs of his family members are much better met with the common family business than when he worked as an engineer.

Hiến's case shows that individuals consider a multitude of factors when making decisions, and rather than going for the highest income, a strategy with which to combine diverse needs of family members is given priority. In contrast to Ngân, Hiến's life trajectory is much appreciated in the village, as he managed to have a high education and a respected job, founded a family and finally returned to the village to perform the various roles of a husband, father and son. These two stories not only shed light on generational relations, but also contain clues about gender roles and expectations in the village, an issue I will turn to in the following section.

Notes

1. Greenhalgh (1994, 749) refers to the position of Chinese family businesses being conducive to economic development due to particular "cultural traits" as "inverse Orientalism".
2. According to official statistics, Ninh Hiệp's rate for third child births is significantly higher than in other communes in Gia Lâm district (UBND xã Ninh Hiệp 2012).
3. Haines (2006, 7) argues, in reference to Alexander (Woodside 1995, 162–163), that on the one hand, Vietnamese women helped their non-Vietnamese merchant husbands in commerce immensely with their local knowledge, and access to raw materials as well as to preserve their wealth, while on the other hand, Vietnamese wives acquired economic skills and formed an entrepreneurial group.
4. According to the Civil Code of Vietnam of 2005, article 676, "heirs at the same level shall be entitled to equal shares of the estate", whereby "the first level of heirs comprises: spouses, biological parents, adoptive parents, offspring and adopted children of the deceased" (Vietnam 2005). However, since inheritance includes a variety of material assets, and daughters (and occasionally sons) already receive significant

pre-mortem payments, it is difficult to assess the equality of inheritance among all children. Yet, the fact that inheritance practices are often the source of conflicts in families in Ninh Hiệp hints at non-equal treatment—real or perceived—among heirs.

5. For an elaborate discussion of different kinds of entrepreneurs in China and how they relate to concepts of class, see Hsu (2007). She distinguishes between cadres who go into business; *getihu*, which is a category for people of low social status earning a living as petty traders; and "good businesspeople", referring to respected and trusted entrepreneurs.

References

Abrami, Regina M. 2002. Self-Making, Class Struggle and Labor Autarky: The Political Origins of Private Entrepreneurship in Vietnam and China. PhD thesis, University of California, Berkeley.

Alexander, Jennifer. 1998. Women Traders in Javanese Marketplaces: Ethnicity, Gender, and the Entrepreneurial Spirit. In *Market Cultures: Society and Morality in the New Asian Capitalisms*, ed. Robert W. Hefner, 203–223. Boulder: Westview Press.

Bélanger, Danièle, and Kate Pendakis. 2009. Daughters, Work and Families in Globalizing Vietnam. In *Reconfiguring Families in Contemporary Vietnam*, ed. Danièle Bélanger, and Magali Barbieri, 265–297. Stanford: Stanford University Press.

Bélanger, Danièle, and Magali Barbieri (eds.). 2009. Introduction: State, Families, and the Making of Transitions in Vietnam. In *Reconfiguring Families in Contemporary Vietnam*, 1–44. Stanford: Stanford University Press.

Bestor, Theodore C. 2004. *Tsukiji: The Fish Market at the Center of the World*. Berkeley: University of California Press.

Brenner, Suzanne A. 1998. *The Domestication of Desire: Women, Wealth, and Modernity in Java*. Princeton: Princeton University Press.

Creed, Gerald W. 2000. "Family Values" and Domestic Economies. *Annual Review of Anthropology* 29: 329–355.

Endres, Kirsten W. 2001. Local Dynamics of Renegotiating Ritual Space in Northern Vietnam: The Case of the Dinh. *Sojourn* 16 (1): 70–101.

Gammeltoft, Tine. 1999. *Women's Bodies, Women's Worries: Health and Family Planning in a Vietnamese Rural Community*. Surrey: Curzon Press.

Greenhalgh, Susan. 1994. De-Orientalizing the Chinese Family Firm. *American Ethnologist* 21 (4): 746–775.

Haines, David W. 2006. *The Limits of Kinship: South Vietnamese Households 1954–1975*. DeKalb: Northern Illinois University.

Hamabata, Matthew M. 1990. *Crested Kimono: Power and Love in the Japanese Business Family*. Ithaca: Cornell University Press.

Haughton, Dominique, and Jonathan Haughton. 1999. Son Preference. In *Health and Wealth in Vietnam: An Analysis of Household Living Standards*, ed. Dominique Haughton, Jonathan Haughton, Sarah Bales, Trương Thị Kim Chuyên, and Nguyễn Nguyệt Nga, 97–199. Singapore: Institute of Southeast Asian Studies.

Hsu, Carolyn L. 2007. *Creating Market Socialism: How Ordinary People Are Shaping Class and Status in China*. Durham: Duke University Press.

Jayakody, Rukmalie, and Vũ Tuấn Huy. 2008. Social Change and Marriage in Vietnam: From Socialist State to Market Reform. In *International Family Change: Ideational Perspectives*, ed. Rukmalie Jayakody, Arland Thornton, and William G. Axinn, 199–222. New York: Lawrence Erlbaum Associates.

Kleinen, John. 1999. *Facing the Future, Reviving the Past: A Study of Social Change in a Northern Vietnamese Village*. Singapore: ISEAS.

Leppänen, Antti. 2007. Neighborhood Shopkeepers in Contemporary South Korea: Household, Work, and Locality. PhD thesis, University of Helsinki, Helsinki.

Leshkowich, Ann Marie. 2014. *Essential Trade: Vietnamese Women in a Changing Marketplace*. Honolulu: University of Hawaii Press.

Luong, Hy Van. 1989. Vietnamese Kinship: Structural Principles and the Socialist Transformation in Northern Vietnam. *The Journal of Asian Studies* 48 (04): 741–756.

Malarney, Shaun K. 1996. The Limits of "State Functionalism" and the Reconstruction of Funerary Ritual in Contemporary Northern Vietnam. *American Ethnologist* 23 (3): 540–560.

N.N. 2015. Chợ Ninh Hiệp – Phụ Nữ Là "Trụ Cột Kinh Tế" [Ninh Hiệp Market—Women Are the "Economic Pillars"]. http://banbuonquanaonam.blogspot.de/2015/04/cho-ninh-hiep-phu-nu-la-tru-cot-kinh-te.html. Accessed 20 April.

Park, Seo Young. 2011. Pace and Passion in Seoul's Dongdaemun Market, South Korea: Time in the 24-hour City. PhD thesis, University of California, Irvine.

Park, Seo Young. 2012. Stitching the Fabric of Family: Time, Work, and Intimacy in Seoul's Tongdaemun Market. *Journal of Korean Studies* 17 (2): 383–406.

Redding, Gordon S. 1990. *The Spirit of Chinese Capitalism*. Berlin: de Gruyter.
Taylor, Philip (ed.). 2007. *Modernity and Re-Enchantment: Religion in Post-Revolutionary Vietnam*. Lanham: Lexington Books/Rowman & Littlefield.
UBND xã Ninh Hiệp. 2012. 'Báo Cáo: Kết Quả Thực Hiện Công Tác Dân Số - KHHGĐ Năm 2012. Nhiệm vụ Trọ ng Tâm Năm 2013 [Report: Results].
Vietnam. 2005. *Civil Code. 33/2005/QH11*. http://moj.gov.vn/vbpq/en/Lists/Vn%20bn%20php%20lut/View_Detail.aspx?ItemID=6595.
Vũ Mạnh Lợi. 1991. The Gender Division of Labor in Rural Families in the Red River Delta. In *Sociological Studies on the Vietnamese Family*, ed. Rita Liljeström, and Tương Lai, 149–164. Hanoi: Social Sciences Publishing House.
Vũ Mạnh Lợi. 2000. Marriage, Family, and Women. In *Social Development in Vietnam: A Sociological Overview in 2000*, ed. Trịnh Duy Luân, 23–32. Hanoi: Social Sciences Publishing House.
Weber, Max. [1930] 2001. *The Protestant Ethic and the Spirit of Capitalism*. London: Routledge.
Werner, Jayne. 2009. *Gender, Household and State in Post-Revolutionary Vietnam*. London: Routledge.
Whitmore, John K. 1984. Social Organization and Confucian Thought in Vietnam. *Journal of Southeast Asian Studies* 15 (02): 296–306.
Whyte, Martin K. 1996. The Chinese Family and Economic Development: Obstacle or Engine? *Economic Development and Cultural Change* 45 (1): 1–30.
Wisensale, Steven K. 1999. Marriage and Family Law in a Changing Vietnam. *Journal of Family Issues* 20 (5): 602–616.
Wisensale, Steven K. 2000. Family Policy in a Changing Vietnam. *Journal of Comparative Family Studies* 31 (1): 79–90.
Woodside, Alexander. 1995. Central Vietnam's Trading World in the Eighteenth Century as Seen in Lê Quý Đôn's "Frontier Chronicles". In *Essays into Vietnamese Pasts*, ed. Keith W. Taylor, and John K. Whitmore, 157–172. Ithaca: Cornell University Press.
Yanagisako, Sylvia J. 2000. Patriarchal Desire: Law and Sentiments of Succession in Italian Capitalist Families. In *Elites: Choice, Leadership and Succession*, ed. João de Pina-Cabral, and Antónia Pedroso de Lima, 53–72. Oxford: Berg.
Yanagisako, Sylvia J. 2002. *Producing Culture and Capital: Family Firms in Italy*. Princeton: Princeton University Press.
Yeung, Henry W. 2000. Limits to the Growth of Family-Owned Business? The Case of Chinese Transnational Corporations from Hong Kong. *Family Business Review* 13 (1): 55–70.

5

The Gendering of Market Trade

The rather ambiguous kinship practices outlined above also inform gender relations and ideas of femininity and masculinity. While women are most often the managers of the family business (*chủ*), men continue to be the head of the household and enjoy a higher symbolic status than women in the village. They are the representatives of the family to the outside, and in this position are supposed to take decisions beyond the household level. This implies that even though women do have a strong economic position within the family, it does not directly translate into a higher status or more recognition. Other scholars share this view for Vietnam more broadly, for example Bélanger and Barbieri (2009), Werner (2009), and Rydstrøm (2010). One of the hamlet chiefs confirmed this point: "Men here [in Ninh Hiệp] don't have economic power, but they lead. The decision to build a house is made by the husband, and before something is bought, the husband needs to be asked. But the finances are managed by the wife; she holds the purse strings (*tay hòm chìa khóa*)".

Shelly Errington (1990) put forth a similar point, warning that "power" and "status" should not be confused in the Southeast Asian context. She notes that "we in Euro-America tend to identify power

E. Horat, *Trading in Uncertainty*,
DOI 10.1007/978-3-319-55648-2_5

with economic control and coercive force: any status or prestige not linked to it we tend to conceptualize as empty prestige, mere symbolism". In doing so, we fail to understand that "the prevalent view in many parts of island Southeast Asia, however, is that to exert force, to make explicit commands, or to engage in direct activity—in other words, to exert 'power' in a Western sense—reveals a lack of spiritual power and effective potency, and consequently diminishes prestige" (Errington 1990, 5). Suzanne Brenner (1995, 22–23) raises a similar point when drawing attention to the ambivalence of the gendered division of power in Javanese households, where wives are expected to defer to their husband's prestige and authority as the heads of the household, while their de facto economic power outweighs that of their husbands by far. She also highlights the ironic dialectic between power and prestige, when noting that "one of the very characteristics that appears to give women so much autonomy and power in the household—their economic prowess—is also one of the main factors detracting from their prestige. In the central ideologies of Javanese society, there is an undeniable devaluation of the economic activities for which women and traders are known".

The same has long been argued for Vietnam, where direct interaction with money, especially as a marketplace trader, was seen as diminishing to the prestige of a person, as the following quote indicates:

> In Vietnam, as elsewhere in Southeast Asia, market trade traditionally has been something that women do. While their ability to make money through trade could potentially give women economic power, this historically has not been the case in Vietnam. Instead, the significance of women's trade activities has been downplayed by cultural attitudes disdaining trade and traders as immoral and insignificant. […] These attitudes are also reflected in gendered divisions of labor: women take charge of small-scale economic activities, and their dominance of this sector reinforces perceptions of its insignificance. (Leshkowich 2000, 4–5)

In addition to this, there are several related reasons why trade has not been considered a suitable occupation for men in Southeast Asia, especially in countries such as Indonesia and Vietnam. According to

Brenner (1998, 144–146), in Java trade was seen as demeaning for men because of the unrefined language used at the marketplace, the risk of damaging one's status if one loses his temper and the necessity of haggling over prices, which implied paying attention to trivial issues. Moreover, men were seen as more likely to lose self-control and should thus stay away from the temptations money brings about. Since women were of lower status than men, trade posed less of a problem for women, as Brenner points out. Also, the status of a family depended on the man, not on the woman. Therefore, men used to secure their family's status by taking up a prestigious yet not necessarily economically rewarding occupation, while women were less restricted in the kind of work as long as they brought money home.

Yet, the idea of trade having always been stigmatised in Vietnam as is suggested in much of the literature should not be accepted readily. Accounts about trade in the pre-colonial period in Vietnam contain an ambiguity difficult to reconcile: on the one hand, commerce is often depicted as having been of low esteem, usually in reference to the strict division between mental and menial labour (Luong 2003). According to the Confucian hierarchy, educated scholars and officials (*sĩ*) were at the very top, followed by agriculturalists (*nông*), artisans and handicraft specialists, and finally traders (*thương*) at the bottom (Malarney 1998, 271). Nguyễn Quang Ngọc (1993) pointed out that regardless of the many marketplaces and the central role of trade in the life of peasants, trade did not receive recognition, and many people engaged in trade because they had no other alternative to make a living. Later, during the colonial and the revolutionary period, trade was condemned and branded as unproductive and exploitative (Malarney 1998, 280). Thus, according to this view, trade has been an activity of low prestige throughout Vietnam's history. Sometimes, the fact that most traders were women is used as a validation that trade must have been a low-status occupation.

On the other hand, trade is described as a crucial and very popular economic activity across Vietnam and among different social strata. A hint that trade may not have been as stigmatised as is often suggested lies in the fact that in trade villages, social categories were not separate, but inclusive (see Nguyễn Quang Ngọc 1993). Only a few people were pure traders, while most villagers combined different activities. Therefore, traders did not figure as an independent class in trade villages.

This seeming contradiction may stem from a difference in perspective, that is whether an author pays more attention to the formal structure or to the lived experience of people. As George Dutton (2013) made clear in his article on women in early modern Vietnam, in most historical accounts, especially official reports, women were hardly represented, and if, it was not the common woman, but only a few outstanding ones belonging to the elite. Furthermore, the majority of these accounts take Confucian ideologies as the reality without questioning the impact of these ideas and norms on the lives of people.[1] Dutton called for particular attention to commerce and the role women played in it. At the same time, a focus on ordinary women as opposed to the usual elite and literati women that dominate existing historical studies is needed. According to Dutton, the fact that women were involved in commercial activities belies the idealised Confucian notion of women as confined to the "inner" realm of the family and instead points to a high degree of agency women could exercise outside of their homes. Thus, instead of uncritically accepting and replicating the statement that merchants have always been of low esteem, attention should be paid to the opportunities traders could seize precisely because of their commercial activities, for example making contributions to the village and travelling to other places.

In a similar vein, Leshkowich (2014, 57–58) states that trade in twentieth-century Vietnam has been vastly feminised not primarily due to cultural reasons, but even more because of political reasons. She argues that during the high socialist period, women were under less strict control regarding economic class struggle and could therefore engage in trade more easily than men. Although Vietnamese people, both women and men, readily relate commerce to women's "natural" characteristics needed in the marketplace, such as patience, sweet-talking and skilfulness, it would be misleading, according to Leshkowich (2014, 48–50), to take this as the motivation for women to become traders—rather, the political and economic conditions during and after the high socialist period drew women to trade.

Women traders then used essentialist notions of gender that were also replicated by state officials, in particular the idea of women's aptitude to trade, to keep a low profile.

Hy Van Luong's (1998) study on gender and entrepreneurship in an ancient ceramic village in the Red River Delta also relates to the topic. He argues that the trend in this village and more generally in northern Vietnam in the twentieth century towards men increasingly managing small craft enterprises was due to ideology and political economy. Referring to bureaucratisation as the main reason for men to manage small-scale businesses instead of women, he explains that the bureaucratic system during the colonial period favoured men for these positions as they had privileged access to education. Later, during the high socialist period, a similar pattern emerged because the command economy was also highly bureaucratised. In addition, leading a cooperative included a lot of travelling and was therefore difficult to combine with the domestic chores of women.

When comparing my data with Brenner's, Leshkowich's and Luong's accounts, the strategic use of particular notions of gender essentialism put forth by Leshkowich seems to resonate with my work the most. The trend of men increasingly becoming traders in Ninh Hiệp may indicate that the socialist legacy shaping gender roles long into the post-reform period is finally vanishing. This challenges Brenner's account that tends to overemphasise the impact and resilience of cultural logics and neglect the dynamic notions of gender and changing trade practices. Luong's explanation is interesting, especially because the trend of men assuming managerial positions is happening in Ninh Hiệp as well. Yet ceramic production and clothing trade have different historical trajectories, and even more importantly, clothing trade in Ninh Hiệp is by far less bureaucratic than Luong claims for the village he studied. In the remainder of this chapter, I will present an ethnographic exploration of the intersections of gender and neoliberal governance. As a first step, I will shed light on how men found their way into trade and what it means for their sense of mascu linity.

The Making of the Man Trader

As a matter of fact, men rarely worked as traders in the past. A high proportion of Ninh Hiệp men, who are now in their late fifties and above, served as soldiers during the Second Indochina War and the subsequent intervention in Cambodia and other places, and some of them came back physically disabled and/or traumatised. Those men whose health condition was good or at least sufficient used to work for the commune's agriculture cooperative or for the local government. As part of an emancipation programme, women were integrated into production outside the home and were thus employed as the members of the agricultural cooperative to work alongside men. Paradoxically, the cooperative system in Vietnam encouraged the expansion of the family economy, and women were again held responsible for various tasks that had to be carried out in or around the house, as Christine White (1982) has shown in detail. In Ninh Hiệp, women did not only work for the cooperative, but also engaged in trade as a side occupation. With the growth of the village economy and the expansion of the marketplace, trade became the main source of income and women thus slipped into the role of the main breadwinner. Men increasingly stayed at home and carried out different jobs in a flexible manner, yet doing household chores was not seen as men's work.

Although newspaper articles and people outside the village often make comments about how men in Ninh Hiệp are lucky (*sướng*) because their wives earn enough to support the family, many men are not content with the situation. When I asked a hamlet chief what he thought about the current division of labour, he answered: "Why should we men be lucky? What is lucky about finding an exhausted, angry wife at home whom I have to ask for money if I want to go out to drink a tea, or attend a banquet (*ăn cỗ*)?" Yet, as has been mentioned before, it is not new to Vietnam that wives earn more than their husbands in households that are based on agriculture and petty trade. What is crucial, though, is *how much more* money women earn in relation to men in Ninh Hiệp, especially when the wife's income is enough to sustain the whole family. The hamlet chief thus continued: "Our wives earn a lot of money on a single day, and after a few days they have already made as much as we earn in one month. When the wife earns enough money, the [professional] future of the husband is not protected. Husbands stay at home because their wives earn enough (*đạt thành quả*) already".

My findings are very similar to the ones of Trương Huyền Chi (2009), who also highlighted the ambiguity of men's attitude of being dependent upon their wives, mothers and daughters as the main source of income. On the one hand, the financial contributions of women to the household are acknowledged, yet on the other hand, the unease about the asymmetry can barely be disguised. To deal with the embarrassment the situation provokes, men often mock themselves and their male friends for being dependent on their wives and taking over tasks normally assigned to women. Trương Huyền Chi therefore argues that the group of men she studied redefines masculinity as "being able to rise to the challenge of putting up with female tasks" (Trương Huyền Chi 2009, 322).

Nowadays, there are basically three options for men in Ninh Hiệp: first, to stay at home to do housework and assist in the background, while their wives conduct business; second, to do another job, such as a motorcycle-taxi driver (*xe ôm*), farmer, day labourer, teacher, public servant, and so on, even if the salary is most probably lower than that of a trader; third, to join the business. While the first two options were preferred by men of the pre-Đổi mới generation, men of later generations, who experienced the boom of the marketplace, often decide for the third option. Interestingly, these men are not only much more involved in the family business, but also carry out tasks which were previously assigned to women, such as selling at the market and managing the budget. Especially since the establishment of the new markets in 2011, it is no longer uncommon for young men to even become marketplace vendors. A very important condition for this change is the fading of the negative connotation of money in the aftermath of Đổi mới (Bélanger et al. 2012). In the context of the socialist-oriented market economy, men, who are successful in earning money and are able to afford a certain lifestyle, are more and more being looked up to. As Minh T.N. Nguyen (2014) put it: "Money-making power or any kind of power that facilitates wealth generation represents an important post-Đổi mới benchmark for being a man".

Seen in the wider context of Vietnam, there may be two reasons for the trend of men becoming traders: on the one hand, there is, according to Knodel et al. (2004), a general tendency in Vietnam for men to increasingly take part in managing the household budget, which in Ninh Hiệp means to be actively involved in the family business. The authors suggest that the reason for this trend to emerge in the post-Đổi mới era is because the disposable income has risen considerably and thus there are significant amounts of cash to manage. Ninh Hiệp with its flourishing textile trade may be a similar case, attracting men to become traders because it is not about insignificant amounts any longer—a fact which turns trade into a financially and culturally legitimate occupation for men.

On the other hand, the study by Philip Martin (2013) about the changing notions of masculinity among different generations in Vietnam suggests that many young men, who grew up in post-Đổi mới Vietnam, oriented themselves towards their mothers rather than their fathers. This, he explains, was because men generally had more difficulties to deal with a changing society than women.[2] While the mothers of the young men in his sample seized the opportunity to go into business and became thriving traders, their fathers were far less dynamic. When recounting the memories of their parents, the young men often did not consider their fathers to be role models, but instead their mothers, because they were dynamic and more successful in getting along with the social and economic mobility induced by the reform process. Accordingly, risk-taking was associated with mothers, while fathers were seen as risk-averse and not being able to manage to stay relevant to present-day society in general and to one's family in particular—not only financially, but also as somebody to give advice on difficult decisions in life (Martin 2013, 215). Martin argues that this phenomenon strongly affected young men's ideas and practices related to masculinity, pointing to the ambiguity of the son's perception of their fathers being strong and authoritative when their mothers were actually preeminent at home.

His study offers a useful perspective on the current developments in Ninh Hiệp. Based on the observation of young men increasingly becoming marketplace traders, it seems that they orient themselves more towards their mothers than towards their fathers, and in this way try to seize the opportunities the new economic structure offers. Interestingly, what is considered masculine—dynamism, risk-taking and decisiveness—is most closely embodied by traders in Ninh Hiệp. Although men of current generations see themselves as head of the family (*chủ gia đình*) like their fathers, at the same time they do not see their active participation at the marketplace compromising their masculinity, but rather enhancing it.

However, this does not imply that female and male traders do their work in the same way or under similar circumstances. When looking at male traders at the marketplace, the differences between them and their female counterparts are easily detectable. While the old market is an almost exclusively female zone, nearly all men traders sell at the two new markets. This is no coincidence, as Hạnh, a young woman vendor at the old market, whose husband sells at the new market, stated:

> Because the clothing sold at the new markets is more expensive and mainly men's wear and bargaining is less common, it is suitable for men to sell there. And here [at the old market], cheaper clothing is sold, and we have to sit like this [pointing to herself squatting on a piece of cloth on the floor], that's why mostly women sell here. It is reasonable (*hợp lý*) like this.

In contrast to the many inconveniences of the old market, including very small stalls standing cheek by jowl, stuffy air as a consequence of the low ceiling and lack of air circulation, and unbearable hot temperatures in the summer, the new markets are modern buildings, which provide a convenient environment for trading activities. Not only can traders sit on chairs thanks to the generous stall size, but it is also much brighter and there is always a breeze of fresh air in the aisles between the stalls. These aisles are large enough to easily transport the goods to the stall, and around the markets is space to drive as close as needed with the kind of small trucks used in the village to transport the wares.

Furthermore, the new markets are very clean, especially the newly built sanitary facilities. Finally, the atmosphere is much less busy and loud, and drinks can be ordered conveniently by phone from the café just next to the market building. All in all, the conditions at the two new markets make the life of traders comfortable, which stands in stark contrast to the old market.

Not only do the conditions that frame trade experiences differ between women and men, but so do their trade practices. The most noticeable difference is that women are more likely to be drawn into haggling with potential customers, whereas men avoid this situation at (almost) any cost. Within the village, young men traders do not risk being perceived as less masculine, but rather as dynamic, aspiring men with the ability to seize chances and deal with the challenges of the rapid changes the economic system poses. Although they do the kind of work usually associated with women, they do it in a modern and clean environment and have more expensive merchandise on offer than most of the women traders.

Angie Ngoc Tran (2004), who examined masculinity among male workers in the garment industry, presents similar findings. She notes that the male workers she studied, who were doing what is commonly considered "female jobs", defined their roles in the female-dominated garment industry by highlighting their masculine skills to perform the job. Such qualities include self-determination and technical, managerial and leadership abilities. She concludes that the decisive factor "is not so much the types of work, but rather the extent to which they measure up to social expectations of masculinity" (Tran 2004, 226). Nguyen (2014) made very similar observations during her research among male migrant waste traders. In order to distinguish themselves from female waste traders, men tend to highlight the stark contrast between their work and the work carried out by female traders. Their work, they argue, concerns electronic appliances that require a particular knowledge and a set of skills, whereas the task of women traders, on the other hand, is merely to collect and resell cheap waste for little return. This line of reasoning typifies the ways in which men try to convince others—and perhaps even themselves—that their work is a distinctly masculine domain that falls outside a woman's scope of competence. This helps keep their sense of pride intact.

Seeing as most urban planners as well as government officials in relevant positions are men, it is not surprising that the vision that guides the process of market modernisation is also heavily influenced by a distinctly male flair. But this dynamic also extends beyond the market's physical design. As the experience in Ninh Hiệp indicates, even redeveloped and newly established markets eventually turn into spaces where men are overrepresented. The end result is a marketplace where mostly male vendors cater to the needs of other males who happen to be their customers. In the same way as the new markets are conceptualised as modern compared to the old market, vendors at the new markets are seen as behaving in a "civilised" way. In contrast to the image of the uneducated, lower-class, female vendor, men at the new markets seem to be creating a new male trader by incorporating neoliberal ideals of knowledge, entrepreneurship and money. They give this impression by reading the newspaper, counting big bundles of money in public and carrying it visibly in their trouser pocket. During the day, they take breaks to meet each other at the nearby café, which is also run by a man (Quân, who I introduced at the very beginning). Thus, the fact that men sell where it is clean, bright and relatively quiet adds positively to their image.

This does not mean that selling at one of the new markets is everyone's wish—especially long-term women vendors at the old market often said that due to their good relations with their stall neighbours, the relatively modest stall rent fee, and the fact that their regular customers can find them easily, they had no intention to move. These practical considerations and Hạnh's earlier statement reaffirming gender stereotypes could be read against the backdrop of Leshkowich's argument of the strategic use of gender essentialism. Possibly, other labour and space division would turn out less efficient for the family in terms of economic return and the use of available capacities. For instance, if men would not work as vendors, fewer stalls could be operated; if men and women switched stalls, then their clientele might be lost, etc. Yet, even if this were true and women could exert agency by reassuring their essentialising gender role, it would not better their situation in terms of having to work fewer hours or in a more comfortable environment, or enhancing their social status.

All in all, the neoliberal turn shaping the redevelopment of marketplaces seems to have been particularly important for men in Ninh Hiệp, as they not only found a source of income, but also a new position in the village society. By becoming traders, they prove that they are dynamic and able to participate in rapidly changing circumstances. Also, with their increased purchasing power they can take part in consumption and thereby enhance their sense of masculinity. The next step is to turn to the role of women and notions of femininity to examine their situation in more depth.

Civilising Women

In Vietnam, women are first and foremost seen as wives, mothers, daughters and daughters-in-law, but they also have a long tradition of being part of the labour force. As Tran (2008, 60) points out, the women's role promoted by the state and the Vietnamese General Confederation of Labour is one of a compliant female worker, who carries the double burden of work and home. This image is expressed in the labour union's slogan "Good in national affairs and good in domestic affairs" (*giỏi việc nước, đảm việc nhà*)—in peacetime, however, "national affairs" means wage labour. As Trương Huyền Chi (2009) and Bélanger and Barbieri (2009) note, expectations towards women in contemporary Vietnam are very high. While they are under pressure to contribute financially to the household economy, discourses on women in Vietnam convey the message that they are also responsible for the well-being of their children, husbands and parents-in-law. In comparison with the high socialist time, when the ideal of women as labourers was strongly propagated, the role of women in the aftermath of Đổi mới was mainly linked to the domestic chores and the family. As Leshkowich (2012a, 101) noted, subordinating one's needs and desires to the welfare of the family—and in nationalist discourses, to the state—in other words, to sacrifice (*hy sinh*), is essential for being a woman.

According to Ashley Pettus (2003), "civility" is often used in state discourses targeting the family, as this is where economy and morality come together. She traces the notion of civility back to 1994, where it appeared in a nationwide campaign run by the Women's Union to promote the "Prosperous, Egalitarian, Progressive, and Happy Family" (Pettus 2003, 84). Targeting the family is synonymous with targeting women, as they were seen—throughout the Vietnamese history—as responsible for the domestic domain. The call to create and maintain family happiness did not only demand from women to do whatever it took to keep the relations between the family members harmonious, but they should also be preoccupied with every dimension of the conjugal life, including their husband's sexual pleasure, as Nguyễn-Võ Thu-Hương (2008) writes. This aspect was especially propagated among urban middle-class women as a way to reduce the temptation to visit sex workers, and hence to combat "social evil"—as sex work was classified—in society. Thus, efforts in the name of "civility" were directly related to the "advancement" of women.

In the aftermath of Đổi mới, the urban educated and affluent middle class became the standard of "civility" and was most closely embodied by female civil servants living in the centre of the city (Pettus, 84). Having had access to the Women's Union during her research, Pettus was able to attend contests in three districts of Hanoi. There, women dressed up like in beauty pageants were tested about their knowledge of the principles of "civilised" family life. Questions ranged from birth control, health care, child development and domestic life to women's beauty and Vietnamese femininity. Pettus noticed not only the absence of female entrepreneurs and merchants at these events but also the different set of questions in each contest, depending on the expected level of knowledge. In the third contest she attended, which was held in a village about as far away from the centre of Hanoi as Ninh Hiệp, and known for agriculture and handicraft production, she recognised that the questions implied the population's lack of knowledge about the principles of the state-defined "civilised" family life. This perceived lack was dealt with "by instilling in them [contestant participants] an awareness of their inferiority vis-à-vis the urban feminine standard and their need for conscientious self-improvement in the domestic domain" (Pettus 2003, 103).

My findings seem to resonate with her argument that respectability and deviance in current times very much depend on women's cultural and spatial distance to the ideal femininity. As Ninh Hiệp is geographically not in the centre of Hanoi and has a comparably low percentage of female civil servants, women's knowledge of, or at least compliance with, the principles of a "civilised" family life could be expected to be low. And indeed, in a conversation with Mrs. Giang, who works for the

Women's Union in Ninh Hiệp, the seeming lack of knowledge among women was raised multiple times. "Because they are traders", she said, "they don't know". Drawing my attention to what appeared to her like a paradox, she continued:

> Ninh Hiệp's economy is growing, but the proportion of malnourished children is very high. Why? (…) Because they are traders, they lack knowledge. They only know going to the market, earning a lot of money. They buy foreign products for their baby to drink, although this foreign milk is very expensive. Instead of breastfeeding the baby in the first six months, they go back to the market soon after giving birth and hire a maid to take care of the baby. But how can a maid know how to take care of their baby?

According to this statement, not only the traders lack knowledge, but also their maids, who often come from rural provinces. Thus, again, the spatial and cultural, respectively, class distance of the maid to the idealised urban middle-class woman is taken as explanation for—and even evidence of—her lack of knowledge. Implicit in her statement is also a critique towards women traders to be occupied more with making money than with pursuing a female ideal.

The second issue causing Mrs. Giang a headache was third (and more)-child births. Asking her what the possible reasons for the relatively high number of women with more than two children in Ninh Hiệp could be, she answered:

> I found out that in reality women don't like to give birth to many children. But Confucian values are still ingrained in the mind of people. Ninh Hiệp is a place with a developed economy, but besides this the customs of the people are still feudal (*phong kiến*), they haven't changed. For example weddings and funerals are still very feudal, they don't have a civilised character. Funerals are lavish, they are still done according to the old procedures. Because the customs are feudal, women want to give birth to a son. The people in Ninh Hiệp want a son to worship the ancestors and continue the patrilineage. When the economy grows and people have a lot of money, they wish to have a son even more so that he can manage the assets, because there is still the conception of the past that daughters will leave the house when they get married.

Mrs. Giang went on telling stories of women who already had four or five children, but as all of them were girls, they still wanted to have more in the hope to have a boy. When she talked to them, they said that they were not respected in the husband's family as long as they had not given birth to a son. Yet, as they are not employed by the state but work independently, they cannot be restrained. "The only solution is education, advocacy and campaigning—if they want to hear, they hear, if not, we can't do anything", Mrs. Giang said. Apparently, the policy that restricts the number of children per woman is not strictly enforced in Ninh Hiệp, but is handled like a target towards which the commune should strive. As it is the responsibility of the communes to abide by the national target, the number of children per couple could be mentioned in the village convention (*quy ước, hương ước*). Yet, the leaders of Ninh Hiệp decided not to do so, although the district leaders as well as Mrs. Giang advised them to.

Comparing this situation to Nguyễn-Võ Thu-Hương's (2008) conception of freedom and coercion helps to identify the tensions that emerged in the context of market liberalisation. The opening of the economy did not only allow to choose one's occupation, but also lead to the revitalisation of ideas that run counter to the state's vision of modernity. In Ninh Hiệp, the traders' independence from the state in terms of employment as well as their ability to earn money made it possible—and, according to Mrs. Giang, even desirable—for villagers to choose to have three, four, even five children and let them be brought up by a maid, instead of having the wife or her mother-in-law staying at home to look after the children. Although defining family planning targets in the village convention was advised, the commune leaders did not endorse it. Instead, another solution was suggested, namely to bring about change through education. While the women's hard work and skills in trading were played down by phrases such as "all they know is making a lot of money", their seeming deficit of knowledge about a "civilised" life and the need to improve this situation were emphasised. The problem of education, respectively, the lack thereof was not only expressed by Mrs. Giang and mentioned in internal governmental reports, but also in newspaper articles on Ninh Hiệp, where women traders were blamed for immoral behaviour. Thus, rather than coercion, the more subtle techniques of self-governance through educating women on how to behave were applied.

"Wife's Property—Husband's Labour"?

From the perspective of villagers, women in Ninh Hiệp are expected to be skilled in business (*giỏi làm kinh tế*) in order to provide for the family. Conversations with villagers revealed that the skills to conduct business, the ability to manage the family and the readiness for hard work and sacrifice for the family were the most important attributes of a wife or daughter-in-law. Upon asking Mrs. Giang what women in Ninh Hiệp consider to be their most important task, she answered: "This is very difficult to say, because women in Ninh Hiệp head for more than one thing; they want a family, children, and a business". She then continued by pointing out what was special about Ninh Hiệp women:

> The characteristic of this place is the local trade, wherein women participate a lot. Women mainly provide the household economy. In Ninh Hiệp, the roles are reversed [compared to most other parts in Vietnam]: Women are the pillars of the family, of course not completely, but to seventy or eighty percent. Trade in the village is one thing, going to China to buy merchandise another. Women also cross the border to go to far-away markets. They go for three, five, seven days. Men stay at home, mainly taking care of housework, looking after children, caring for the family and events with the relatives, like anniversaries, Lunar New Year… This is the special feature of Ninh Hiệp.

This quote reaffirms the newspaper article in the previous chapter, which also adverted to the strong economic position of women in the family and the particular division of labour. Nevertheless, women are not seen as equal to men, as Diệp, a young woman and owner of a day nursery, remarked. Referring to the "village nature" (*tình chất làng xã*) that, according to her, strongly influences the notions of masculinity and femininity, she said that "women in Ninh Hiệp need to be patient (*nhẫn nhịn*) and suffer (*chịu đựng*), and not having a husband is a scandal". Yet, she also mentioned that women nowadays do not accept everything and increasingly get a divorce, just as she did: "It is only a small percentage, but there are women who stand up because they cannot bear it anymore. Like me. I felt there was no harmony (*hòa hợp*) anymore, no happiness (*hạnh phúc*), and so I let it be". Her statement supports the view that in spite of women's particularly strong economic position, gender-specific expectations are not different from those in the rest of Vietnam.

Although women's involvement in trade allowed them to make substantial financial contributions, their reduced participation in physical care for members of the family and family-in-law was sometimes criticised. In particular, some elderly people in Ninh Hiệp bemoaned that due to marketisation, their children and grandchildren visited them less and spent only little time with them, resulting in a loss of sentiments (*mất tình cảm*). Yet, even though the general belief that money impacts negatively on sentiments was quite commonplace, material comfort was acknowledged. Money was not only used to make life more convenient by buying air conditioners and rebuilding the house, but also to create family time by travelling to beach cities and other places in Vietnam with the whole family, including grandparents.

How the multiple household-related tasks are met differs in each family. In some cases, practical care work is smoothly divided among family members, so that, for example, grandparents or husbands look after small children, or bring them to the day nursery or school in the morning and take them back in the afternoon. Such was the case with the family of Mr. Thâm. However, not every family arranges it this way, and some women carry the full burden of moneymaking, housework, and child and elderly care, as was the case with Chi, whose story I am going to recall now.

Chi is a young, pretty woman trader, who I met several times at her stall in the old market. One day she invited me for dinner when I visited her late in the afternoon. It was ten minutes to five, and as the market would close at five, she started to take the displayed clothes from the hangers, piled them all on the neatly arranged stock inside the stall and finally put a piece of fabric on top to cover the merchandise. I was told to wait at the market gate while she went to collect her motorbike at the nearby parking space. On the way home, we stopped at the local fresh market where she bought half of a duck including the heart and some herbs for the dinner. When we reached the house where she, her husband Nam and their four-year-old son lived, we found Nam and a friend of him sitting on the living room floor, drinking beer and watching TV. Chi poured me a glass of water and invited me to take a seat, while she went to fetch her son from the day nursery. Upon coming back, the son sat down to watch television and ate some snacks, while she immediately started to clean the floor. Meanwhile, Nam's friend left and Nam went upstairs to his room, where he had some work to do, he said. After tiding up the mess Nam and his friend had left in the living room, Chi started to prepare dinner without taking a minute of break.

The tired look in Chi's face could not be overlooked, and thus it did not come as a surprise when she sighed and said she was completely exhausted day by day. While I washed the herbs and she prepared the duck, she continued to lament how hard her days were, starting in the early morning with making breakfast for her son, dressing him and bringing him to the day nursery before going to the market to open her stall. Working at the market all day is physically and mentally demanding as it implies sitting uncomfortably, haggling with customers who sometimes ask an unreasonable price, being exposed to a noisy environment, and constant worrying about the business. When closing down the stall in the late afternoon, she has no time to do sports with other traders, but has to do the household chores and look after her son. Sometimes, she would go to visit her parents-in-law and make sure they were well and had everything they needed.

Nam was not seen until Chi called him for dinner. During the meal, he explained that he had just founded an IT company with a friend, and as soon as the dinner was finished he left the table to go back to his room. After bringing her son to bed, Chi did the washing up and cleaned the kitchen. Shortly thereafter, I left the place as Chi announced to go to bed immediately due to her fatigue.

The kind of complaints Chi raised concerned the high workload and the stress of being in charge of fulfilling work and family-related tasks simultaneously. However, there was no open reproach towards her husband, who apparently did not help her with the household chores or with the business, and was also not able to support the family financially as his company was not yet making money. Although Chi was clearly overworked and stressed, she did not reject the gender role but conformed to the notion of femininity by being a hardworking and caring wife and mother.

Recalling the proverb introduced earlier in its reversed form—"Của vợ công chồng"—it is certainly fits regarding the strong economic position of women. Yet, to which extent their husbands fulfil the second part of the proverb—"công chồng"—by supporting them with their labour differs from family to family, as I have shown with the cases of Huy and Chi. Also, even if the labour division in Ninh Hiệp may differ from what is considered the norm in Vietnam, ideas about how men or women should be and behave are not markedly different from those in other areas in Vietnam.

Overall, women are in charge of the productive and reproductive tasks in the household and are expected to hold the family happily together. Remarkably little has changed regarding the role of women since White's article in 1982, where she pointed to the paradox between the state's ambition to integrate women into production outside the home as a means for emancipation, and the continued expectation of women's family responsibilities. Thus, while women in Ninh Hiệp are under pressure to juggle the many demands of work and family and, as a result, are exhausted and often suffer from back pain and stress-related illnesses, men struggle to redefine their position in the family and in society more broadly. They seem to face less clear expectations, which can be an advantage as it means more freedom, but it can also make men feel dispensable when their financial and practical contributions are reduced to "assistance", or, as Martin (2013) put it, when they have difficulties to "stay relevant". For some men, however, the recent marketisation process has had a positive effect as it created opportunities for work, earning money and thus enhancing their sense of masculinity.

It is important to emphasise that not only the possibilities to make money and even become rich have multiplied in the post-Đổi mới era, but also attitudes towards money have changed substantially. This process is intertwined with the changing notions of femininity and masculinity. Unlike in the past when men were not supposed to be directly concerned with money, in contemporary Vietnam the ability to earn money and display it in certain ways is becoming an important part of masculinity. Interestingly, whereas becoming a marketplace vendor would have been almost unthinkable or at least very unpopular for men in the past, young men in Ninh Hiệp nowadays do not object to selling at the market and are actively involved in managing the family business. Changing trade practices, especially less bargaining, a modern environment and the presence of male customers reduced the cultural obstacles for men to become traders. Although the trend of men getting into business leads to a new division of labour in families, it does not necessarily mean a release for women, as it often implies an expansion of the business by acquiring a new stall. For women in Ninh Hiệp, being a skilful trader in order to provide for the family is important, but earning money does not attribute to femininity in the same positive way as it does to masculinity. While financial contributions are acknowledged, femininity is still very much tied to the domestic sphere and the family. Money and gender thus stand in an ambiguous relationship—while money is not to be equated with power, it nevertheless has powerful consequences in regard to gender relations.

By demonstrating the close link between family and business, this and the previous chapters defy simplistic assumptions of money poisoning social relations. This is in line with Viviane Zelizer's (2011) argument that intimacy and economic actions are mutually constitutive. It also supports Park's (2011) and Leshkowich's (2011) findings that material comfort, as a result of hard work at the marketplace, does not impact negatively on intimate relations but is seen as a necessary precondition for family happiness. Seo Young Park suggests that instead of the traditional notion of "care", implying domestic labour and direct interactions, the way traders care for their family is through hard work at the marketplace (Park 2011, 51).

Just how central familiarity is in the market will be illustrated in the next chapter when I examine traders' myriad social relations. How is the local economy organised, not just within a family, but on the village level? Arguing that the creation of long-term trade relations is a way to cope with uncertainties, the next chapter attempts to shed further light on the nature of these relationships.

Notes

1. This broader question of to what extent Confucianism impacted on Vietnam needs critical examination, as many writers differ significantly in their take on that matter. For more elaboration, see for example Shawn McHale (2004, Chap. 3) who reflects the accounts of three Vietnamese writers in the time between 1920–1945 and points to the tendency to essentialise Confucianism and overexaggerate its role in Vietnam's history. According to McHale, although certain Confucian notions and practices, such as the "four virtues"(*tứ đức*) and "three submissions"(*tam tòng*), found resonance in the Vietnamese society, there is no evidence for Confucianism having been understood by a majority of people as a coherent set of beliefs (McHale 2004, 76).
2. This argument does not contradict other studies that point to the fact that more women than men lost their jobs in the process of downsizing state-owned companies in the aftermath of Đổi mới. Martin builds on the same premise and extends it by saying that the increased job-related uncertainty borne by women actually triggered their resourcefulness and the ability to deal with rapidly changing circumstances.

References

Bélanger, Danièle, and Magali Barbieri. 2009. Introduction: State, Families, and the Making of Transitions in Vietnam. In *Reconfiguring Families in Contemporary Vietnam*, ed. Danièle Bélanger, and Magali Barbieri, 1–44. Stanford: Stanford University Press.

Bélanger, Danièle, Lisa B. Drummond, and Van Nguyen-Marshall. 2012. Introduction: Who are the Urban Middle Class in Vietnam? In *The Reinvention of Distinction: Modernity and the Middle Class in Urban Vietnam*, ed. Van Nguyen-Marshall, Lisa B. Drummond, and Danièle Bélanger, 1–17. Dordrecht: Springer.

Brenner, Suzanne A. 1995. Why Women Rule the Roost: Rethinking Javanese Ideologies of Gender and Self-Control. In *Bewitching Women, Pious Men: Gender and Body Politics in Southeast Asia*, ed. Aihwa Ong, and Michael G. Peletz, 19–50. Berkeley: University of California Press.

Brenner, Suzanne A. 1998. *The Domestication of Desire: Women, Wealth, and Modernity in Java*. Princeton: Princeton University Press.

Dutton, George. 2013. Beyond Myth and Caricature: Situating Women in the History of Early Modern Vietnam. *Journal of Vietnamese Studies* 8 (2): 1–36.

Errington, Shelly. 1990. Recasting Sex, Gender, and Power: A Theoretical and Regional Overview. In *Power and Difference: Gender in Island Southeast Asia*, ed. Jane M. Atkinson, and Shelly Errington, 1–58. Stanford: Stanford University Press.

Knodel, John E., Vũ Mạnh Lợi, Rukmalie Jayakody, and Vũ Tuấn Huy. 2004. Gender Roles in the Family: Change and Stability in Vietnam. PSC Research Report 04-559.

Leshkowich, Ann Marie. 2000. 'Tightly Woven Threads: Gender, Kinship, and "Secret Agency" among Cloth and Clothing Traders in Ho Chi Minh City's Ben Thanh Market'. PhD Thesis, Cambridge, MA: Harvard University.

Leshkowich, Ann Marie. 2011. Making Class and Gender: (Market) Socialist Enframing of Traders in Ho Chi Minh City. *American Anthropologist* 113 (2): 277–290.

Leshkowich, Ann Marie. 2012. Finances, Family, Fashion, Fitness, and… Freedom? The Changing Lives of Urban Middle-Class Vietnamese Women. In *The Reinvention of Distinction: Modernity and the Middle Class in Urban Vietnam*, ed. Van Nguyen-Marshall, Lisa B. Drummond, and Danièle Bélanger, 95–114. Dordrecht: Springer.

Leshkowich, Ann Marie. 2014. *Essential Trade: Vietnamese Women in a Changing Marketplace*. Honolulu: University of Hawaii Press.

Luong, Hy Van. 1998. Engendered Entrepreneurship: Ideologies & Political-Economic Transformation in a Northern Vietnamese Center of Ceramics Production. In *Market Cultures: Society and Morality in the New Asian Capitalisms*, ed. Robert W. Hefner, 290–314. Boulder: Westview Press.

Luong, Hy Van. 2003. Wealth, Power, and Inequality: Global Market, the State, and Local Sociocultural Dynamics. In *Postwar Vietnam: Dynamics of a Transforming Society*, ed. Hy Van Luong, 81–106. Lanham: Rowman & Littlefield Publishers.

Malarney, Shaun K. 1998. State Stigma, Family Prestige, and the Development of Commerce in the Red River Delta of Vietnam. In *Market Cultures: Society and Morality in the New Asian Capitalisms*, ed. Robert W. Hefner, 268–289. Boulder: Westview Press.

Martin, Philip. 2013. I Want to Take Risks, like My Mother: Memory, Affect, and Vietnamese Masculinities—The Legacy of Gendered Variations in Socio-Economic Mobility during Đổi Mới. *Norsk Geografisk Tidsskrift-Norwegian Journal of Geography* 67 (4): 210–218.

McHale, Shawn F. 2004. *Print and Power: Confuscianism, Communism, and Buddhism in the Making of Modern Vietnam*. Honolulu: University of Hawaii Press.

Nguyễn Quang Ngọc. 1993. Markets and Villages. The Rural Markets (chợ Làng) of North Vietnam. In *The Traditional Village in Vietnam*, 315–368. Hanoi: The Gioi Publishers.

Nguyễn-Võ Thu-Hương. 2008. *The Ironies of Freedom: Sex, Culture, and Neoliberal Governance in Vietnam*. Seattle: University of Washington Press.

Nguyen, Thi Nguyet Minh. 2014. Tiền Bạc, ăn Chơi và Phiêu Lưu: Chuyển Biến Nam Tính Trong Một Cộng đồng Kinh Doanh Phế Liệu ở đồng Bằng Sông Hồng [Money, Risk-Taking and Playing: Shifting Masculinity in a Waste-Trading Community in the Red River Delta]. *Tạp Chí Dân Tộc Học* [*Anthropological Review*] 186 (3): 37–49.

Park, Seo Young. 2011. Pace and Passion in Seoul's Dongdaemun Market, South Korea: Time in the 24-Hour City. PhD Thesis, University of California, Irvine.

Pettus, Ashley. 2003. *Between Sacrifice and Desire: National Identity and the Governing of Femininity in Vietnam*. New York: Routledge.

Rydstrøm, Helle (ed.). 2010. *Gendered Inequalities in Asia: Configuring, Contesting and Recognizing Women and Men*. Copenhagen: NIAS Press.

Tran, Ngoc Angie. 2004. What's Women's Work? Male Negotiations and Gender Reproduction in the Vietnamese Garment Industry. In *Gender Practices in Contemporary Vietnam*, ed. Lisa Drummond, and Helle Rydstrøm, 210–235. Copenhagen: NIAS.

Tran, Ngoc Angie. 2008. Contesting "Flexibility": Networks of Place, Gender, and Class in Vietnamese Worker's Resistance. In *Taking Southeast Asia to Market: Commodities, Nature, and People in the Neoliberal Age*, ed. Joseph Nevins, and Nancy L. Peluso, 56–72. Ithaca: Cornell University Press.

Trương Huyền Chi. 2009. A Home Divided: Work, Body, and Emotions in the Post Doi-Moi Family. In *Reconfiguring Families in Contemporary Vietnam*, ed. Danièle Bélanger, and Magali Barbieri, 298–328. Stanford: Stanford University Press.

Werner, Jayne. 2009. *Gender, Household and State in Post-Revolutionary Vietnam*. London: Routledge.

White, Christine P. 1982. Socialist Transformation of Agriculture and Gender Relations: The Vietnamese Case. *The IDS Bulletin* 13 (4): 44–51.

Zelizer, Viviana A. 2011. *Economic Lives: How Culture Shapes the Economy*. Princeton: Princeton University Press.

6

Trust and Entrepreneurialism

Strolling through the market on a cold, gloomy winter day in the peak season just a few weeks before the Lunar New Year, I came across Thu and Ly, two dynamic young women selling socks in the Fashion Street. Thu was in her early thirties and, as it turned out in the conversation, the aunt of Ly. They grew up in a neighbouring village, and while Ly was still living there, Thu had moved to Ninh Hiệp once she got married to Trung, a man from a rather well-off family. Instead of renting a stall or shop, Thu and Ly simply displayed the colourful socks on a piece of cloth on the sidewalk at the edge of another shop. Being on good terms with the shop owner and the vendors nearby, it was not difficult for Thu and Ly to make an informal agreement to rent this tiny space for a modest sum of money. With only a few hundred pairs of socks as stock, it was a truly small-scale business compared to others in the village. Yet, by purchasing socks from a wholesaler in the village and reselling them at retail price to customers, they could make enough to make a living, they said.

It was the first year for Thu and Ly as traders in Ninh Hiệp, and as the Lunar New Year approached, they planned to move to another place in the market. When I visited the markets after the New Year's break, I found

E. Horat, *Trading in Uncertainty*,
DOI 10.1007/978-3-319-55648-2_6

Thu at her new place, just a few meters away from the old place. The selling space still belonged to the same shop as she had only moved from the edge to the front of the house, yet the new stall was bigger and more convenient since there was even enough space for a small chair to sit on while waiting for customers. Moreover, instead of socks, she had started to sell fashionable women's clothing, which she arranged nicely on clothes hangers and on two mannequins. However, the most noticeable change was that she had established a family business along with her sister, her sister's husband and her two sisters-in-law. From then on, labour was divided, and hence, Thu took over the task to travel to China in order to import women's clothing, while the other members of the business stayed back in the village to attend to the shop. The turnover was quite remarkable and thus, after just a few weeks of being in business, Thu signed a contract to rent a second shop in the same street to sell men's fashion as well.

In addition to importing ready-made clothing from Guangzhou in order to supply the two shops, Thu also buys fabrics with the purpose of producing certain designs that, according to her, have the potential to be sold well in the village. Because she has only recently started to produce clothing and does not have much time, she only produces one design per week, which her sisters-in-law sell next to the imported clothes. Four days per week she is not in China, but devotes her time to making clothing patterns at home. The inspiration for her work is drawn from diverse sources. Sometimes, it is from fellow designers in her village or from exposure to the works on display in Chinese markets. Other times, she browses the Internet for new ideas. After drawing the pattern on paper, she brings it together with the fabric to Hoa, the wife of her husband's brother, who lives close by and has a workshop for sewing. Thu decided to do so because it is faster and more convenient than to outsource this step to a factory outside the village, as other traders tend to do. Nevertheless, Thu would complain about the problem of her designs being copied by Hoa and thus losing the competitive advantage in attempting to set a new trend. Since Hoa is a relative, Thu tries to avoid conflicts with her. At the same time, Thu also hesitates to change to another sewing workshop, not only because she would have to renegotiate the price and time for sewing and the payment methods, but also, and perhaps even more importantly, because of the high likelihood of the designs being copied by another workshop as well. As such, while the arrangement with Hoa is not ideal, Thu accepts the situation.

Remarkable about this case is, first of all, its manifestation of entrepreneurship as it depicts a trader—Thu—starting from a truly small-scale business that she is able to develop into a thriving business involving four more family members. Her resourceful personality and her skills to lead and organise stand out as the decisive factors for her entrepreneurial drive. Furthermore, the case captures some of the advantages and disadvantages of particular social relations in business and sheds a glance at how individuals make decisions by considering different factors. It also touches upon the dilemma that familiarity and intimacy are the preconditions for trust, but at the same time reduce the ability and willingness to sanction. The relation between Thu and Hoa is exemplary in that it shows how Hoa seizes the chance to copy Thu's designs, while Thu benefits from Hoa's fast and convenient sewing service, even if at the cost of losing the competitive advantage. Although Thu knows that Hoa copies her designs, she continues to rely on her, simply because she expects that any possible alternative would leave her equally bad or even worse off. Hoa, who knows that Thu does not consent to her copying the designs, is aware of Thu's position and therefore perceives the risk of losing Thu as a customer or of provoking a conflict between the families as low.

Flexible Stability

As illustrated in the ethnography above, flexibility is a crucial feature of the organisation of trade in the village due to the rapidly changing environment. In addition to the fluctuations in the global market, shifting international clothing trends and changing trade policies and regulations, micro-level changes have to be taken into consideration as well, such as local consumer preferences, the development of the village economy and the marketplace, and dynamics in the family. Nevertheless, traders do not merely adapt to a changing environment, but also trigger changes by resorting to different strategies. In regard to trade relations, for instance, newly made contacts may evolve into longer-term relationships. Over time, they have potential to morph into regular customers and suppliers. Meanwhile, the importance of well-established relationships may erode over time or lose its significance entirely. Moreover, owing to their receptiveness to trends and customer demands, traders switch from one type of clothing to another, or, for instance, from Chinese imports to made-in-Vietnam products. Thus, when speaking of flexibility in the organisation of trade, I am referring to the readiness of traders to change the merchandise, the shop location, and the supply and distribution channels, including the corresponding relationships.

In the literature, flexibility in small-scale production has been examined critically by asking what the costs of flexibility are and whom flexibility benefits (Green 1997; Rothstein 2005). Frances A. Rothstein (2005), who has conducted research on small-scale garment manufacturing in a rural Mexican community, investigates the new relationship between the residents of the community and global capitalism. She claims that, in this context, "flexibility and control at the local level are largely illusions that hide a reality of greater control by fewer people at the global level". Based on a detailed analysis of the involved actors, she concludes that while retailers, manufacturers and retailer/manufacturers in the community can reap short-term benefits, the arrangement works to the disadvantage of workers, owners and worker/owners of small businesses. In the context of Ninh Hiệp, I argue that flexibility is not just a passive reaction to the consequences of global capitalist formations, but part of a strategy for family businesses to deal with changing circumstances and a way to shape globalisation from below (see Mathews et al. 2012). Moreover, instead of understanding flexibility in terms of instability, as Rothstein (2005, 67) seems to imply, I suggest to conceive flexibility and stability as two complementary strategies which traders use selectively. Traders may want more flexibility in one aspect, and more stability in another. From this view, relationships are the tools to regulate the degree of flexibility and stability in a business.

In the case of Thu and Ly, they were both newcomers and had started off together on a very small scale. After the first year, they both switched to other locations, products and business sectors. While Thu established a business with her sister and in-laws, and started to import and produce clothing in addition to only selling, Ly moved to a stall at the old market, where she started to sell underwear, just like her mother had done in the past in Đồng Xuân market in Hanoi. "It's boring here", Ly said when I visited her, "but the stall rental fee is very low compared to the Fashion Street. Now that it's only me, I cannot afford to sell anywhere else". When asking her why she decided to sell underwear, she replied: "The trends for underwear don't change much. I can keep the assortment of underwear for a longer time without having to run after or create new trends. It's a stable business". Because her husband works as a driver and is not at home often, and there is nobody else who could look after Ly's stall, she decided to sell underwear because it also meant that she would not be required to go to China herself and could instead restock her stall with goods her sister-in-law bought for her from China. "Buying from her, I know that I will get the commodities at a good price", Ly would say.

Thus, while Thu applies flexibility as the predominant strategy, for Ly stability is important. Ly relies heavily on her sister-in-law as a trustworthy supplier and sells her goods mostly to regular customers. She neither has the capital to invest in renting a shop at a more frequented location, nor family members with whom she could establish a business. Coming from a nearby village, Ly is not well connected with Ninh Hiệp and therefore cannot expand her business in any way. Although she can still participate in the market and make what she considers a decent living, her business is not as thriving as Thu's, who has married into a Ninh Hiệp family and is also living there. Thu established far more diversified relations as a result of her business strategy, which relied heavily on multitasking. For instance, Thu's customers are wholesalers and retailers, and while her supply channels in China are flexible, she prefers to have a stable relation with the sewing workshop in the village. Having a vast social network that allows for a combination of stability and flexibility is crucial as it helps businesses to cope with changing situations and to use one's resources efficiently. Last but not least, Thu's impressive character and business acumen shape the way she conducts business.

Price-Fixing, Specialisation and the Informal Banking and Credit System

Social networks are of crucial importance to deal with business-related uncertainties. While relations with local officials do not have the same significance as they used to have in the past, the relationships between traders and customers as well as the relationships among traders themselves continue to be essential in the marketplace. One reason is the sharing of business-related information in the interest of reducing risks and uncertainties, especially through price-fixing. Mr. Thá, an elderly villager, told me that:

> In business we can only survive if we unite, because if I sell something at a price and you sell it at another price, we will destroy the price. That's why we should exchange information about prices and what to buy and sell on a particular day. In commerce we need to unify, to help each other…We have to do business together. If one drifts away he will die [economically], because he is not able to develop his business. Without information one['s business] dies.

Price-fixing is done informally by coordinating prices for a certain piece of clothing with neighbouring traders, friends and relatives who also sell at the market. While there might be an incentive to ignore a previously agreed price in order to make a quick sale, the incentive for being on good terms with neighbouring traders is far greater to most sellers and they usually avoid luring customers away from others by offering lower prices. Regular customers, however, often enjoy more flexible prices. The exchange of information with stall neighbours, not only about prices, but also about the products themselves—e.g. trends, origin—is crucial. In addition, the information on the trustworthiness of particular providers and customers is highly sought after as it helps traders to avoid potentially negative and troublesome experiences.

Rather than trying to expand one's business and becoming more independent, family businesses tend to specialise in one step of the production and marketing chain according to their available resources—capital, labour, relations, skills and experience. When performing the steps that fall outside their immediate professional focus, they rely on others. For example, most villagers who produce clothing buy the fabric at the market in Ninh Hiệp from traders who go to China on a regular basis (Fig. 6.1). Some villagers specialise in cutting cloth, while others cut, sew and sometimes decorate the clothing, and finally, vendors sell their own or other people's products at the marketplace. Only a few family businesses do not collaborate with other businesses directly. If one family business relies on another business, priority is usually given to relatives. However, this does not suggest that traders are entirely confined to doing business with relatives, as will be shown later. In many cases, they choose their partners according to the goods or services offered.

Traders in Ninh Hiệp usually focus on one type of clothing—either women's or men's clothing, and either for children, young adults or middle-aged people—but change the selection according to the four seasons.

Fig. 6.1 Cloth section inside the old market

This sometimes entails a change of the source of supply as well, because simple clothing, worn in the warm months, can be produced in the village or bought in Ho Chi Minh City, whereas more sophisticated clothing, and especially winter clothing, is often imported from China.[1] In the following paragraphs, I will illustrate Mrs. Huyền's business, which is quite typical in that she specialises in one part of the production process in combination with selling, but relies on other businesses for importing fabrics, and outsources the sewing to a factory outside the village.

Mrs. Huyền and her family, that is her husband and two of their four adult children, live in a spacious yet modestly decorated two-storey house. It is located a few hundred metres from the old market where Mrs. Huyền sells colourful fabrics in a corner of the oldest part of the market. The pieces of fabric are piled on a wooden board, weighed and then sold to mainly retail customers. Mrs. Huyền does not travel to China by herself but instead buys leftover fabric stock from different wholesale traders in the village at a reduced price when the patterns are out of fashion. Her second daughter Trang, who still lives at home, sells infant clothing a couple of metres from her stall. While the fabric trade of Mrs. Huyền is rather slow and not very lucrative, the home-produced infant clothing can be sold in large amounts to wholesalers, and in smaller amounts but at a higher price to retail customers.

Mrs. Huyền is in charge of most of the production-related tasks, which she carries out in the morning before attending to her stall at the market, or, alternatively, in the evening after dinner. Trang is responsible for buying fabric and selling the ready-made infant clothes at the market. Although she goes to China to buy fabric every now and then, most of the time she buys fabric for home production from wholesalers at the market in Ninh Hiệp. The first and the third daughters of Mrs. Huyền are married and thus have separate businesses. Both sell accessories such as belts, hats, sunglasses, hair clips and bands. Sometimes, they go to China together in order to buy the merchandise. Other times, only one of them goes and makes the necessary purchases for both of them. The son, who is the youngest of the four children and does not have his own business yet, helps his mother and sisters in their respective businesses.

When I visited Mrs. Huyền at home on a sunny, but cold, day a few weeks after the Lunar New Year celebrations in 2013, she invited me to come up to the second floor to see the first step of the production of infant clothing. The first thing I noticed when I entered the room was the dusty air—a very common feature of this type of work, as I realised during my subsequent visits. In the back of the room, there were four old sewing machines, which Mrs. Huyền had bought in the early days of the business when she had managed to hire a few labourers for sewing clothing. Yet, having faced several problems related to the lack of space for accommodating the workers, insufficient management skills and, finally, loss of trust when the workers stole from her during her absence from the workshop, she decided to narrow down the scope of her business and focus on cutting cloth. Although three of the four machines were still functioning adequately, they had hardly been used in recent years, except for the rare occasion when Mrs. Huyền or somebody else in the family needed to sew something for herself.

On the floor lay squares of fabric, each about one-and-a-half square meters, tidily on one another. "With this fabric", Mrs. Huyền explained, "I can make 1000 pieces of infant clothes within two days, each consisting of a pair of shorts and a shirt". After having inscribed all necessary parts with the help of paper patterns on the cloth on top, she took an electric jigsaw and cut out the parts, which took no longer than fifteen minutes. Afterwards, she bound the parts together with a textile band and prepared them for transport to a nearby factory outside the village, where the parts would be sewn together. Usually, Mrs. Huyền needs an entire day for the preparations, the most time-consuming task being the piling of square pieces of cloth. When the ready-made infant clothes are brought back the next day from the factory, Mrs. Huyền lays them out on the living room floor so that she, her husband, her son and Trang have space to assemble pairs of shorts and shirts, fold them and finally put them into plastic bags. This is usually done in the early morning so that the clothes can be taken to the market before it gets too crowded.

One obvious advantage of specialisation is that businesses save time and money due to the focus on one or two steps and products. Another important, yet less apparent, advantage of specialisation and hence collaborating with other businesses in the village is the access to the informal intra-village banking and credit system. In the import–production–marketing chain, goods are usually passed from one business to another without any cash payment until the goods leave the village. At this point, the money travels back from the last person in the chain through several hands until it reaches the first person who often is a large fabric dealer. Thus, the villagers, who rely on each other for supply, production or distribution, are linked by credit relationships in which trust is crucial. The central role of mutual trust and good will in credit relations, generated by long-term and repeated business interactions, has been stressed in the earlier studies of peasant marketing systems in different parts of the world (Mintz 1961; Dewey 1962; Geertz 1963; Davis 1973) and in South Vietnam (Barton 1977). In order to establish the relationships of trust, the spread of information and the possibility to apply sanctions in case of misconduct are important. In Ninh Hiệp, living in the village and being a member of the community through one's own family or through marriage is therefore essential to be eligible to participate in the informal intra-village banking and credit system.

Thus, thanks to the informal banking and credit system, it is relatively easy to start a new business and even to operate on a larger scale, as Mr. Thành pointed out. A gentle-speaking man in his mid-forties, Mr. Thành was eager to discuss economic theories he had first learned about at university and later by himself. Being the owner of one of the biggest workshops in Ninh Hiệp, he employs fifteen young labourers who carry out tasks ranging from cutting cloth, sewing the pieces together, decorating and finally wrapping the product to sell it in the village. To accommodate his workers, most of whom come from far away provinces, he rented a house close by. His wife, Mrs. Xuyến, manages the business accounting, and she is also in charge of making patterns for new fashion designs. The designs look very similar to the ones imported from China—the differences are small and sometimes hardly noticeable. Mr. Thành and Mrs. Xuyến produce more elaborate types of clothing than other workshops, such as dresses in summer and coats in winter, with zippers, pockets, buttons, imprints and rhinestones, and apply other sewing techniques than only a plain seam. The workshop is integrated into their house and occupies the entire third floor for sewing and the ground floor for decorating and wrapping. In addition to their own stall at the new market where a niece is in charge of sales, they supply several other stalls in the area with clothing. Operating on a large scale, it is crucial for Mr. Thành to be able to purchase fabric on credit (*được nợ* or *được mua chịu*). He considers himself very lucky to be located in "one of the nation's biggest raw material warehouses", as he refers to Ninh Hiệp, and that, for instance, he can allegedly buy cloth for 500 million Vietnamese Đồng (around 23,000 USD) on credit because he is a member of the village community and has built up a good reputation over the years. The fact that he comes from a respected family also contributes to his repute. He regards the access to the informal banking and credit system as one decisive factor for his business success. On another account, he specified that not money itself was the crucial factor to be able to establish a business, but trade relations:

> Trade relations don't suddenly appear [out of nowhere]. If somebody opens a shop, his father and his siblings will refer customers to him. This is the primary capital, much more important than money. It's like if somebody goes fishing: If you give him a fish, he'll only have enough for one meal. But the crucial capital you pass on to your children are the relations for doing business. Economically, relationships are money, they are the capital. Someone who has good relations does not need capital to do business. What we inherit from earlier generations are relations.

As became clear in the story of Mr. Thành, relationships in general and the informal banking and credit system in particular are very beneficial for villagers. Establishing credit relations is most important to the businesses that place emphasis on production because they depend heavily on the possibility to purchase raw material on credit. Hence, they have to invest in machines for the shop floor, raw material for production and wages for the workers, but returns are not immediate because the buyers in the village who distribute the products also expect to be offered credit.

Yet it is not only the bigger workshops who benefit from the informal banking and credit system, but also smaller workshops and vendors. They can usually not pay the supplier immediately but wait until the products are sold to a customer from outside the village who pays in cash. Asking a young man, who recently established a sewing workshop together with his wife, when the market vendors selling his products pay what they purchased from him on credit, he replied: “The traders, who sell my products, pay their debts (*thanh toán nợ*) every 2 weeks, or at the end of the month. They pay when they have money”. Thus, the payment of debts does not adhere to a strict deadline like bank credits, but should be met in accordance with the agreement both parties have negotiated previously. To not pay one's debt will result in a bad reputation in the community and may lead to the exclusion from the informal banking and credit system, itself a costly penalty.

Apart from debts in trade relations, borrowing money from family members and friends for business-related matters is common. While a few informants mentioned having taken out formal bank loans in the past, the majority expressed a strong preference for informal credit. A common way to save money and have access to credit is through revolving credit associations, the local term of which is *hụi*. It is not only popular in Ninh Hiệp, but in Vietnam more generally, and local variants of the same principle are to be found in most parts of the world.[2] In addition to family, friends and through participation in revolving credit associations, credit can be obtained from moneylenders. Although they charge a higher fee than the standard bank interest, most villagers prefer this private service to the bank, because large amounts of money can be borrowed almost immediately and paid back with a flexible schedule. Taking out a loan from the bank involves a complicated, time-consuming and formal procedure, and must be done in accordance with the strict terms and conditions of the bank. Allison Truitt (2012) notes that economists and bankers refer to Vietnam as “one of Asia's most ‘underbanked’ economies”, meaning that the availability of mainstream banking services is still very limited. Yet, she argues that “the problem of ‘under-banking’ has been complicated not only by the lack of access to banking services, but also by popular mistrust of the predominantly state-owned banking sector” (Truitt 2012, 131). Thus, the unpopularity of formal banking services among most Ninh Hiệp people may not only stem from practical considerations, but also from a lack of trust in banks.

A major advantage of informal money-lending services in Ninh Hiệp is that they are negotiable and "custom-tailored" for traders. One particularly popular service private moneylenders in Ninh Hiệp offer is the transfer of money to the bank accounts of Chinese assistants shortly before the actual shopping trip to Guangzhou takes place.[3] Once Ninh Hiệp traders arrive in Guangzhou, the Chinese assistants, with whom the traders had prearranged to meet, hand them out the money in Chinese currency they had received via Ninh Hiệp moneylenders in advance. Ninh Hiệp traders pay back the debt to the moneylenders when they finally have money in their hands from selling the Chinese-imported merchandise, often in more than one go. Hence, in not only advancing money on loan, but also transferring it directly, moneylenders serve two important purposes at the same time: one is to enable traders to buy as much merchandise as they need at once; the other is to facilitate and make the business trip safer so that traders do not have to carry and exchange large amounts of cash and do not get into trouble during the journey from Ninh Hiệp to Guangzhou.

Nordstrom (2000) emphasises that international informal networks, or "shadow networks" as she calls them, are not small-scale, low-income, low-tech, subsistence-level activities and marginal, but are actually central to the world's economies and politics. She mentions the informal banking systems in Asia as an example of how "cash, goods and credit flow along these banking lines", and that "this system may be non-formal, and the 'banks' little more than storefronts, but the system is both vast and powerful, transmitting untold fortunes through family and ethnic linkage, business partnerships and triad associations" (Nordstrom 2000, 45). An interesting finding of her research is that these shadow networks are not entirely distinct or in opposition to states, but intersect with or work through formal institutions at times, and that they are very coherent. In regard to the informal banking and transport system Ninh Hiệp traders use when making business with Chinese traders in Guangzhou, it is noteworthy that they are considered safer, cheaper, more efficient and more trustworthy than formal channels. This observation is supported by Caroline Grillot's (2014) work on informal trade across the Sino–Vietnamese border.

While the organisation of trade in terms of specialisation and the informal banking system is advantageous for villagers, at least as long as agreements are kept and debts are paid, traders coming from outside the community to conduct business find it difficult to establish trade relations in Ninh Hiệp. Even though technically everybody can start a business in Ninh Hiệp, it is a challenge to participate in the textile and clothing trade in the absence of credit relations with local traders. Those traders who come from outside and are not married or related to anybody from Ninh Hiệp need to have capital to invest in the business and usually pursue a different strategy than local traders. One of them is Mrs. Ngọc, who originally comes from a north-eastern Vietnamese province:

Mrs. Ngọc, a fashionably dressed trader in her late thirties, operates two stores for women's clothing at the new market. Before moving to a town close to Ninh Hiệp and establishing a business together with her husband, she lived in Hanoi, where she supplied sewing workshops with cloth and thereby acquired expert knowledge on textiles. When she heard of the new markets that were going to be built in Ninh Hiệp, she and her husband decided to pursue self-employment by establishing a family business. Not only Mrs. Ngọc's look—high heels, make-up, stylish clothing—distinguishes her from the other traders at the market, but also her business strategy: instead of selling cheap merchandise like most of the traders in Ninh Hiệp, she decided to offer clothing of better quality at a slightly higher price. By explaining the quality difference and thereby proving her knowledge of fabric and clothing, she gains the customer's trust—a very important condition for doing business, she says. As she would point out, her business strategy is to be different and unique in terms of the clothing designs she sells: "I am the only person who sells this pattern in the market". In addition to her different designs, Mrs. Ngọc's business differs in another central aspect: her husband is Chinese, which means that she has access to supply channels that most traders in Ninh Hiệp do not. Unlike Mrs. Ngọc, they must rely on themselves when organising business trips to other marketplaces in China. Furthermore, Mrs. Ngọc uses an alternative transport route to send the goods to Ninh Hiệp, which includes a cargo ship until Hải Phòng, and from there an overland transport to the village. Upon asking her about her position in the market, she reassures that running a store here as an outsider is not a problem at all. Her stall neighbours were friendly, she said, and often invite her to play cards with them in the afternoon.

While Mrs. Ngọc is accepted in the market and spends time with other vendors, she is clearly not a member of the community and therefore does not have access to the informal banking and credit system unless somebody from the village would act as a guarantor for her. However, as she has enough capital, very good knowledge of the garment industry as well as on how to run a business, and on top of that, is in an advantageous position regarding the Chinese market thanks to her husband, the fact of her not belonging to the community does not form an obstacle for her participating in the market. A particularly interesting point about her is that she does not try to gain the customer's trust primarily by offering a just price or creating a personal relation, but by showing her knowledge about clothing.

Trade Relations Among Ninh Hiệp Traders

As demonstrated thus far, collaboration with relatives is a common practice among family businesses in Ninh Hiệp. However, this does not entail that traders automatically turn to kin when doing business. As Leshkowich points out, resorting to kinship ties for the purpose of conducting business is not to be taken as "an essential fact of market life" in Vietnam, but rather as a "logical response to concrete circumstances" (Leshkowich 2014, 90–91). In the context of Leshkowich's own research in the 1990s in Ho Chi Minh City, these circumstances were the outcome of economic reforms and included "un- or underemployment, political suspicion of private entrepreneurship, and the need to forge personalistic business relations in a volatile environment" (Leshkowich 2014, 91). Leshkowich made sense of her observation of the performance and intentional use of kinship terminology among small-scale traders—even when there was no actual kinship relation—in seeing it as a strategy to obtain security and referring to it as "strategic familism". In line with Leshkowich, I also recognise the crucial role of kinship in the organisation of trade. Nevertheless, instead of applying the notion of "strategic familism", I will focus on the situational use—and at times avoidance—of actual kinship ties. Furthermore, I will stress the importance of business relations between traders who are not related. Thus, in what follows, I shall attempt to explain how traders in Ninh Hiệp combine relations with kin and non-kin to carry out their business. This strategy is fittingly captured by the concepts of flexibility and stability introduced earlier.

Looking back at the time I spent in Ninh Hiệp, the marked significance of kinship ties in business would often stand out as a recurrent theme throughout the stories of Thu, Ly, Mrs. Huyền and Mr. Thành. They all collaborate with immediate and distant family members and relatives, be it siblings, aunts, uncles, nieces, nephews, cousins, or in-laws. Generally, more immediate family members are perceived as more reliable than distant ones and may be preferred over acquaintances in certain situations. This is in line with Luhmann's (1988) and Adler and Kwon's (2000) claim that familiarity is a precondition for trust, and also with Dasgupta's (1988) argument that being able to estimate the likelihood of certain actions of others is crucial. Usually, one is more familiar with immediate family members than with distant ones and can more easily estimate the actions of the first than the latter group. Moreover, the strong moral obligation towards immediate family members to not cheat adds to cooperation, which in turn enhances the level of trust. Another aspect to take into consideration is the consequences resulting from cheating. In severe cases of cheating among close relatives, the price to pay would be very high, assuming it leads to a serious conflict in the family. Yet, as both sides may not want to get into a conflict, the situation could be exploited by one side to a certain degree, as was the case with Thu and her sister-in-law Hoa, illustrated at the beginning of this chapter.

In interactions between traders, trust is of utmost importance, since deals are brokered based on oral agreements only, rather than written contracts. The oral nature of the agreements renders the deals as legally non-binding. Yet, despite the advantage of being trusted more readily, kinship ties may also slow down and restrict traders' actions, especially when disagreements or conflicts arise. Therefore, members of the extended family or in-laws are not necessarily one's most desired business partners. Although kinship ties are an integral part of the village economy, business relationships within the community are not restricted to familial ties, because the success of traders largely depends on their flexibility and how fast they react to the demand of customers.

Thus, Ninh Hiệp traders sometimes choose acquaintances rather than kin for business transactions. The category "acquaintance" in this context refers to people with whom one is neither related nor friends. Here, the two individuals know each other as a result of their belonging to the village community. Most of the family businesses that collaborate with other businesses in the village employ a mixed strategy of specialisation and diversification: while they usually specialise in one step of the production and marketing chain and in one type of merchandise, they often use diverse channels for supply and distribution. Often, their business network consists of both kin and acquaintances. For those transactions where choice is important and prices are easily comparable, it is common to engage with anyone who offers the sought product. Buying fabric for home production is usually done in this way. For example, when Trang, the daughter of Mrs. Huyền, goes out to buy fabric, she does not care about a potential kin or non-kin relationship with the vendor, but buys whatever material she likes in terms of colour, pattern and quality. The fact that there is a standard village price for the kind of fabric she needs for the infant clothes means that transaction costs are low and she thus does not need to establish a relation with the vendor to get a good price. Whether or not credit is offered depends on the vendor and how well he or she evaluates the customer's credibility in the village in terms of timely payment. Therefore, a reputation of being trustworthy is fundamental in the village community. A bad reputation has a negative impact on one's ability to establish new and maintain existing relationships, especially those related to credit.

In transactions where stability and reliability are desirable for both parties, traders usually choose kin as business partners. This is often the case in the link between production and marketing. Businesses that either produce or sell normally depend on relatives for accomplishing complementary tasks. In these transactions, the goods are sold at a price composed of the material and production costs plus a minimal profit. Finally, if one sells ready-made clothing from China but, for whatever reason, cannot go there in person to import, he or she simply buys the goods from close relatives, which generally tend to be one's own siblings or in-laws, to sell these goods at the market.

It should be stressed that the above-described transactions among kin and between acquaintances are always seen as relating to business and thus payments are expected to be met according to a previously reached agreement between buyer and seller. As Davis (1973) observed in a Philippine marketplace, kinship relations do not necessarily result in a "burden of dependency", but can be profitable and perform economically significant functions if they are handled well.

In addition to business relations with kin and acquaintances, traders' networks contain social relations, which do not involve transactions, but are relevant for the exchange of information. According to Mark Granovetter (1973), networks consist of different types of social relations—strong, weak and absent—with distinct functions. He argued for the importance of relations between groups, which do not interact closely and frequently, or, put differently, for the cohesive power of "weak ties" in a community. Following his line of argumentation, weak ties are particularly significant in regard to the spreading of information. Based on the definition of the strength of a tie as "a combination of the amount of time, the emotional intensity, the intimacy (mutual confiding), and the reciprocal services which characterize the tie", Granovetter (1973, 1361) argued that people linked by strong ties tend to share friends and thus information circulated through these ties stays in a rather small group of people, whereas information passed through weak ties can reach a larger number of people and traverse greater social distance. While traders share what relates to their own business within the family and close friends, they usually talk about other people's business with other traders. This finding is of great importance to the case of Ninh Hiệp, where information is usually kept confidential within a group of people who interact closely with one another, like the family and a few close relatives. Yet, in order to obtain new information it is crucial to have access to other groups of people. One such opportunity is the travel to China where traders, who do not interact with one another on a regular basis, spend time together and thus get information they would otherwise not be able to access.

Finally, there is a fourth type of relationship, which is not seen by traders as created for business, but is nevertheless crucial in their everyday life at the marketplace. These relationships, which are typically established between stall neighbours, are referred to as "tình cảm" (*sentiment, affection*) relationships and have a recreational and emotional effect. By offering each other small snacks and drinks, and sharing stories and personal problems, traders cultivate *tình cảm* relationships. Although these intimate ties are seen as distinct from or even opposed to business relations, they are important for traders, primarily in doing small favours for each other such as watching each other's stall during a short absence, and sometimes sharing experiences and business-related information. One kind of business-related information exchanged in such relationships is, for example, other traders' level of trustworthiness. Thus, even though *tình cảm* relations are not created with the intention to perform better in business, they may be beneficial. Not only do they have emotional value, but they also enable the flow of information about fellow villagers and their financial situation, which can be important when it comes to decisions whether to offer credit. *Tình cảm* relations are morally loaded and structure the interactions between the involved parties. While in the daily life at the market mutual moral obligations moderate ruthless competition and conflicts and generally lead to fair play, *tình cảm* relations may also be used to create solidarity and to organise collective actions when common interests are threatened.

Even though many family businesses apply a strategy of specialisation and coordinate the workflow with other businesses in the village, some family businesses do not directly collaborate with others. One of these businesses is the one of Hạnh, a young woman trader selling women's clothing in the old market, and her husband, who recently started to sell fashionable men's clothing in one of the new markets. Once they have sold most of their goods or need new designs, Hạnh travels to China to buy ready-made clothing for the two stalls. In good times, she may go as often as once a week, while at other times only once a month or even once in two months. Thus, the business model of Hạnh and her husband consists of importing clothing from China and selling it directly to wholesale and sometimes retail customers. Yet, even this type of business is not completely self-reliant as Hạnh uses the commonly organised means of transport to China and other related services. Perhaps most importantly, even if she does not collaborate with other businesses, she maintains *tình cảm* relationships with other vendors selling close by in the market and creates ties with other traders during her travels to China and thus has access to valuable information about trends in the marketplace and the businesses of other traders.

In the face of rapid social change and economic restructuring, social relationships have remained essential in contemporary Vietnam in all areas of life. As Philip Taylor (2016) and Hy Van Luong (2016) note, a core question is to what extent connections are equally accessible for people of different social backgrounds. In Ninh Hiệp, relationships are used to navigate between flexibility and stability as well as between cooperation and competition in order to cope with rapidly changing circumstances. Relations are at the heart of businesses and allow traders to manage the daily market life. Yet, a comparison of the businesses of Thu, Ly, Mrs. Huyền, Mr. Thành and Mrs. Ngọc reveals that their ability to forge relations is quite uneven. Although cultural capital resulting from higher education may attribute positively to someone's trustworthiness, even more important is the respectability of one's family. A good reputation is not built overnight, but in a long-term process, as with Mr. Thành, who "inherited" his reputation from his father. This points at the potency of the legacy of the past and its influence over current relations of power and influence. In terms of status, there has not been a disruption but a rather seamless transition from the pre-to the post-Đổi mới period. However, this is not the whole story. In order to build a successful business in contemporary times, entrepreneurial acumen is of great relevance. Even people who are relatively new to trade but were able establish a network relying on their own capacities could see their businesses thriving. Management skills as part of entrepreneurialism stood out positively in the cases of Thu and Mr. Thành, yet was experienced as a disadvantage when not fully developed as with Mrs. Huyền. While Thu and Mr. Thành possess the necessary conditions and indeed have flourishing businesses, Mrs. Huyền only fulfils one while Ly has none of them and consequently fares much less well. Mrs. Ngọc, who is not a community member, is not able to latch on the intra-village network, but has money, experience and entrepreneurial skills to organise her business.

It is not necessarily the size of one's network—the sum of all relationships—that is decisive, but the diversity of the network, resulting from a combination of different sorts of relationships with trade partners as well as stall neighbours. However, although relations are an important resource for traders, and the tightly knit trade community is beneficial in many respects, traders may also find themselves trapped in some relations. This may be the case with certain kin relations because they contain moral obligations. Moreover, some relations may not be entirely beneficial or even partly destructive, but are nevertheless maintained if they fulfil at least partly the purpose, as we have seen with Thu and Hoa. Quitting a relationship also involves costs, most importantly time that need to be invested to look for another trade partner and negotiate the terms and conditions, and social costs, likely to arise when the two people are related. Finally, establishing and maintaining relationships is not the result of pure calculation, but also include factors such as sympathy, emotions and even coincidence for getting to know one person and not another.

Social relations are not only important for conducting business, but strengthen the cohesion of society and foster solidarity in the trade community. Especially *tình cảm* relations bear potential to solidarise with one another and to organise collective actions in order to protect common interests, as was the case with the protests against the privatisation of the old market in 2010 and the new market project in 2014 (see Chap. 3).

Navigating Between Cooperation and Competition

In her study on a marketplace in the Philippines, Cristina Szanton Blanc (1972, 129–131) distinguished between economic and social motives to cooperate. Economic motives can result from the concern of traders to maximise profits by a tacit agreement on a price instead of price competition, or because they need help in their business, or to increase security. As social motives, Szanton Blanc mainly refers to the "right to survive" , which means that every vendor should at least be able to make a living from selling, and if necessary, vendors should help each other out. However, in Ninh Hiệp, the notion of "helping each other" (*giúp nhau*) is more complicated. When asked whether they help each other in business, about half of the traders replied positively while the other half denied that this was the case. The notion of helping each other is problematic because it is not clearly defined and can be applied to a very broad range of areas, ranging from financial help to practical help in another's business to the sharing of information and experience, and many other forms of help. When asked more precisely how and whom they help, it turned out that the most common way was indirect help, and that more important than to help was to not purposefully cause harm to others. At times, indirect help can imply offering basic advice during a business trip to China to less experienced traders from the village. However, it does not include direct intervention such as helping a fellow village trader bargain in a market in China if his or her Chinese language skills are not sufficient. Generally, the closer one is to somebody, the more practical support is offered. In a family, for instance, lending money is common practice, and also assisting in each other's shop if needed. Thus, it is noteworthy that businesses do not only collaborate directly to accomplish complementary tasks, but also help each other in various ways. Even businesses considered as self-reliant depend on other businesses, like Hạnh who travels with other traders to China and uses the jointly organised services and benefits from the experiences of others.

However, the local economy is not only marked by cooperation, but also competition. A noticeable feature of the markets in Ninh Hiệp is that traders usually do not compete openly with one another in the marketplace, but in rather subtle ways. Moreover, competition in Ninh Hiệp is non-destructive because most traders follow the moral guidelines, including not taking away each other's customers and not undermining prices in the village. This is consistent with what (Gambetta 1988, 215) argues, namely to be able to compete in a non-destructive way, one needs to trust one's competitors comply with the rules. Thus, non-destructive competition is prevalent in Ninh Hiệp because the level of generalised trust is high according to villagers, and there is a possibility to sanction traders who do not abide by the rules. For instance, if a vendor steals her neighbours' potential customer by offering a lower price, she puts the relationship with her neighbours at stake, which may not only put paid to the emotional bond, but also cut the flow of information useful for conducting business. One day, as I was sitting with Hạnh and her friend Thảo, they started chatting about another trader a few metres down the aisle, whom they—and apparently many other traders around—seemed to dislike. Upon asking them why they used so harsh words when talking about that vendor, Thảo answered: "I want no truck with her, it's her own fault. Mrs. Bình [the vendor they were talking about] is the kind of person who betrays others to make her own gain. For example, when everybody sells at the same price, she suddenly makes a lower offer to strike a deal". Hạnh chimed in: "Or, she randomly accuses other traders for luring away potential customers and thereby sabotaging her business. Quite generally, wherever Mrs. Bình goes, a conflict emerges shortly thereafter. Everybody around her ignores her, except for her husband, who is the only person with whom she talks in the market". Thus, by defying the rules of fairness and appropriate behaviour, Mrs. Bình disqualifies herself from the social life at the marketplace.

In order to attract new customers, traders use different strategies, such as displaying their freshest designs on a mannequin in front of their shops and making sure the designs are being replaced frequently, offering older designs on sale, and sometimes decorating the shop, for example with wallpapers. For traders who have their shops at much frequented places and pay a high shop rental fee, timing and innovation are crucial factors for being competitive. Several times a month, new designs emerge, and it is most profitable being the first vendor to sell a certain design. However, many traders imitate designs they see at the market, rather than coming up with their own innovations. Although the creator of a design can make a high profit at the beginning, if the imitators are fast and the design becomes popular among customers, the imitators can also make a gain. Interestingly, the more a design is imitated and displayed in shops, the more it is perceived as the latest fashion, and thus the better it is sold. Therefore, innovation and imitation go hand in hand and represent two mutually constituent aspects of the functioning of the market. Hạnh, whom I have just mentioned, employs both of these strategies, yet imitating others seems to be the dominant strategy:

> When I have time, I check designs on the Internet as an inspiration for the clothes I produce. If I set a new trend, I can make a high profit in the first few days. But most of the time, I follow the trends of others. When I go to China to buy merchandise, I usually buy what others buy. I am afraid of not being able to sell, so I don't buy too much at a time.

In addition to attracting new customers, traders try to keep wholesale customers over a longer time by treating them favourably. This can include offering advantageous terms of payment, arranging transportation services, reacting to customer's demands, taking their orders and giving price reductions, either by directly lowering the price or by giving a free sample. In turn, to become a preferred customer, customers have to qualify primarily as reliable partners in terms of regular purchases and payment. Each trader has his or her strategy to treat regular customers in a special way. Hạnh, for instance, built a relationship of trust and mutual help in using one of her regular customers as accomplice:

> One of my regular customers, whom I trust most, keeps me updated about new fashion trends in Hanoi. She comes here every week, sometimes even twice, and reports what she could sell well in her boutique and what customers look for. When she comes here for shopping, I ask her to look around what other vendors sell well and buy some samples of these designs for me. This gives me an idea of what customers like. I will then tear the sample apart to use it as a pattern for sewing. I cannot go around alone, because I have to attend to my stall. And what's more, the other vendors in the market know me and won't sell anything to me. Of course I offer her a good price, and I keep the goods she wants to buy until she comes to pick them up.

Because Ninh Hiệp traders are suspicious of each other in regard to imitating designs, they usually do not sell their merchandise to each other. Most disputes that arise in the market are provoked by traders who go around in search of new fashion trends. Therefore, using a customer to accomplish this job is a safe way to not get into trouble, at least as long as the customer is not suspected to cooperate with her. In addition, being informed about prices and consumer preferences of the end customer is helpful for traders to set prices and make buying decisions.

One fundamental aspect I have touched upon in several sections of this chapter is the role of trust in the organisation of trade in Ninh Hiệp. Closely associated with the concept of trust is trustworthiness, or more precisely, the reputation to be trustworthy. As Gambetta (1988, 233) has noted: “It may be hard to bank on altruism, but it is much harder to avoid banking on a reputation for trustworthiness: as all bankers (…) know, a good reputation is their best asset”. This statement can be applied to traders, as a reputation for trustworthiness is key to participate in the village trade. The fact that information about the reputation of others is well accessible within the community is a strong incentive for traders to cooperate with others and comply with agreements. In cases where somebody is indebted, another family member would repay the loan, or the indebted person would sell part of its property. In any case, it is difficult to escape the sanctions as long as one lives in the commune. In turn, traders who do not live in Ninh Hiệp are usually not trusted—not because they do not appear as trustworthy, but because they are not seen as belonging to the community and can escape potential informal sanctions without great difficulties. This predominance of relations of trust and generalised trust on the village level are decisive factors to understand the development of the markets in Ninh Hiệp.

In the next chapter, I will delve into the role of trade relations reaching beyond the community, including both suppliers and customers. Being rooted in an ancient trading village, people from Ninh Hiệp had established trade relations throughout the country from early on. However, I will only briefly describe the historical dimension of trade relations with Hanoi and Ho Chi Minh City and direct my focus on contemporary trade relations, including a detailed ethnographic account of a trip to the markets in Guangzhou.

Notes

1. I differentiate "simple" and "sophisticated" clothing in regard to the production process and the machines and skills required to produce a certain design or type of clothing. The simplest type is infant clothing, whereby two pieces of textile are sewn together by applying a plain seam. T-shirts and other casual clothing are also considered simple clothing, while coats, dresses and pants are usually produced in a more elaborate way.
2. See Leshkowich (2014, 112–113) for a detailed example of how *hụi* works at Bến Thành market.
3. The traders I spoke with were reluctant to divulge information regarding matters such as the exact mode of money transfer or the identity of the moneylenders. However, a cursory search on the internet is enough to find plenty of informal service providers that offer Vietnamese customers fast and easy money transfer to Chinese recipients.

References

Adler, Paul S., and Seok-Woo Kwon. 2000. Social Capital: The Good, the Bad, and the Ugly. SSRN Scholarly Paper ID 186928. Rochester: Social Science Research Network.

Barton, Clifton G. 1977. Credit and Commercial Control: The Strategies and Methods of Chinese Businessmen in South Vietnam. PhD Thesis, Ithaca: Cornell University.

Dasgupta, Partha. 1988. Trust as a Commodity. In *Trust: Making and Breaking Cooperative Relations*, ed. Diego Gambetta, 49–72. New York: Blackwell.

Davis, William G. 1973. *Social Relations in a Philippine Market: Self-Interest and Subjectivity*. Berkeley: University of California Press.

Dewey, Alice G. 1962. *Peasant Marketing in Java*. New York: Free Press of Glencoe.

Gambetta, Diego. 1988. Can We Trust Trust? In *Trust: Making and Breaking Cooperative Relations*, ed. Diego Gambetta, 213–237. New York: Blackwell.

Geertz, Clifford. 1963. *Peddlers and Princes: Social Change and Economic Modernization in Two Indonesian Towns*. Chicago: University of Chicago Press.

Granovetter, Mark S. 1973. The Strength of Weak Ties. *American Journal of Sociology* 78 (6): 1360–1380.

Green, Nancy L. 1997. *Ready-to-Wear and Ready-to-Work: A Century of Industry and Immigrants in Paris and New York*. Durham: Duke University Press.

Grillot, Caroline. 2014. Navigating across Beilun River. Chinese Adjustments to Border Trade Shipment Practices in Vietnam. In *Conference 'Traders in Motion: Networks, Identities, and Contestations in the Vietnamese Marketplace'*. Halle/Saale, Germany.

Leshkowich, Ann Marie. 2014. *Essential Trade: Vietnamese Women in a Changing Marketplace*. Honolulu: University of Hawaii Press.

Luhmann, Niklas. 1988. Familiarity, Confidence, Trust: Problems and Alternatives. In *Trust: Making and Breaking Cooperative Relations*, ed. Diego Gambetta, 94–108. New York: Blackwell.

Luong, Hy Van. 2016. Social Relations, Regional Variation, and Economic Inequality in Contemporary Vietnam: A View from Two Vietnamese Rural Communities. In *Connected and Disconnected in Vietnam: Remaking Social Relations in a Post-Socialist Nation*, ed. Philip Taylor, 41–72. Acton: Australian National University Press.

Mathews, Gordon, Gustavo L. Ribeiro, and Carlos Alba Vega (eds.). 2012. *Globalization from Below: The World's Other Economy*. London: Routledge.

Mintz, Sidney. 1961. Pratik: Haitian Personal Economic Relationships. In *Proceedings of the 1961 Annual Spring Meeting of the American Ethnological Society*.

Nordstrom, Carolyn. 2000. Shadows and Sovereigns. *Theory, Culture & Society* 17 (4): 35–54.

Rothstein, Frances A. 2005. Flexibility for Whom? Small-Scale Garment Manufacturing in Rural Mexico. In *Petty Capitalists and Globalization: Flexibility, Entrepreneurship, and Economic Development*, ed. Alan Smart, and Josephine Smart, 67–81. Albany, NY: State University of New York Press.

Szanton Blanc, Cristina. 1972. *A Right to Survive: Subsistence Marketing in a Lowland Philippine Town*. University Park: Pennsylvania State University Press.

Taylor, Philip. 2016. Introduction: An Overture to New Ethnographic Research on Connection and Disconnection in Vietnam. In *Connected and*

Disconnected in Vietnam: Remaking Social Relations in a Post-Socialist Nation, ed. Philip Taylor. Acton: Australian National University Press.
Truitt, Allison. 2012. Banking on the Middle Class in Ho Chi Minh City. In *The Reinvention of Distinction: Modernity and the Middle Class in Urban Vietnam*, ed. Van Nguyen-Marshall, Lisa B. Drummond, and Danièle Bélanger, 129–142. Dordrecht: Springer.

7

The Spatial Organisation of Trade

Thanks to the short distance and convenient transport connection between Ninh Hiệp and Hanoi, trade relations have been in full swing since long ago. Several of the famous streets in the Old Quarter in Hanoi, once dominated by craft guilds, are said to have a lot of Ninh Hiệp people as shop owners, namely Lãn Ông street (herbal medicine), Hà Trung street (leather products and gold exchange) and to a certain extent Hàng Da market (leather and a variety of other products), before it was turned into a modern shopping centre in 2011. Cloth traders from Ninh Hiệp used to sell their products at Đồng Xuân market, because it was known as the biggest wholesale cloth market in northern Vietnam. Yet, while Đồng Xuân market is right in the midst of the city and its spatial growth is therefore very limited, the number of markets and traders in Ninh Hiệp are still on the rise and in recent years has surpassed Đồng Xuân market in terms of size, variety and cheapness of goods. Most of the traders who still keep a stall at Đồng Xuân market commute between the village and the market every day.

Yet trade relations with Hanoi are not confined to people who originate from Ninh Hiệp and went to Hanoi to become shop owners in the old streets and traders at the markets just mentioned. Relations are also created with tailors, owners of boutiques and market vendors of various origins, all

E. Horat, *Trading in Uncertainty*,
DOI 10.1007/978-3-319-55648-2_7

currently located in Hanoi. Students should be mentioned as an additional category of customers who foster the connection between Hanoi and Ninh Hiệp to some extent, because they are particularly attracted by the cheap prices of the merchandise. Although they do not buy large amounts at once, they come frequently to take several pieces of different designs and sell the clothing and accessories (belts, hats, scarves, bags, purses and the like) at students markets, on the university campus and in dormitories. Some students are quite professional and even advertise the products on websites and take orders from other students.

The second important trade link is the one connecting Ninh Hiệp to Ho Chi Minh City in southern Vietnam. According to the villagers, a group of Ninh Hiệp people migrated to Ho Chi Minh City at the beginning of the twentieth century and established a small leather processing and trading community there. They maintained the relationships with their native place (*quê hương*) primarily by regular visits on the occasion of worshipping the lineage ancestors.

However, the connections between Ninh Hiệp and Ho Chi Minh City were also used as trade links. The importance of Ho Chi Minh City for the businesses of Ninh Hiệp traders has been sustained until the present day. If they do not have relatives in Ho Chi Minh City, traders from Ninh Hiệp travel there hoping to be able to establish new connections with producers and traders. One significant characteristic of these relations is that goods flow in both directions, in contrast to trade relations with Guangzhou (China) where Ninh Hiệp traders always perform the role of customers and in trade relations with all other places in Vietnam where they are always suppliers. The most common goods Ninh Hiệp traders buy in Ho Chi Minh City are sport clothing, jeans, winter jackets and sometimes fabric, although it is said that the selection of fabric in Ho Chi Minh City is not comparable to China. Traders in Ho Chi Minh City are mainly interested in Chinese fabrics, because of the variety in terms of colour, pattern, material and quality compared to the fabric produced in and around Ho Chi Minh City.

One of the many shops dedicated to selling sportswear in Ninh Hiệp is run by Hiến, a 31-year-old male trader at one of the new markets (see Chap. 4). Specialising in men's sportswear produced in and around Ho Chi Minh City, his shop is mostly visited by customers from rural areas.

He had attracted his regular customers, who enjoy the option of buying from him on credit, during the 15 months he had been in business and considers them as vital to his business. Hiến has never been to Ho Chi Minh City but obtained the contact details of the distributor from a relative and places orders by phone. The same is true about his customers: although customers come to his shop from time to time to browse through and have a look at the clothes displayed in his shop, his regular customers usually make their orders by phone. "Within Vietnam", he said, "placing orders by phone is convenient and uncomplicated", quickly adding "to order from China by phone is possible, too, but more complicated because of the language and the payment procedure". Many Ninh Hiệp traders I spoke with also agreed that when it came to dealing with Chinese traders, conducting business via face-to-face interactions was far more preferable than over the phone. While the practical reasons stated above were important for this preference, the lack of trust in Chinese traders was another factor, to which I will return later.

Although trade relations are predominantly established with the two biggest cities, Hanoi and Ho Chi Minh City, connections also exist between Ninh Hiệp traders and their counterparts in cities in Central Vietnam, like Đà Nẵng and Hội An. Đà Nẵng is the fourth biggest city in Vietnam and, being located almost exactly midway between Hanoi and Ho Chi Minh City, is an important trade node in the area. The big market in the centre of the city, called Cồn Market, comprises an extensive fabric section on the second floor. Hội An, a smaller town about thirty kilometres south of Đà Nẵng, is a tourist magnet, not only because of its historical and cultural heritage, but also because of its specialisation in tailor-made clothing. In the centre is a clothing market with tailors waiting for foreign customers, and in the streets in the old town tailor shops are next to one another. While fabric traders at Cồn Market in Đà Nẵng mainly purchase their goods from traders in Ho Chi Minh City and to a lesser extent in Hanoi, and sometimes Ninh Hiệp, fabric traders and tailors in Hội An tend to buy the material mostly in Ho Chi Minh City and Đà Nẵng, rarely in Hanoi. Only very few buy cloths in Ninh Hiệp, according to Mr. Minh, a large-scale fabric trader from Hội An, who frequently comes to Ninh Hiệp to buy cloth. When I met him on a grey day in April 2013 near the old market, he told me that he does not only supply tailors in Hội An with cloths, but also customers in various other cities in southern Vietnam, including Nha Trang and Ho Chi Minh City. In addition, he is the owner of a shop floor, where he produces clothing for tourists. Upon asking him why only few traders from Hội An come to Ninh Hiệp to buy cloth, he answered: "One reason is that most traders in Hội An don't know about the fabric market in Ninh Hiệp, and the second reason is that it needs a lot of money because we have to pay immediately in Ninh Hiệp, while our customers in Hội An expect to buy on credit from us".

In the past, Mr. Minh used to buy fabric in Ho Chi Minh City, but 5 years ago he decided to switch to Ninh Hiệp because of the greater choices and lower prices. Together with his wife, he travels regularly to Ninh Hiệp to see whether there is suitable fabric in terms of material, colour and pattern for his workshop. If they cannot find anything they like, they sometimes continue their way to Guangzhou where there are many more fabric markets. Before going back to Hội An, they usually pass by Mr. Minh's brother in Hanoi for a short visit. Apparently, Mr. Minh did not establish relations with Ninh Hiệp traders, or at least not to a degree that would allow him to buy on credit. In our conversation, he emphasised having particular ideas of the fabric he wanted, and that he needed to see the material with his own eyes and therefore never ordered by phone. Thus, for Mr. Minh it is more important to be able to choose fabric from various shops than to be confined to one, even if this means not being able to purchase on credit (Fig. 8.1).

In addition to supplying markets and shops in urban areas, Ninh Hiệp traders also provide the Vietnamese countryside with fabric and ready-made clothing. My conversations with traders and customers in Ninh Hiệp revealed that buyers come from virtually every part of the country. Mr. Liên, a former soldier who served in the army from 1967 until 1975, said that during these years relationships were established by Ninh Hiệp villagers, who were stationed as soldiers all over Vietnam. When the war ended, these relationships were revitalised and used as trade relations. The fact that villagers got around a lot as soldiers or traders at that time had a beneficial effect on the creation of trade relations and the promotion of Ninh Hiệp as a centre for fabric and clothing. However, most traders in Ninh Hiệp said that their relations with customers were established in the last few months or years, the longest relationship I heard of was 10 years. Thus, even if the relation between two traders is often not maintained for more than a generation, knowing about the connection of the two places in terms of trade relations is important.

One relatively new customer is 24-year-old Duy from Hưng Yên province, about 60 km south of Ninh Hiệp. Several times a week in the early morning, Duy comes to Ninh Hiệp by motorbike and buys as much as he can carry. He does not have personal trade relations with vendors in Ninh Hiệp but buys the clothing he likes and is offered a reasonable price. Because he sells at spontaneous, so-called frog markets (*chợ cóc*)[1] to a rural population consisting of mostly farmers and workers, he needs to sell cheap. When he has finished his shopping in Ninh Hiệp, usually at around 10 or 11 a.m., he goes back to his hometown to sell the newly acquired merchandise. When I met him for the first time at a tea stall in front of the old market, two women from the same hometown accompanied him. They were market vendors and took him along. It was also through them that he first got to know about Ninh Hiệp's markets.

Another wholesale customer, who keeps coming to Ninh Hiệp for 5 years, is Mrs. Lan and her niece, Mai Anh. They both live in Vinh city in Nghệ An province and travel the 300 km to Ninh Hiệp two to three times per month, each time for only one entire day. After a shopping tour at the markets in Ninh Hiệp, they usually visit Đồng Xuân market in Hanoi to buy what they cannot obtain in Ninh Hiệp, for example watches and more expensive clothes. In contrast with Duy, who sells simple clothing at rural markets, they have a fashion store in the provincial capital and sell trendy clothing for young people.

In sum, within Vietnam, transactions can either take place personally at the marketplace or over the phone. According to conversations with wholesale customers who said they did not have trade relations with traders in Ninh Hiệp, their main reason was that they preferred to buy what and where they wanted without obligations and restrictions. This seems to be related more to fabric traders than to traders dealing in ready-made clothing, presumably because the colour and quality of cloth cannot be transmitted by a picture in contrast to the design of clothing. Having outlined the spatial reach and the diversity of trade relations within Vietnam, the remainder of the chapter will give a more in-depth view on the way trade with China is organised.

Trade with China

China is Vietnam's largest trade partner. However, the two-way trade is not balanced due to a trade deficit on the Vietnamese side (The Economist 2012; WTO 2015). Regarding imports, China is clearly ranked as trade partner number one, with a continually rising volume of trade in recent years, while for exports China is on rank three, after the USA and Japan (GSO Vietnam 2015). Accordingly, China is the main supplier of fabric and clothing for Ninh Hiệp traders. While some traders had already crossed the Chinese border to import goods prior to the abrogation of the sanctions in the early 1990s, the number of Ninh Hiệp traders crossing the border for import has continuously been on the rise ever since.

Except for a few traders who have their own supply routes in China, the majority of the traders from Ninh Hiệp buy the goods at the big cloth markets in Guangzhou. However, many of them stated openly that they were reluctant to trust Chinese traders and said that this was one of the reasons why they would travel to Guangzhou. They claimed that when placing an order by phone and making advance payments to a given Chinese supplier, they could not be entirely sure whether they would ever actually see the ordered merchandise. They feared Chinese suppliers could simply decide not to ship the goods and claim later that the order had been lost en route to Vietnam.

When going to Guangzhou for shopping, the Vietnamese traders hand over the wares to transporters whom they entrust with the shipping. These transporters guarantee to bring the goods complete and within the agreed time to the destined place. Traders may not have full trust in these transporters, but it seems to be the best possible solution in this situation. This is in line with what Gambetta (1988) noted, namely that even if there is only a low level of trust in a relationship, actors may still try to maintain the relationship if alternatives are expected to be worse. Another concern shared by the Vietnamese traders was that even if the Chinese goods reached the Ninh Hiệp customer, there was always the possibility that what was received and what was originally ordered would differ significantly in terms of colour, quality and quantity. Generally, the geographical distance and cultural differences, including language and business practices, were perceived as major obstacles in Sino–Vietnamese trade relations. In order to deal with this challenge, Ninh Hiệp traders rely on Chinese assistants to a large extent.[2] These assistants can be of both sexes and any age, and have usually spent a considerable amount of time throughout their lives in Vietnam.[3] Some of them were married to Vietnamese nationals and maintained close relations to Vietnam while living in Guangzhou. The following account of a 3-day business trip with village traders during my field research is aimed at situating the assistants' role in the wider context of trade relations between the two places.

During what felt like a simmering hot afternoon in April 2013, I stood eagerly next to a small tea stall along the street between the old and the new markets, anticipating the arrival of a group of traders who had been planning to leave for China that same day. The arrangement had been made possible thanks to Thu, the trader I had come to know earlier (see previous chapter). She had agreed to take me along with her and the rest, altogether about thirty people. Most of the traders had been brought there on a motorbike by their spouse or parents, and carried big suitcases. As it turned out later, the suitcases were filled with defective clothing they had bought in their previous trip to China and intended to return. The traders, who gathered in small groups of three to four people, were of both sexes and their ages ranged from 20 to 44. Two young girls, who had just graduated from a university in Hanoi, had come along for the first time. To avoid the midday sun, they squeezed under the parasol erected above the tea stall, waiting impatiently for the bus to come soon. The bus is privately operated and runs several times a day between the main bus station close to the centre of Hanoi (Gia Lâm) and the Chinese border. Everyday around noon, the bus would deviate from its standard route to pass by Ninh Hiệp in order to pick up a group of traders. When the first bus with a passenger capacity of around ten people eventually arrived, some of the traders stowed their luggage in the back of the bus under the last row of seats and quickly got in. Soon, two more buses, which had been ordered by the driver of the first bus, would arrive. Within a few minutes and after everyone had boarded the buses, we finally headed towards the Chinese border.

Thu, I noticed, had brought along another young female trader who was making the journey for the first time and needed some guidance. Despite being penned up uncomfortably in the bus, the men in the last row lifted the group's spirits by making jokes and appeared to be making the best of the journey, until, at some point, they suddenly fell asleep. As it was silent in the bus now, Thu could talk to me about her previous trips to China. She assured me that it was safe and really well-organised. She had been travelling to China once a week for a few months and had never experienced serious difficulties or losses, she vaunted. Although the loud men at the back were sound asleep, our conversation would still be interrupted by occasional phone calls from her sister, one of the two sister-in-laws, her son's teacher and a customer in Ho Chi Minh City. They all needed to talk to her urgently, either to arrange things for her son who had caught an eye infection and needed to be brought to the hospital, or to deal with business-related issues. Even though she had to organise and give instructions on several urgent matters, she kept a cool head and went on to check off one task after another, without a trace of unease.

After being on the road for three tiring hours, our bus arrived in Lạng Sơn and dropped the traders off at the border crossing for passport and customs control. All passports were taken at once, checked and then returned one by one. This control did not pose any problems for the traders, who had all used the same informal visa service available in the village, whereas my visa, which I had obtained at the Chinese Embassy in Hanoi, was inspected more thoroughly. On the other side of the border, just a few hundred metres further, two night buses were parked, with half an hour to go till departure time. Thu purchased the tickets that she had booked before the journey, as did the other traders. This was to ensure that they would have a seat. Behind the small ticket stand was a restaurant suitable for a quick dinner before getting on the bus. Thu reminisced that on her first trip, her cousin had forgotten to book a seat for her, and it was only a matter of luck that she was able to get the last available seat. And indeed, as in the small bus before, every seat was taken, and there would not have been another possibility to go to Guangzhou from there on that day, because the buses only run if they have been reserved in advance.

The bus line is operated by a private bus company, which belongs to the Chinese–Vietnamese couple that also manages the restaurant. When they settled down, they first opened the restaurant, and after a while realised that direct buses from the Vietnamese border to Guangzhou were in high demand. They bought four modern buses and employed drivers, who drive the buses back and forth between the border and Guangzhou at night. Thu and some of the other traders seemed to know the couple well and were on friendly terms with them as could be understood from the conversation they had during dinner.

When most of them had finished their meal, it was time to go onto the bus and start the next leg of the journey. The bus had three double rows of bunk beds, two along the windows and one in the middle. While the middle-aged traders took their seats and lay down immediately, some of the young traders gathered on a seat to chat, listen to music together and eat some snacks. Shortly after departure, a Chinese-border official stopped the bus and controlled our passports again. It took only a few minutes and did not lead to any complications. Afterwards, everybody lay down and tried to get some sleep, knowing well that the next day was going to start early and would be exhausting.

At 5'o clock in the morning, the bus arrived in Guangzhou. Everybody got up quickly, took their suitcases and went off in small groups to different directions. It was still dark and a bit cold, and felt as though it had just stopped raining. Thu headed straight to the flat of her assistant, which was only a few 100 metres away in a grey, run-down apartment block. She knocked on the door, and a middle-aged woman in pyjamas opened. As it turned out later, she was the mother of three daughters, who, along with their father, all worked as assistants for Ninh Hiệp traders. Inside the flat were already four other traders who had been on the same bus. One was a woman aged 44, who often talked in a loud and determined voice. She was the one who initiated the contact with the family and introduced them to the others. It was also her who helped Thu during her first trip to China to get the last seat on the night bus. Since this incident, they slowly created a *tình cảm* relationship, which prompted Thu being introduced to this family. Furthermore, there was another man and a woman of about 35 years of age. Both of them had started to buy goods in Guangzhou quite recently and were thus not as experienced as the other woman, who had been a professional trader for many years. Finally, there was a young, dynamic man, who travels to Guangzhou on a regular basis to buy goods for the stall he has with his wife, who was pregnant and had therefore stayed in Ninh Hiệp.

The three-room flat, which consisted of two bedrooms and a living room with a kitchen, was small and only scantily decorated. On the living room floor was a mattress to sit or lie on while waiting to use the bathroom. For her breakfast, Thu cooked the instant noodles that she had bought at the border restaurant the evening before. In the meantime, the husband of the woman who had opened the door got up, made tea and started to hand out Chinese currency to the traders. Each trader received the amount of money she or he had transferred to the couple's bank account beforehand, which ranged roughly from 70 million VND to several hundred million VND. Thu got an amount equal to 100 million VND (around 5000 US Dollar), which she found appropriate for 1 week's shopping. To be able to estimate how much one will be able to sell in 1 week is very important for traders. In case they buy too much at once, they die on their goods, because fashion trends change very quickly, and clothes from the last week are not sought after one week later. But if they buy too little, they have to go back to China earlier when the trends have not changed yet, and also, the travel to China is very tiring and includes travel expenses. Making the right, or best possible buying decisions, is therefore crucial and needs experience.

Using the bathroom, eating a quick breakfast and receiving the money was done in a different order by each so as not to lose time. The markets are open only until noon, and the earlier one gets there the better. It was decided in advance who would go with whom, and when all were ready to leave at around 6'o clock, the daughters came to pick up the traders. Hương, Thu's assistant, was the oldest of the three daughters. She was 30 years of age and lived with her Vietnamese husband whom she had gotten to know during her stay in southern Vietnam a few years ago. Her Vietnamese husband was almost at the level of a native speaker. Even more impressive was her in-depth knowledge of the markets in Guangzhou and the trading practices. The way she led Thu through the markets left no doubt that she knew them inside out.

The group of traders and assistants left the flat and took a taxi which dropped them off at the square where the wholesale markets were located. It was not even 7'o clock when Thu and Hương finally entered through the main door, but the market was bustling as traders and transporters surged into the market hall. After having a quick look at the clothes on the ground floor while heading to the escalator, they went up to the first floor in order to exchange the defective clothes for new ones. Going up the first floor, Thu navigated through the small alleyways between the stalls unerringly and had no difficulties in locating the sellers from whom she had bought clothes the other week. Thanks to the notes she kept in her small notebook, she remembered exactly what, which amount and at what price she had bought from whom. When she took the clothes out of the bag to return them to the seller, she didn't even have to explain in which way they were defective, but the seller would take it back without the slightest hesitation and offer her the same clothes or a new style, depending on what she preferred. These exchanges were done in a quick and efficient manner, without talking too much. Even with her rather limited knowledge of Chinese, Thu could manage these deals without having to consult the assistant. When all defective clothes were given back, the shopping tour started.

Thu was also interested in detecting new trends. Just as important as buying merchandise was to fish for inspiration for potential future products she would end up producing and selling in the village. For this purpose, she took pictures of the clothes she found suitable in terms of material, style and skill needed in the production process. The simpler a piece of cloth can be produced the better, because it saves time and money, which are the crucial components in the competitive game. Furthermore, according to her experience, her customers generally prefer modest clothing. Taking pictures was not an easy undertaking because it is seen as stealing an idea, and therefore Thu had to do it secretly and move around the market constantly.

When a dress or a shirt caught her attention, she stopped and had a closer look at it to check whether it was suitable for her shop and whether she would be able to sell it. Sometimes, she asked the assistant for her opinion before she started a discussion with the seller about a deal. Hương assisted her patiently like a friend, but also professionally when offering her knowledge about current fashion trends in China and their suitability for Vietnamese tastes. Thu knew the demand of her customers quite clearly and was therefore able to make on the spot decisions about what and how much to buy almost instantly. When buying something, Thu paid the amount in cash and kept the receipt. Sometimes she tried to bargain a bit, using the Chinese phrases she knew. Instead of carrying around the merchandise with her the whole time, she handed it over to the vendor who deposited the goods in a bag, which was then sent to a warehouse somewhere in town later that day for further checks. Once the checks have been carried out, the products are shipped to her stall back in the village. This was common practice, I observed. Considering the large amounts of goods wholesale traders buy at these markets, it could hardly be done otherwise.

On each floor of the market, a particular type of clothes was being sold. The ceiling was very low and the narrow alleyways were crowded, forcing one to follow the flow of people in only one direction. The air was stuffy and hot, and there was no natural light since there were no windows at all. After going from the ground to the top floor of the first market, Thu and Hương went to the second market building just next to the first one, where they repeated the procedure. A few times, they ran into other traders from Ninh Hiệp, who were on the bus the night before. They greeted each other briefly, but would not get dragged into longer conversations. This time, they went through the stalls faster than at the beginning because they were running out of time. Even before the market closed at 11'o clock, some sellers started to pack their things and shut down their stalls. When there were no more chances to buy anything, they left the market and sat down at a place outside the market, where big vans were being packed with bags of clothes. The bags were about to be shipped to a warehouse in another place of town, where they would be checked and wrapped before being sent off to customers.

While taking a short break, one of Hương's sisters came by and asked about the shopping success. After having a conversation with her about the experiences in the morning, Thu and Hương went to another corner of town, not too far away, which had plenty of shops for men's fashion. As these shops were open all day, there was no need to rush. Unlike the wholesale markets from the morning, the clothes here were sold in boutiques located along an expensive-looking commercial street. The fashion was not designed for a rural clientele as was mostly the case in the markets, but seemed to attract rather young, urban customers. Thu decided to buy some T-shirts and trousers from the same collection she had bought the week before, but only a moderate amount.

As noon passed, it became hotter and hotter, and the level of exhaustion reached its peak. When Thu finally found that she had bought enough, we went for lunch in a small noodle stand not far from the last shopping area. After lunch, Thu and Hương took a taxi back to the house of Hương's parents, where the other traders were already taking a rest. Some of them were sleeping while others discussed their experiences with Chinese sellers and the markets more generally. They would also reminisce about life back in the village and exchange stories, which bordered on gossip at times, about their common friends or acquaintances there.

Thu and Hương did not have much time to rest and refresh because they had to be at the warehouse at 4'o clock. While being indiscrete from the outside, the warehouse was rather dark inside, and the dreary unpainted walls and the worn state of the floor added to the shady atmosphere. The floor was cluttered with bags of clothing when we got there, and the place was filled with Ninh Hiệp traders, as well as a few Chinese workers. When Thu finally found the bags filled with the merchandise she had bought in the morning, she checked whether it was complete, and then handed her bags over to the Chinese workers, who pressed and vacuumed the bags. Afterwards, the bags were all loaded onto a van and were sent back to the village, where they arrived 2 days later. The traders from Ninh Hiệp, however, left Guangzhou in the evening of the same day and on the same bus, without any luggage except for a few personal belongings and the empty suitcases.

Most remarkable besides the extremely time-efficient organisation of the trip was the crucial role of the assistant, who does not only translate, but also changes money, accommodates and cooks, guides from home to and through the markets and back, and gives advice about material and style. Moreover, the assistant's knowledge about the markets, products, prices, vendors and Chinese business practices more generally gives traders from Ninh Hiệp a significant advantage over other Vietnamese traders who travel to Guangzhou on their own and unattended. Ninh Hiệp traders usually go with the same assistant each time and thereby establish a relationship of trust—not only through repeated interactions in the form of the shopping trip at the market itself, but also due to the fact that they are being introduced to the family and taken to their home. In short, the assistant's help is invaluable for the traders and involves much more than just translating from Vietnamese into Chinese and vice versa. Another interesting fact is that in the case of Hương, the whole family works as assistants, and that they actually work every day for different traders from Ninh Hiệp. This suggests that, although trader–assistant relationships are personal to some extent, it is a paid service and does not include an exclusive commitment to one trader. Therefore, while Hương's assistance is of great value for Thu, Hương also accompanies other Ninh Hiệp traders, who are likely to be Thu's competitors.

For Ninh Hiệp traders, relations with partners from outside the community are crucial, because they allow, to a certain degree, for stability and calculability. According to conversations with traders, long-term relations with customers outside of the village are of fundamental importance, so much so that traders say they account for 90% of total sales. Whereas purchase on credit can, but not necessarily, be part of such a relation between Vietnamese traders, buying on credit is out of the question in relations between Chinese and Vietnamese traders. According to conversations with my informants, most of them are not able to build relations of trust with Chinese traders, mainly because of language difficulties and thus lack of direct interaction. It could be argued that this, together with a certain cultural or even political distance, could prevent traders to reach a level of familiarity that would be necessary to develop a trusting relationship. Other reasons may be time pressure at the marketplace, and the fact that for Chinese traders Vietnamese customers are not of great interest if they do not buy large amounts of goods on a regular basis. Finally, many Vietnamese customers like to shop around without being bound to a certain trader.

Notes

1. Spontaneous markets are usually held once or twice a day on the street, with vendors selling fresh vegetables, fruits and herbs on the footpaths. Sometimes, clothing is sold as well, lying in a heap on a piece of fabric or plastic. This kind of market is not official and thus meets spontaneously to avoid police inspection (Higgs 2003, 83). However, this does not mean that the place and time this type of market is held is completely random.
2. Traders from Ninh Hiệp use the term "người phiên dịch", literally meaning "interpreter" to refer to these assistants. However, considering the wide range of tasks they carry out, the term "interpreter" does not do justice, and I therefore use the broader term "assistant".
3. There may be a possibility that some of these assistants belong to the Hoa people, one of the largest overseas ethnic Chinese communities in Southeast Asia. The Chinese have expanded southwards to Vietnam early in history, and greatly increased their number over the centuries, especially in southern Vietnam were they were successful in commerce. However, shortly after reunification in 1975, most Hoa people fled the country as they faced the closing down of their businesses and a general atmosphere of hostility.

References

Gambetta, Diego. 1988. Can We Trust Trust? In *Trust: Making and Breaking Cooperative Relations*, ed. Diego Gambetta, 213–237. New York: Blackwell.

GSO Vietnam. 2015. International Merchandise Trade Vietnam 2013. In *General Statistics Office of Vietnam*. https://www.gso.gov.vn/default_en.aspx?tabid=780.

Higgs, Peter. 2003. Footpath Traders in a Hanoi Neighbourhood. In *Consuming Urban Culture in Contemporary Vietnam*, 75–88. London: Routledge Curzon.

The Economist. 2012. Vietnam's Trade with China: Fellow Travellers, Fellow Traders. *The Economist* June 30. http://www.economist.com/blogs/banyan/2012/06/vietnams-trade-china.

WTO. 2015. *Country Profile Vietnam*. WTO. http://stat.wto.org/CountryProfile/WSDBCountryPFView.aspx?Language=E&Country=VN. Accessed 10 Oct.

8

Morality and the Making of a Community

It is almost a general rule that wherever manners are gentle (moeurs douces) there is commerce;
and wherever there is commerce, manners are gentle.[1]
(Montesquieu [1749] 1961, Vol. 2, p. 8 cited in Hirschman 1982, 1464)

Instead of being lauded for its booming clothing market, which has contributed to a strong local economy since 2002, Ninh Hiệp has been consistently vilified in media reports and became a symbolic target for journalists writing about the corrupting influence of money on society. Recent newspaper articles criticised Ninh Hiệp traders not only for becoming wealthy too easily, and through dishonest business practices, but also for the way they spent their money. In one article, which caused quite a stir in Ninh Hiệp, two journalists decried children discarding small bills of money and the rampant demand for consumer goods, so that, for instance, virtually everybody had a smartphone, while education was neglected (An Nhiên and Nguyên Trang 2013).[2] In short, traders in Ninh Hiệp are portrayed as money hungry,

E. Horat, *Trading in Uncertainty*,
DOI 10.1007/978-3-319-55648-2_8

privileging the market over the pursuit of knowledge and higher education. Reinforced by proliferating media reports, this image of Ninh Hiệp is widely shared and reproduced among those in neighbouring villages and in Hanoi.

For traders in Ninh Hiệp, however, morality (*đạo đức*) as a shared understanding about how things ought to be done forms a core element of their actions. During my research, I came to acknowledge the crucial role morality played in interactions among traders as well as between traders and customers. From an anthropological point of view, markets are not only sites for economic exchange, but social institutions deeply pervaded by moral evaluations and power relations. Roy Dilley (1992, 4) contends that "moral evaluations of trade and commerce must be viewed empirically as arising from a context of changing politico-economic relations". He further notes:

> The relationship between morality and commerce cannot simply be derived from the structure of a peasant ideology. Moral evaluations, whose forms are always culture specific, result from the processes of contestation within, and over, exchange relations. In the hands of exchange partners—perhaps for the lack of any other means—morality is a weapon in the attempt to address potential imbalances of power relations which arise from and are articulated through the extension and development of "market" relations. (Dilley 1992, 6)

That morality and power relations are tightly enmeshed, as the statement above indicates, is also palpable in the Vietnamese context. Traders in Vietnam have especially been confronted with the issue of morality during the high socialist period, as trade was considered unproductive and therefore an immoral activity. The seeming contradiction between the portrayals of the Ninh Hiệp traders in newspaper articles as money-oriented, in contrast to their self-understanding as having a strong moral fibre, epitomises this contestation. This points at the intertwining of morality with the political and to morality being an important element of governance (Fassin 2005, 2012). In the mid-1990s and early 2000s, the state-led "social evils" campaign was a strong force to promote moral values and to "demarcate the boundaries between acceptable, or 'normal' (*binh thuong*), vis-à-vis non-acceptable, or 'abnormal', behaviors" (Rydstrøm 2009, 119). In recent years, however, government campaigns are dominated by the pursuit of modernisation (*hiện đại hóa*) and civilisation (*văn minh hóa*). Similar as in contemporary China, where "modernity as an ethic of 'how one should live' is being proposed" (Ong and Zhang 2008, 16), I suggest taking a closer look at the ways modernity and civilisation are proposed as a moral guideline in Vietnam.

This chapter sheds light on the complex intertwining of the economic and moral transformation processes in Ninh Hiệp. As Kate Jellema (2005, 235) argues, "deeply held moral principles shape economic practices even as changing economic exigencies gradually transform deeply held moral principles". While the emerging market opportunities in the aftermath of Đổi mới are widely embraced, an undertone of anxiety is present in daily conversations and media reports on the negative consequences of new capitalist relations, such as the corruption scandals of leading politicians, or the rise of "social evils", ranging from drugs, gambling and prostitution to theft and violence. Jellema (2005, 235) aptly summarises the dilemma: "At the heart of Vietnamese anxiety about the post-revolutionary age is not the novel availability of wealth per se or even its unequal distribution, but rather deep uncertainties about how to be at once wealthy and good". Ong and Zhang (2008, 16) have pointed to the same dilemma in China, namely "how the life of goods can be linked to the good life".

The concerns that Jellema as well as Ong and Zhang identify are vibrantly present in Ninh Hiệp, where traders responded rapidly to the new incentives of the socialist-oriented market economy. While they were often able to make a decent living pursuing commerce, they were also among the first to be cast as morally dubious. In the context of the state-led discourse that denigrates traders as immoral and undeservedly wealthy, Ninh Hiệp traders developed a specific set of moral values around which they produced their own local discourses and social practices. Declarations stressing that they sold at a "fair price" did not just aim to counter state-propelled discourses that throw a bad light on them. They constitute a performance of very specific local identities. Attempting to examine what traders in Ninh Hiệp perceive as moral, I start from the individual and its moral subjectivity. Individual ideas on morality are then negotiated in interactions with others, and as harmonised values disseminated in the form of moral discourses. The validity of moral values in these discourses is constantly renegotiated, contested and reaffirmed through social actions, in this case particularly through actions concerning the use of money. While the chapter aims to show how moral discourses structure the social life within the community and thereby help recreating the communal identity, it should be stressed that one needs to be cautious to not overestimate conformity with values (Heintz 2009, 10–11). Put differently, in reality there are often situations of moral dilemmas, where individuals have to choose between contrasting moral values, and by adhering to one value they may go against another.

Earlier studies on moral subjectivities of petty traders in northern and southern Vietnam provide a background for the examination of contemporary articulations of small-scale entrepreneurial morality in Ninh Hiệp. Regina Abrami (2002), for instance, who conducted research in Ninh Hiệp in the 1990s just as trade mushroomed as a consequence of the economic opening, noticed a rhetorical insistence of merchants on downplaying the magnitude of their commercial transactions and their affiliation to trade and commerce. Instead, they preferred to continually refer to themselves as peasants. As she points to traders' emphasis on their smallness and the economic insignificance of their businesses, she wonders why the economic transformation did not result in a change of identity. She then analyses this phenomenon in the light of the socialist legacy, suggesting that traders use the norms of a socialist economy to make moral claims upon the state. By adopting the label "small traders", merchants hope to keep the state regulators at a distance, in order to be able to accumulate wealth.

Ann Marie Leshkowich (2014), who conducted ethnographic research among small-scale traders in Bến Thành market in Ho Chi Minh City in the 1990s, made similar observations about merchants' tendency to highlight the smallness of their businesses. Being struck by the traders' adoption of an essentialist notion of petty trade as insignificant, marginal and backward, Leshkowich sets out to understand how particular forms of essentialism may be meaningful for creating certain identities and making room for agency. She thus argues that female stallholders strategically use these essentialist depictions of the petty trader to develop their businesses away from the gaze of the state. As she explains, trade in Vietnam in the 1990s was "an act of speculation" (Leshkowich 2014, 20–21), because the development of market socialism was in its early stages and traders were not sure if they would need protection when engaging in commerce. Therefore, narrating and performing an identity that resembled the official stereotype was a strategy to not attract attention while making considerable profit. While traders in the Bến Thành market played down the issue of how wealth was produced, their consumption practices aimed at upgrading their lifestyle and buttressing their belonging to the middle class. Interestingly, the research I conducted almost 30 years after the Đổi mới policy was first implemented shows that the moral identities of petty traders have not changed much in spite of the country's thorough socio-economic transformation. In contrast to simple explanations for standardised economic and moral changes that assume a causality between a liberal economy and the freedom to make choices in production and consumption, the downplaying of one's commercial activities as well as the moralising of consumption practices to be found in Ninh Hiệp suggest a more complex relation between economic and moral changes.

To get a grasp of this complexity, the study of Ashley Pettus (2003, 186–189), in which she elaborates on the ethics of small-scale traders, simply referring to them as having a "*buôn bán* ethic",[3] is helpful. She differentiates moral subjectivities among two generations of women merchants in Hanoi: while elderly traders portrayed themselves as the bearers of the authentic *buôn bán* ethic—most important of which is to be honest and trustworthy—younger generations of women strategically used the *buôn bán* ethic with customers, but admitted to the researcher that if they were honest, they would not be able to make a profit. Pettus also found that older generations of traders tended to emphasise the economic insignificance of trade and referred to it as an extension of their domestic responsibilities. Younger women, in contrast, did not proclaim their selling activities as unimportant, but rather stressed the challenge of meeting the contesting demands of family and business, especially their duty to support the family financially. To pick up on this issue, I will discuss three local moral discourses—about honesty, patriotism and peasantry—that are central in shaping traders' identities. Presenting themselves as honest, traders emphasise their good business practices, for instance by selling at a fair price so as to establish and maintain a reputation for trustworthiness. The discourse on patriotism implies following closely the aims of the "Buy Vietnamese" campaign and thus to reduce the dependency on others, particularly China. Finally, values typically related to the peasantry, such as hard work, modesty, community spirit as well as a strong emphasis on agriculture are subsumed under a "peasant discourse" .

Following Nguyễn-Võ Thu-Hương's (2008, xiv) argument that techniques of governance in Vietnam consist of the promotion of market freedom on the one hand, and the employment of measures of repression on the other hand, I propose to conceive the performance of moral identities of traders as a way of dealing with the ambiguous economic and political situation they find themselves in. Yet not only do traders perform a moral identity to voice their claims and address power imbalances, as Dilley's aforementioned statement has indicated, but techniques for governance have a moral dimension itself. In the name of a "good life", that is a modern and civilised life, the Vietnamese state has put the renovation, privatisation and new establishment of marketplaces high on its agenda. How this vision of a "moral modernity" has impacted on and been dealt with in Ninh Hiệp will be examined in the following pages.

Moral Discourses in Ninh Hiệp

The Honest Trader

To start with, Ninh Hiệp is known as a place where bargaining is rarely practiced, and goods are sold at the "right price" (*giá đúng*). Traders emphasise this to potential customers at every opportunity and declare they are honest (*thật thà*) and upright. What the right price is, i.e. how much profit is legitimate, is a crucial, yet highly complex question.[4] In political economic literature, a just price is often seen in relation to the labour and costs involved in the production process, as in Marx's labour theory of value, while in capitalist societies prices are usually set in relation to demand. In the present context, a just price seems to imply that it is enough to make a living, but not necessary to enrich oneself. As Richard Tawney ([1926] 1961) already noted long ago, a level of wealth acquired to sustain one's livelihood was legitimate, but more than that pointed to avarice. One day in Ninh Hiệp, as I was talking to Mr. Cường, an elderly villager, about attitudes to wealth, he recited the maxim written on one of the pillars of the old market gate to stress the importance of virtue and morality.[5] More than once, he used the term "civilised commerce" (*thương nghiệp văn minh*) in this context:

> By selling at a fair price and delivering goods reliably, Ninh Hiệp traders create trust and prestige. This reputation [of civilised trade] is one decisive reason why Ninh Hiệp market is able to attract so many customers from all over Vietnam.

To sell at the right price is relevant not only in situations involving customers from outside the community, but also in deals made among traders within the community. When I asked Trang, a young trader, from whom she usually buys cloth for her production site, she answered: "I buy the kind of fabrics I like, it doesn't matter from whom. It's the same price everywhere. I know the prices. If it's different, I don't buy it". Thus, "the right price" represents a careful balance between what is considered appropriate by both customers and other traders. Customers should not be excessively overcharged, and it is also important to respect what the majority of traders in the community perceive as the right price, so that as stall neighbours they do not engage in price wars and wantonly seek to devalue it and instead adjust to the dynamics of competition in the marketplace. Stealing each other's customers is not considered appropriate behaviour.

In fact, forging and maintaining *tình cảm* relationships is very important for traders, especially between those in nearby stalls and those who interact on a daily basis. Often in the afternoon, when business is not that brisk, they sit together and chat, play cards and share food and drinks. Thus, trade is as much an economic activity as it is a

Fig. 8.1 Food stalls and street cafés between the old market and the Fashion Street

social practice that is deeply embedded in the web of community life (Fig. 8.1). In the conviviality of the group, traders share information and support one another. Conflicts or tensions do not figure prominently in the marketplace, or are prevented from spilling into it. The few conflicts I encountered broke out between traders and customers when the latter tried to steal something, or between traders when one had copied the other's clothing designs.

Mrs. Hiền, an elderly trader, used the metaphor of a bowl of rice for the market (*chợ như bát cơm*). With that she meant that the market had to feed everybody and served as a means of subsistence for the whole community, thereby implying that a strong sense of fairness and equality persisted among traders. This bears close resemblance to Cristina Szanton Blanc's (1972) findings at a fish market in the Philippines, where she came across a strong emphasis on the "right to survive", in the sense that every vendor had to be able to make a living.

Inherent in this discourse is the belief that the "morally good" begets what can be considered "economically good". Mrs. Nguyệt, the wife of Mr. Cường whom I cited at the beginning of this section, shared her experiences from the time when she was a trader:

> It is important for traders to remain true to their skills (*bản lĩnh*), abilities (*khả năng*) and level of knowledge (*trình độ hiểu biết*) instead of copying others. In Ninh Hiệp, unlike other villages, insiders and outsiders are not differentiated.[6] Everybody can come and do business. If one is serious-minded (*đứng đắn*) and does business in a true (*chân chính*) and legitimate (*chính đáng*) way, the business will be successful. If one is not serious, the business will fail. We have seen both cases here many times.

This is reminiscent of the "gentleman's path" that Richard Lufrano (1997, 113–126) describes in his study about merchants in late imperial China. Instruction manuals written for merchants emphasised the value of acting virtuously and morally. Traders should prove to be reliable and hospitable as well as flexible, generous, trustworthy and confidential. Kirsten W. Endres (2015) makes a similar point in the context of contemporary Vietnam, arguing that economic success among small-scale traders is seen as the result of *lộc*—a concept relating to fate, fortune and divine benevolence. In a similar vein, Ann Marie Leshkowich (2012, 101–103) stresses the importance of the concept of Buddhist fate among traders, who must use their individual skills and talents to cultivate virtue in order to achieve business success.

Notwithstanding the significance of the cosmological dimensions of success, the importance of morality among traders is far from discounted. I argue that this is the case because acting in accordance with and respecting moral values is perceived as enhancing one's trustworthiness, which then becomes the basis for generating the kind of individual success the trading community desires. It is not my intention to invoke the myth of a perfectly harmonious moral community, but to highlight the extent to which James Ferguson's description of "communal solidarity" is factored into the pursuit of success: "Actual 'communal solidarity' is not built solely out of egalitarian relations of cooperation and altruism, but just as much out of interested and often competitive relations of exchange. Both a wholly disinterested sharing and a purely asocial calculation are fantasies; real sociality always unites sharing and self-interest in a single act" (Ferguson 2014, 119). In this sense, morality helps traders navigate between competition and cooperation. The following statement, made by Mrs. Nguyệt, explains its value and wisdom:

> It is not that traders are just gentle, but they imitate each other in the way they do business. Customers don't buy from hot-tempered and sharp-tongued vendors but from the ones who treat them in a nice way.

Ninh Hiệp traders explained that it was as important to be trustworthy as it was to be gentle and serious. In their perception, the market could only have expanded in that measure because people in the community trusted each other and lent money to one another. However, the credit and banking system only works as long as traders treat each other fairly and repay their debts, because such transactions cannot be legally enforced. Thus, traders do not only bring up the topic of honesty towards their customers, but also reassure each other that they are honest.

The Patriotic Trader

Stimulated by the increasing political tensions between China and Vietnam, the image of the patriotic trader has taken on immense importance in the moral discourse. In the early years of socialism, petty traders were categorised as patriotic labourers and organised into commercial cooperatives in line with the state's aim to use their contribution to "serve production" by providing supply inputs through state purchasing channels (Abrami 2002, 95–96). Even if the situation has changed considerably with Đổi mới, as private trade is allowed and traders no longer work for a commercial cooperative, traders continue to identify with patriotic values on many levels, such as acting for the good of a collective at the local level or contributing to the national cause by selling domestic instead of foreign products. Propelling this discourse is also the so-called Buy Vietnamese campaign, launched by the Ministry of Industry and Trade together with the Ministry of Communication in 2009 (Huong Ly 2014). As the name suggests, Vietnamese products have to be given preference over foreign, especially Chinese, goods. In addition to quality concerns (particularly safety when it comes to food), the campaign has clear economic and political intentions, which are to strengthen the domestic economy and reduce dependency on imports. The campaign is also morally charged, as buying and selling Vietnamese products is considered "good", while giving preference to Chinese goods symbolises betrayal of the Vietnamese nation. The impact of the campaign on the shopping habits of consumers should not be underestimated, at least when domestically produced goods are available and affordable. For example, in June 2014, buyers boycotted Ninh Hiệp traders for several days as a way to penalise them for selling Chinese instead of Vietnamese clothes.[7]

Ninh Hiệp's markets have the reputation of being dominated by Made-in-China clothes—so much so that collectively they are referred to as the "hypermarket for Chinese apparel" (*đại siêu thị may mặc Trung Quốc*). This is not without reason, as the majority of clothes indeed are cheap, low-quality imports from Guangzhou. The association between Ninh Hiệp's markets and Chinese goods was evident in my own personal interactions while conducting fieldwork. On one occasion, after having explained to a Vietnamese friend that my research was devoted to Ninh Hiệp's traditional cloth market, she suggested in a somewhat chastising manner that I should go to China instead if I was interested in Chinese trade. This was by no means an isolated incident during my time in Vietnam outside the village. Nearly all my interlocutors in Hanoi knew about Ninh Hiệp's wholesale market, and almost everybody mentioned, at least as a side note or an afterthought, the visible predominance of Chinese goods. Yet, in the light of the complicated and emotionally charged relationship with China in the past, as well as today, these are not neutral and casual comments, but, rather, a harsh criticism. Therefore, political propaganda and the heightened awareness of the readiness of the people and the traders to adapt to these requests (or at least pretending to do so) have supported the emergence of the discourse of the patriotic trader.

This discourse is also linked to the discourse of the honest trader, in a way that traders are expected to provide clear information about the country of origin for their merchandise. Even though the campaign has already been in full swing for a few years now, only the recent rise in the popularity of Made-in-Vietnam clothes has had a decisive impact on Ninh Hiệp traders to prioritise home production. According to a newspaper article, some traders take this step very seriously and invite potential customers to their production site in order to provide proof of the country of origin for their garments (Diệp Sa 2014). However, not everybody owns production facilities. For traders who do not have the means to improve their economic strategy, the "right to survive" weighs heavier than their patriotic duty to comply with the motto "Buy and Sell Vietnamese". Although the "right to survive", driven by its own moral logic, may appear as though it could challenge the discourse of the patriotic trader, in recent protests a rhetoric of patriotism—referring to the socialist principles anchored in the Constitution of Vietnam and prominent in state propaganda—was used to support claims of the right to make a living. Thus, while the state called for patriotic commitment from its citizens through giving preference to domestic products, Ninh Hiệp traders instrumentalised their performance of a patriotic identity to voice their claims towards the state.

This discourse touches upon two important points: on the one hand, going back to the introductory section of this chapter, morality is a core aspect of state-led campaigns and thus an important element of governance. On the other hand, it gives an example of how traders play with discourses: they may or may not act according to the "Buy and Sell Vietnamese" campaign, but they repeat similar slogans so as to hold the state accountable to its own rhetoric when their interests are threatened, as happened in recent protests.

The Peasant Trader

In addition to these two specific trade-related discourses, there is a third, more general moral discourse related to the images of the peasantry. Many traders speak of farming as their main occupation and trading as an ancillary activity. This statement may seem paradoxical at first glance, in view of the fact that most traders use hired help to work their fields, and, in turn, dedicate most of their time to trade, which is their main source of income.

This rhetorical insistence on magnifying one's agricultural roots instead of aligning with one's trading pursuits falls in line with what Regina Abrami (2002, 102) encountered during her fieldwork. Based on her own observations, she argues that this narrative is part of the socialist legacy of production and virtuous labour. By framing trading activities as tangential to an agricultural household, the focus is shifted to productivity rather than gain. Abrami explains traders' continuous emphasis on the smallness of their businesses by pointing to the fact that the ideas of the socialist economy have not completely disappeared, and that wealth as such is not glorified in Vietnam, as if to preserve social unity.

A crucial yet seemingly oppositional dimension of this rhetoric is to refer to trade as the traditional occupation of the village (*nghề truyền thống của làng*), in order to emphasise stability and continuity, and at the same time to render it legitimate. Yet the rhetoric of continuing the village tradition of selling at the market conceals the actual extent and form of contemporary trade, the major part of which is dealing with Chinese textiles and garments for wholesale.

The emphasis on hard work and making "just enough" to make ends meet is also part of this discourse. A sentiment I often heard from traders was that the money from trading was just enough to meet their basic daily needs—"to buy vegetables and fish sauce" (*buôn bán thế này chỉ đủ tiền rau mắm hàng ngày thôi*). As for their external appearance, an inconspicuous style is seen as appropriate. Wearing dresses, high heels, make-up and jewellery at the village marketplace is frowned upon and therefore not, or very rarely, found there.

Furthermore, people in Ninh Hiệp do not hesitate to express their pride in the rich history and culture of their village. Not only are a multitude of officially recognised historical sites maintained until the present day, but villagers also remember a number of famous scholars from the village, whose names are inscribed on the steles at the Temple of Literature in Hanoi. The appreciation for Ninh Hiệp's culture is expressed in poems and songs composed by the local villagers. Similarly, education is highly valued, as demonstrated by the initiative taken by some elderly people to teach *Nôm* to children. In addition, the rhetoric about the importance of education was prominent in the protests against the privately funded market project on the secondary school premises at the village centre in January 2014 and December 2015 (see Chap.3).[8] The idea that the planned market would displace the school was perceived as unacceptable, because it openly degraded education and privileged private over public interests. This event contradicts the concerns generally voiced by journalists, as the planned market project clearly does not reflect the villagers', but the state's interest in furthering the marketisation process in the commune.

Finally, villagers strongly emphasise Ninh Hiệp's rural character by contrasting it with Hanoi, although Ninh Hiệp is located in Gia Lâm district, and thus formally belongs to Hanoi. For instance, villagers often stress the importance of social relations and solidarity, as in the following statement made by an elderly villager:

> This is the countryside. Activities are still carried out with community spirit (*tính cộng đồng*), unlike in urban centres, where 'nobody cares when the neighbor's house burns down' (*cháy nhà hàng xóm thì bình chân như vại).* It's not like this in the countryside. If something happens, people gather to ask and care for each other. The community relations (*quan hệ cộng đồng*) are tighter [than in cities].

Even though Ninh Hiệp is a trading village, its reference point is the capital city of Hanoi, which is perceived as urban and modern, while Ninh Hiệp is considered "not modern" (*không hiện đại*). A young female trader in the old market said: "People in Ninh Hiệp think about money in a traditional way, they don't know how to spend it. Most villagers don't like to go to a café because they consider it a waste [of time and money]". She then continued by pointing to the discrepancy, as she perceived it, between money and modernity in the village: "Although iPhones are common nowadays, we still wear jeans, not dresses" (*nhưng mà làm gì có iPhone mặc váy, vẫn iphone mặc quần bò*), referring to the different dress codes in the city and the countryside.

The tension between gaining wealth and simultaneously maintaining traditional customs was an issue often raised in my conversations with the villagers. While young people tended to be more concerned with consumption and modernity, as the trader just mentioned, elderly people often brought up the question of values and the meaning of a good society. Moral anxiety and the fear of bad habits indirectly framed these conversations, as in the statement of an elderly villager: "The economy is developing too fast, society has no time to accommodate these changes" (*kinh thế phát triển quá nhanh, xã hội không có kịp theo*). This tension also contains a class dimension, as "(…) middle-classness seems to have become very effectively normalized as simply 'modern'" (Bélanger, Drummond, and Nguyen-Marshall 2012, 9). Constructing a "traditional" village identity, as in Ninh Hiệp, connotes a rejection of urban middle-class consumerism, which is deemed immoral. Thus, drawing an ideological, and ultimately moral, demarcation line between one's own village and the perceived Other remains a common modality for self-identification. The discourse of the peasant trader illustrates this point by revealing contrasting juxtapositions—agriculture versus commerce, rural versus urban, solidarity versus anonymity and tradition versus modernity.

Spending Practices

Due to the expansion of the market and the enormous growth of the local economy, Ninh Hiệp became one of the wealthiest communes in the Red River Delta. Crucial factors for the proliferation of trade businesses are not only liberal policies and a climate of supra-contractual trust, but also the social acceptability of profit-seeking. According to Malarney (1998, 285), the stigma attached to commerce and wealth-making during high socialism is diminishing in the Red River Delta since Đổi mới. Yet, although wealth itself does not necessarily pose a moral problem, the way money is accumulated and spent certainly is a moral issue. In this section, I shall examine how social practices, particularly the use of money, are shaped by and again reinforce—and sometimes contest—the moral discourses outlined above.

Quite generally, although many Ninh Hiệp people could possibly engage in the kind of middle-class consumerism spreading in urban centres in Vietnam, most do not do so, or if, only inconspicuously. The majority of villagers adhere to the ideals of the peasant discourse that in the end boils down to modesty. In the everyday life, traders spend money with great care. For instance, when choosing what to eat at noon, most traders go for a cheap meal, boiled rice with vegetables and sometimes meat (*cơm bình dân*). Mr. Trung, a male trader with a very successful business, used to eat plain bread. On one occasion, when I wanted to order bread with paté for the two of us, he insisted on eating bread without anything "because it's cheaper." When traders need to acquire something for the purpose of smoothening the way for their business (e.g., means of transport, telecommunication technology, etc.) they make their purchases throughout the year. Motorbikes, especially the less expensive models of Honda Dream and Honda Wave, are popular. They are essential not only to commute quickly between the home and the marketplace, but also to transport rolls of fabric and bundles of clothes back and forth. Fabric traders with customers in the region find it useful to have a car to deliver the goods by themselves. A mobile phone is a standard accessory for every trader to keep in touch with other traders, customers, producers and other people related to their business.[9] Among young people, smartphones are common with which they can access the Internet and check new fashion trends, share information through social media and, most important of all, take pictures to copy fashion designs of others. This careful spending of money is in accordance with the peasant mentality of saving money. Consequently, buying securities, such as agricultural land, gold and use rights of market stalls, as back up in bad times is a widespread practice.

Although wealth as such is not despised, it only takes on social value when deployed in an appropriate way. Walking through Ninh Hiệp, I became aware of the many renovated and newly built houses, especially in comparison with nearby villages where grey, one- or two-storey houses were prevalent. While there are still a few traditional bamboo houses from the beginning of the twentieth century and some houses from the 1980s and 1990s, many houses in Ninh Hiệp were renovated or newly built since the 2000s and especially during the last couple of years. These new houses are big, have three, four or even five floors, and are often painted in bright colours. Some of the very new, spacious houses are almost empty except for the standard furniture—a massive and richly decorated ancestral altar and at least one big TV set. Others are filled with precious Chinese and European antiques such as wood-carved furniture, vases, china ware, clocks, paintings, and so on. In front of some of the houses are forecourts where bonsais of different sizes are grown and cages with singing birds are hung.

Renovating one's house by adding storeys or building a new house is very important for Ninh Hiệp traders because the house symbolises success, which again is seen as the result of hard work, good business skills and *lộc*. I was reminded of the paramount importance of renovating or rebuilding a house for traders while conversing with a villager, Mr. Công, and his wife, Mrs. Hằng. She originally comes from Central Vietnam and started to work as a trader after settling down in Ninh Hiệp. Mr. Công and Mrs. Hằng have been discussing for some time whether or not to build a new house and finally agreed to start construction by the end of the year. When I asked Mr. Công about the reasons for rebuilding the house, he answered:

> Since we moved to Ninh Hiệp and my wife started to sell at the market, she turned into a veritable trader. She spends a lot of time with the friends she made at the marketplace and adopted the mentality of Ninh Hiệp. In the 4 years my wife has been working as a trader, she was able to save some money and now wants to build a new house. I don't care much about money, I just want to have enough for a stable living and for covering the needs of my family. If it was up to me, I wouldn't build a new house because I don't think it's necessary. But since it's important for my wife, I agreed to her wish to build a new house after long hours of discussion.

This conversation shows that although Mr. Công was not in favour of building a new house, he eventually gave in to the plan, because it was important for Mrs. Hằng to position herself and her family in the village. Although having just a small stall at a not much frequented location, and only selling goods she buys from other traders at a cheap price (*hàng thanh lý*), Mrs. Hằng was able to earn money due to hard work and *lộc*, as she explained to me. Her story suggests that money itself is not the ultimate goal—far more important is recognition by the community, even more so as she was new and had to start from scratch. Towards the end of the conversation, Mr. Công mentioned that the new house would be big enough for a workshop to produce clothes. It is noteworthy that most houses in Ninh Hiệp are not only used as residence, but also include workshops and storage rooms, and sometimes even offer space to accommodate labourers. In this case, the new house would serve two purposes at one time: first, to gain recognition in the community by showing that Mrs. Hằng was a successful trader; and second, to have space for a workshop in order to expand the family business in including Mr. Công and hire a few labourers.

Another way to gain recognition is by sponsoring sport events held in Ninh Hiệp, such as the annual volleyball tournament that was included in the traditional festival dedicated to the village's founders in 2012. The volleyball competition attracts famous teams because the prize money, which consists entirely of donations by villagers, is higher than the prize money of the national championship (Tuoi Tre [Youth] News 2015).[10] While 120 villagers have donated between 500,000 VND (24 USD) and 40 million VND (1900 USD) for the tournament in 2015 and have gained appreciation by the village community, especially the larger sponsors will be remembered for their generous financial contribution, which is conducive to their reputation in the village. According to villagers, hosting and funding competitions in various disciplines is a tradition in Ninh Hiệp and includes Vietnamese sumo (*vật cổ truyền*) and Chinese chess (*cờ tướng*) besides the volleyball tournament.

The way money is used for consumption and entertainment is also strongly influenced by the peasant discourse. Here, the gender bias is most pronounced. Whereas typical male forms of entertainment, such as drinking and gambling, are accepted as part of the "traditional culture", there are no appropriate ways for women in Ninh Hiệp to spend money on consumption. Going to a spa or buy luxury articles, such as expensive clothes, bags and perfumes, is considered unnecessary and therefore wasteful. As drinking and gambling are accepted, they are often done in public and are thus easily visible. Other hobbies many men pursue are collecting expensive antiques, singing birds and bonsai trees. In contrast, female ways of entertainment are inconspicuous, because they are not perceived as legitimate. For instance, only Mrs. Oanh, a trader who lived abroad with her two daughters for 20 years and returned to the village in 2012, told me about herself indulging in beauty treatments or shopping, while all other women traders said that going to the spa was something "other people" do. Gambling among women, which is said to be no rarity in Ninh Hiệp, is seen as equally inappropriate as spending money on one's physical appearance. As a consequence, most women traders conform to a modest look, except for those who do not come from Ninh Hiệp, or have lived abroad for a long time. For instance, when on one occasion the son of Mr. Trung came along for a chat with Mrs. Ngọc, the trader from another province, his first comment after our conversation with her was that she was not from here. Asking him why he knew that, he replied that her style was very different from the way inhabitants of Ninh Hiệp dress. Another trader whose appearance stood out was the aforementioned Mrs. Oanh: with her short dresses, colourful make-up and dyed hair she looked markedly different from the other vendors. As a contrary example, when I thanked a young woman trader at the new market for helping me with the questionnaire, I gave her a small make-up case that she only took hesitantly. Blushing, she said that it was nice, but that she had no use for it.

In Ninh Hiệp, women are expected to sacrifice time and money for the well-being of their family, not for their own pleasure, while for men hanging out with friends and spending money is socially accepted. Thu, the clever and hardworking female trader mentioned in Chaps. 5 and 6 did not make a secret of her husband's habits to drink, gamble and chase other women. In one of our many conversations, she declared:

> He gamed away almost all land and properties we inherited from his family. In addition to that, he lost an expensive watch I bought for him, and sold his smartphone when he was short of pocket money. Of course I don't like my husband wasting money, but drinking and gambling is what men do. There is not much I can do—even if he does not have cash in his hands, he can gamble by incurring debts that I have to clear in the end.

Thus, consumption in the form of entertainment and accumulation of material goods is moralised in a strongly gendered way. Many scholars suggest that gender is an important aspect when it comes to money and morality. Jennifer Alexander (1998, 213) and Suzanne A. Brenner (1998, 140) made similar observations when investigating sites of commerce in Java where most traders were women. They found that money and its association with material desires was commonly thought of as threatening to the moral integrity of a person. For Vietnam, Ashley Pettus (2003, 5) makes a compelling case that the "media's scrutiny of female choices, attitudes and conduct communicated the tenuous divide between national development and cultural degradation and defined the moral angst of a nation caught on the edge of capitalist transformation". In a similar vein, Leshkowich (2011, 283) demonstrated that woman traders in Vietnam are often portrayed in newspaper articles and even academic publications as obsessed with money and therefore not suitable as the moral pillar of the family.

In this part, I have shown how the use of money is moralised in Ninh Hiệp by revealing spending practices and the reasons that render them (il)legitimate in the eyes of villagers. To sum up, rather than spending money, traders save or invest it in things important for their businesses, such as means of transport and communication. Because bringing money to the bank is uncommon in Vietnam, especially among people in the countryside, land and antiques are acquired as securities. In addition, it is popular to build or rebuild houses as they have a symbolic and a practical function. Regarding consumption, it is expected, especially of women, to use little money for themselves while spending it generously for the family. This relates back to the findings in Chap. 4, where I stated that women's standing is still largely defined by the way they care for the family. Although women literally have money on hand, they are supposed to consult with their husbands about how to use bigger amounts of money before they actually spend it.

The moral prescriptions outlined above are sometimes violated, for example, by individuals buying cars of luxury brands instead of just good enough cars to transport goods to their customers. Yet, importantly, nobody would drive with this kind of car through the village, but instead park it at the entrance of the village, in the empty halls of the

Baza market. Thus, while villagers do engage in consumption, they do so in inconspicuous ways. Being aware that it is a fine line between what is considered useful and wasteful things, my point is precisely that what constitutes moral behaviour, and thus legitimates certain purchases and possessions but not others, must be contextualised within a concrete, local context.

In a similar vein, while honesty and patriotism are promoted as important values, they are not always acted upon closely. On some occasions, traders would say to me: "Of course as a trader you cannot be honest, or else you don't make a gain". Or, when asked about their stance on maintaining or ceasing business ties with Chinese traders, they would say that it did not matter whether or not they liked or trusted the Chinese as it was "just business" (*làm ăn thôi*). Therefore, what people value, what they say they value and how they act is not necessarily consistent. This relates again to the strategic use of a moral identity.

Moral Modernities

Abrami makes a valid point when acknowledging the powerful legacy of ideas of the socialist economy. Yet in addition to that, the paradox of the current configuration of a market economy under the guidance of a socialist state evokes confusion about how to be wealthy and moral at the same time. This leads to the creation of "new moral in-between spaces" (Rydstrøm 2009, 118) and thereby reinforces the vagueness of morality in the post-Đổi mới era:

> If, during the period of high socialism, the Vietnamese state valorized workers and production and officially approved of consumption only in terms of 'needs,' the lines between production and consumption, and between socially moral and immoral behavior, are surely less clear in the market reform period. (Vann 2012, 164)

Moral ambiguity, provoked by the incoherent application of socialist and neoliberal logics, respectively, the "government's simultaneous use of freedom and tradition" (Nguyễn-Võ Thu-Hương 2008, xx), can thus be seen as an aspect of contemporary governing. In the case of Ninh Hiệp, a similar line of reasoning is palpable. By claiming the moral authority to publicly criticise certain people or groups of people as immoral, state representatives seek to render their own actions legitimate. Framed as enhancing the process of "modernity" and "civilisation", market projects come under the banner of promoting a "good life". However, the rhetorical praise for the market projects conceals an awareness of the fact that they may strengthen social inequalities and even undermine other publicly celebrated values, such as education. Thus, the latest market project heavily works to the detriment of the local people.

It is important to note that perceptions of and reactions to modernisation are quite different among the members of the community. While elderly people express fear of change and associate "modernity" with commodification and a possible loss of meaningful social relations, young people tend to emphasise new opportunities, an enhanced standard of living and the freedom of choice. From the state's perspective, modernity is captured in the official slogan "wealthy people, strong country, equal and civilised society" (*dân giàu, nước mạnh, xã hội công bằng, văn minh*). In practice, this implies a broad range of measures to develop the country, the primary focus of which in recent years has not been poverty alleviation or sustainably securing livelihoods, but, rather, creating, tapping into and satisfying the demands of emerging middle-class and upper–middle-class consumers. While Ninh Hiệp was celebrated as a success shortly after Đổi mới due to the rapid growth of its local economy, it is now faulted for not being modern enough. Privately invested market projects—some planned for the near future, others already realised in the last few years—are thus envisioned as a means to transform Ninh Hiệp into a "civilised" place of commerce. Here again, perceptions of the local people and the state differ: While villagers speak of "civilised trade" as a particular set of business moralities, for the state it is a stage in the development process that is related to the ideas of orderliness and cleanliness and is connected to efforts to regain control over rather informally organised economic activities.

In contrast to the traders in Bến Thành market in Leshkowich's (2014) study, Ninh Hiệp traders rejected middle-class consumer practices and instead chose to reproduce the same peasant discourse that Abrami (2002) observed in the 1990s. While the peasant discourse is distinctly strong among elderly traders, young people also contribute to it, but with a slight resentment, because for them, rather than to connote the perils of corruption or bad social behaviour, modern life brings the promise of new opportunities and a lifestyle many find desirable. Living in Ninh Hiệp and working at the market, they find themselves deprived of fully participating in what they consider a "modern life". Thus, the notion of generation-specific moral subjectivities that Pettus (2003) suggested seems highly relevant to the case of Ninh Hiệp. Furthermore, the strategic use of a particular moral identity, as suggested by Leshkowich as well as by Abrami and Pettus, is also a crucial feature I observed in my research. While Ninh Hiệp traders adopt parts of the essentialist notions of a trader in their self-representation, insisting that commercial pursuits were insignificant and only a side occupation of a household, they reject the idea that they are dishonest and immoral. By being—or appearing to be—honest, patriotic traders who uphold the values of the peasantry, Ninh Hiệp traders strive to create a good reputation so as to attract customers as well as to navigate their way around the inquiring gaze of the state. In certain moments, for example, when plans for new private market projects are announced, this identity is used to make moral claims upon the state.

Ambiguities and contradictions arising from rapid social and economic transformation is a common picture in Southeast Asia and elsewhere. As a look at one of Vietnam's neighbours, Cambodia, shows, contradictions brought about by a "modern" urban life versus a "traditional" rural life are central to people's contemporary experiences (Derks 2006, 2008). These perceived contradictions are manifested in the tension between the desire to enhance the material state of the society that is newly available and the concern of losing one's culture and identity (Derks 2006, 202). As Annuska Derks (2008) illustrates, the young women in her study tried to balance the satisfaction of their individual desires, often by behaving in ways that would be seen as "too modern" , with performing an "appropriate" modern identity. Similarly, Ninh

Hiệp traders perform moral identities while consuming inconspicuously. People in both countries seem to make experiences of a similar kind by trying to reconcile various demands and expectations. Instead of rejecting modernisation as such, Ninh Hiệp villagers have their own ideas about what is appropriately modern. While in some respects their ideas diverge from the state's vision, they need not always be in complete contradiction. Interestingly, although the traders wanted to keep the market a public good, they also suggested it should be renovated—yet, under their guidance.

Notes

1. Traders in Vietnam are generally not associated with gentleness, but in my research I came across this notion of the gentle (*hiền lành*) trader as I will show later in this chapter.
2. In the same article, entitled "Bạc tỉ và sự thụt lùi của tri thức" (*Billions and the retrogression of knowledge*), the journalists also wrote that civil servants were not respected because they do not earn as much money as traders, and that sometimes there were not even teachers available because they were selling at the market, too. As a final remark, the journalists wrote that men only eat and go out with their friends, and that never in their life have they seen men as disengaged as in Ninh Hiệp.
3. *Buôn bán* means trading, usually in the form of small-scale trade. When using the term *buôn bán,* Pettus emphasises its cultural meaning, implying that it refers to informal "women's work" (Pettus 2003, 180).
4. Alexander (1992, 91) put forth the point that a fair price is difficult to calculate because the notion of cost is also culturally constituted. Examinations of the "just price" have a long history, starting from Aristotle, Thomas Aquinas, Karl Marx, E. P. Thompson and newer proponents of the moral economy approach. As Chris Gregory (2012, 394) recently stated, "the theory of moral economy is the theory of the just price".
5. The original wording of the maxim was: "Nhi tác nhi tức ẩm hòa thực đức, dư túc dư bố dịch vụ thông công". In English, it means: "Working and resting, eating and drinking, is all done virtuously; trading and farming, buying and selling, of which the essence is fairness".

6. Usually, Vietnamese villages differentiate between residential population (*dân cư*) and migrant population (*nội cư*). After three generations, people, who came as migrants, can claim residential status and are thereby granted all rights and duties of the residential population (Luong 2010).
7. This boycott must be seen in the light of the particularly tense relationship between Vietnam and China due to the territorial dispute that was very intense during those weeks.
8. The project was originally scheduled for 2016, but was put on hold due to the recent protests. For more information, see Tuấn Hợp (2014) and Phương Sơn (2015).
9. In Vietnam more generally, mobile phones have become affordable in recent years and are widely used by Vietnamese people of all socio-economic backgrounds.
10. In the article, a former player of the national team is cited, stating that the prize money of the national championship amounted to 100 million VND (4800 USD) when he played, whereas the prize money of the tournament in Ninh Hiệp was 125 million VND (6000 USD) for the men's category, and half that amount for the women's category.

References

Abrami, Regina M. 2002. Just a Peasant: Economy and Legacy in Northern Vietnam. In *Post-Socialist Peasant?: Rural and Urban Constructions of Identity in Eastern Europe, East Asia and the Former Soviet Union*, ed. Palema Leonard, and Deema Kaneff, 94–116. Basingstoke: Palgrave.

Alexander, Paul. 1992. What's in a Price? Trade Practices in Peasant (and Other) Markets. In *Contesting Markets: Analyses of Ideology, Discourse and Practice*, ed. Roy Dilley, 79–96. Edinburgh: Edinburgh University Press.

Alexander, Jennifer. 1998. Women Traders in Javanese Marketplaces: Ethnicity, Gender, and the Entrepreneurial Spirit. In *Market Cultures: Society and Morality in the New Asian Capitalisms*, ed. Robert W. Hefner, 203–223. Boulder: Westview Press.

An Nhiên, and Nguyên Trang. 2013. Ninh Hiệp - Bạc Tỉ và Sự Thụt Lùi Của Tri Thức [Ninh Hiệp - Billions and the Decline of Knowledge]. *Lao Động Điện Tử* [*Labour Online*], March 4. http://laodong.com.vn/phong-su/ninh-hiep-bac-ti-va-su-thut-lui-cua-tri-thuc-109018.bld.

Bélanger, Danièle, Lisa B. Drummond, and Van Nguyen-Marshall. 2012. Introduction: Who Are the Urban Middle Class in Vietnam? In *The Reinvention of Distinction: Modernity and the Middle Class in Urban Vietnam*, ed. Van Nguyen-Marshall, Lisa B. Drummond, and Danièle Bélanger, 1–17. Dordrecht: Springer.

Brenner, Suzanne A. 1998. *The Domestication of Desire: Women, Wealth, and Modernity in Java*. Princeton: Princeton University Press.

Derks, Annuska. 2006. Khmer Women and Global Factories. In *Expressions of Cambodia: The Politics of Tradition, Identity, and Change*, ed. Leakthina C. Ollier, and Tim Winter, 193–204. London: Routledge.

Derks, Annuska. 2008. *Khmer Women on the Move: Exploring Work and Life in Urban Cambodia*. Honolulu: University of Hawaii Press.

Diệp Sa. 2014. 'Đại siêu thị may mặc Trung Quốc' ở Hà Nội ế ẩm ['Hypermarket for Chinese apparel' in Hanoi unable to find customers]. Zing News, 24 June. http://news.zing.vn/Dai-sieu-thi-may-mac-Trung-Quoc-o-Ha-Noi-e-am-post428589.html.

Dilley, Roy (ed.). 1992. *Contesting Markets: Analyses of Ideology, Discourse and Practice*. Edinburgh: Edinburgh University Press.

Endres, Kirsten W. 2015. Lộc Bestowed by Heaven: Fate, Fortune, and Morality in the Vietnamese Marketplace. *The Asia Pacific Journal of Anthropology* 16 (3): 227–243.

Fassin, Didier. 2005. Compassion and Repression: The Moral Economy of Immigration Policies in France. *Cultural Anthropology* 20 (3): 362–387.

Fassin, Didier. 2012. Introduction: Toward a Critical Moral Anthropology. In *A Companion to Moral Anthropology*,vol. 20, ed. Didier Fassin, 1–17. Malden: Wiley-Blackwell.

Ferguson, James. 2014. The Social Life of Cash Payment: Money, Markets, and the Mutualities of Poverty. In *Cash on the Table: Markets, Values, and Moral Economies*, ed. Edward F. Fischer, 113–131. Santa Fe, NM: School for Advanced Research Press.

Gregory, Chris A. 2012. On Money Debt and Morality: Some Reflections on the Contribution of Economic Anthropology. *Social Anthropology* 20 (4): 380–396.

Heintz, Monica. 2009. Introduction. In *The Anthropology of Moralities*, ed. Monica Heintz, 1–19. New York: Berghahn Books.

Hirschman, Albert O. 1982. Rival Interpretations of Market Society: Civilizing, Destructive, or Feeble? *Journal of Economic Literature* 20 (4): 1463–1484.

Huong Ly. 2014. Impressive Made in Vietnam. *VCCI News Online*, January 29. http://vccinews.com/news_detail.asp?news_id=29974.

Jellema, Kate. 2005. Making Good on Debt: The Remoralisation of Wealth in Post-Revolutionary Vietnam. *The Asia Pacific Journal of Anthropology* 6 (3): 231–248.

Leshkowich, Ann Marie. 2011. Making Class and Gender: (Market) Socialist Enframing of Traders in Ho Chi Minh City. *American Anthropologist* 113 (2): 277–290.

Leshkowich, Ann Marie. 2012. Finances, Family, Fashion, Fitness, and … Freedom? The Changing Lives of Urban Middle-Class Vietnamese Women. In *The Reinvention of Distinction: Modernity and the Middle Class in Urban Vietnam*, ed. Van Nguyen-Marshall, Lisa B. Drummond, and Danièle Bélanger, 95–114. Dordrecht: Springer.

Leshkowich, Ann Marie. 2014. *Essential Trade: Vietnamese Women in a Changing Marketplace*. Honolulu: University of Hawaii Press.

Lufrano, Richard J. 1997. *Honorable Merchants: Commerce and Self-Cultivation in Late Imperial China*. Honolulu: University of Hawaii Press.

Luong, Hy Van. 2010. *Tradition, Revolution, and Market Economy in a North Vietnamese Village, 1925–2006*. Honolulu: University of Hawaii Press.

Malarney, Shaun K. 1998. State Stigma, Family Prestige, and the Development of Commerce in the Red River Delta of Vietnam. In *Market Cultures: Society and Morality in the New Asian Capitalisms*, ed. Robert W. Hefner, 268–289. Boulder: Westview Press.

Nguyễn-Võ Thu-Hương. 2008. *The Ironies of Freedom: Sex, Culture, and Neoliberal Governance in Vietnam*. Seattle: University of Washington Press.

Ong, Aihwa, and Li Zhang. 2008. Introduction: Privatizing China: Powers of the Self, Socialism from Afar. In *Privatizing China: Socialism from Afar*, ed. Li Zhang, and Aihwa Ong, 1–19. Ithaca: Cornell University Press.

Pettus, Ashley. 2003. *Between Sacrifice and Desire: National Identity and the Governing of Femininity in Vietnam*. New York: Routledge.

Rydstrøm, Helle. 2009. Moralizing Female Sexuality: The Intersections between Morality and Sexuality in Rural Vietnam. In *The Anthropology of Moralities*, ed. Monica Heintz, 118–136. New York: Berghahn Books.

Sơn Phương. 2015. Tiểu Thương đóng Cửa Chợ Ninh Hiệp, Vây UBND Xã [Small-Scale Traders Close the Ninh Hiệp Market, Besiege the Commune People's Committee]. *VN Express Online*, January 15. http://vnexpress.net/tin-tuc/thoi-su/tieu-thuong-dong-cua-cho-ninh-hiep-vay-ubnd-xa-2939635.html.

Szanton Blanc, Cristina. 1972. *A Right to Survive: Subsistence Marketing in a Lowland Philippine Town*. University Park: Pennsylvania State University Press.

Tawney, Richard H. 1961 [1926]. *Religion and the Rise of Capitalism*. Harmondsworth: Penguin.

Tuấn Hợp. 2014. Hà Nội: Xây Lại Chợ Ninh Hiệp - Đừng đùa Với Sinh Kế Của Dân! [Hanoi: Rebuild Ninh Hiệp Market - Don't Play with People's Livelihood. *Dân Trí [People's Wisdom]*, January 18. http://dantri.com.vn/xa-hoi/ha-noi-xay-lai-cho-ninh-hiep-dung-dua-voi-sinh-ke-cua-dan-1390551477.htm.

Tuoi Tre [Youth] News. 2015. Professional Vietnamese Volleyballers Now Prefer Amateur Contests Thanks to Prizes, Training Opportunities. March 10. http://tuoitrenews.vn/sports/26583/professional-vietnamese-volleyballers-now-prefer-amateur-contests-thanks-to-prizes-training-opportunities.

Vann, Elizabeth F. 2012. Afterword: Consumption and Middle-Class Subjectivity in Vietnam. In *The Reinvention of Distinction: Modernity and the Middle Class in Urban Vietnam*, ed. Van Nguyen-Marshall, Lisa B. Drummond, and Danièle Bélanger, 157–170. Dordrecht: Springer.

9
Conclusion

By examining the reorganisation of small-scale trade ethnographically in the post-reform era in Vietnam, this work sought to destabilise the metanarrative of neoliberalism. At the same time, I have tried to move away from explaining what is happening in contemporary Vietnam simply in terms of the legacy of socialism. Three decades after the launch of the Đổi mới reforms, a new perspective is urgently needed to appreciate current developments. I started with the assumption that the transformation from a planned to a socialist-oriented market economy did not entail the state's retreat, but led to new governing strategies that are less direct, but by no means less powerful. On the basis of empirical research, I have suggested acknowledging the coexistence of socialist and neoliberal governmentalities, while putting particular focus on how the resulting ambiguities and uncertainties were being received and dealt with.

While there are different areas where the impact of the state can be seen, urban planning and infrastructure projects are perhaps the most visible. The regulation of marketplaces is a matter of concern since the mid-1990s and has been pursued with determination in the last few years with the goal of creating a "modern" and "civilised" nation. Not only were many high-end shopping malls built in urban areas—of which some

E. Horat, *Trading in Uncertainty*,
DOI 10.1007/978-3-319-55648-2_9

have failed and had to close down due to a lack of customers—but also a lot of traditional marketplaces were upgraded or newly established. Yet, much of what is envisioned by the state in the name of modernisation and funded by private investors is not in the interest of most Vietnamese. For traders, this meant that while they experienced freedom to pursue the economic activity they wanted—or could, given their circumstances—this freedom was heavily circumscribed by policies as well as by moral precepts. Far from regulating itself, the market is—and is also perceived to be—a product constantly shaped by human intervention.

Family, Gender and the Market

This work has also contributed to the research on family businesses in East and Southeast Asia and to the scholarship on Vietnam by giving an anthropological account of the operation of family businesses in a trading village in northern Vietnam. While there are a few studies on Vietnamese petty traders and marketplace vendors, family businesses have rarely received scholarly attention despite the fact that it is the most common type of economic organisation in Vietnam. Unlike earlier studies on family businesses in East Asia, I have not been interested in evaluating their economic efficiency nor have I found a view centring on patriarchal dominance and exploitation useful to the case at hand. Instead, I have looked closely at the dynamics within families, paying particular attention to gender and generational relations and notions of femininity and masculinity.

What effect does the combination of socialist and neoliberal governmentalities have on gender roles and conceptions of femininity and masculinity? While petty trade is seen as a female occupation in Vietnam, a remarkable number of young men have become marketplace vendors in recent years in Ninh Hiệp. In contrast to older generations of men who used to work for the local state, farm or support their wife's business in the background, many young men are attracted by the advantages of selling at the market. This trend may indicate changing notions of masculinity and a new set of priorities—rather than a stable and prestigious job in the public sector, earning money to afford a certain lifestyle seems important. Unlike in the high socialist time, when wealth was suspicious, being rich is now considered a marker of success and a precondition for a good life. Gone are the times when men were not supposed to handle money in the domestic sphere, supposedly because the household budget has significantly risen in the last years and managing it is not a minor issue any longer. The increased involvement of men led to an expansion and diversification of businesses. While women contribute to the discourse of trade being a side occupation that only brings an income sufficient to feed the family, the financial aspect of trading is emphasised as a major reason for men to become traders. In other words, while both women and men legitimise being traders in relation to the money they make from it, women—especially the middle-aged and the elderly—carefully downplay the financial profit, whereas men tend to magnify it. The fact that men participate in trade in Ninh Hiệp does not automatically challenge their masculinity. Quite the opposite: as the ability to make money became an important benchmark of masculinity, running a market stall seems like a logical step for men. Interestingly, the cultural obstacles that accounted for trade being a suitable activity for women but not for men melted away fairly quickly in Ninh Hiệp as commerce offered chances to make a decent living.

Yet, although earning money at the market may attribute positively to a men's status, being a trader is not generally valued more nowadays than it was in the past. Instead, the involvement of men in trade has contributed to an emphasis of the difference between women and men, which is reinforced through their association with a particular type of market: While it is considered suitable for male traders to sell at the new markets in a clean, comfortable environment, women traders attend to stalls at the old market where it is crowded and stuffy. This spatial difference evokes the image of women as backward petty traders in contrast to men as modern merchants. However, according to Leshkowich (2014), conforming to essentialising depictions of the petty trader as backward and marginal should not be seen as submission. Rather, through narrating and performing identities that correspond to official stereotypes, women traders have been able to quietly develop their businesses in the uncertain context of market socialism. Leshkowich (2014, 21) argues:

> (…) Powerful political or cultural discourses that seem to limit the possibilities for individuals may in fact afford vulnerable groups opportunities by providing ready-made performative and rhetorical strategies of credible identities to which they can appear to conform. By doing so, such groups can carve out a space for their own actions and develop meaningful forms of personhood while simultaneously shielding themselves from disapproving or dangerous scrutiny.

In this sense, reproducing essentialising identities by acting in accordance with them is a strategy employed by women traders to not attract attention and pursue their businesses aloof from state interference. While I agree with this explanation, I am cautious to not overestimate the positive effect of such essentialisms. Although they may help women in conducting their businesses with less interference, they also contribute to the reproduction of stereotypes that reinforce gender inequalities, which again have very real implications.

While a great part of this book has focused on the horizontal linkage between family businesses, the vertical connection, that is the generational bond, is crucial as well. The majority of young traders said that their parents gave them seed money to establish a business, and in most cases parents continue to be the most important source for credit for years. In turn, it is common for young traders to buy merchandise not only for their own shop but also for their parents when going on shopping trips to Guangzhou. Because these trips are physically very demanding, it is mainly the task of young traders, while middle-aged and elderly traders stay back in the village and attend to their children's stall and take over household-related duties. In addition to money and merchandise, the transfer of knowledge and the sharing of information are crucial in generational relations. Many traders stated that all they knew about trade, they had learnt from their parents and grandparents from early on. The high level of trust within the intimate space of the family means that business-relevant information can be shared without hesitation. The exchange of information between generations can be of great value, because traders of each generation have access to particular social networks where information circulates they may not be able to access elsewhere.

Often, there is not only a close emotional bond and exchange of business-related favours between two generations, but between three or even four. As the age of traders ranges from around 15–70 years, in some families three generations work simultaneously at the marketplace. When traders retire, they usually take care of grandchildren or great-grandchildren, especially in families where men are invested in the family business to a significant amount. Thus, different generations support each other with child and elderly care as well as in business-related issues and thereby foster emotional ties. In this sense, the pursuit of commercial activities in the form of a family business does not lead to the degradation of social relations, but in contrast, is actually constitutive of them. The idea of striving for individual profit as the utmost priority bears no resemblance with reality, where economic and social practices are tightly enmeshed with one another and are steeped in affect. By paying great attention to how economic processes are produced through everyday practices, and by bringing the economic and the social together with an emphasis on the reproduction of human life, this book is written in the spirit of the "human economy" project (see Hart et al. 2010).

Dealing with Uncertainty

As elaborated in Chaps. 6 and 7 social networks are substantial to traders as they serve as the main source for business-relevant information, such as trustworthiness and financial standing of fellow traders, prices and designs, producers and markets, and much more. Moreover, because the way traders manage to participate in the market largely depends on their social relations, having a diverse network that consists of family members, relatives, friends and acquaintances is of great importance. One example I illustrated in depth is the banking and credit system in the village, a salient feature of which is trust: On the one hand, trust is needed when lending money or selling on credit; on the other hand, repeated transactions are constitutive to the recreation of trust. In conversations, traders often mentioned a general atmosphere of trust in the village and also said that being perceived as trustworthy was crucial for business success. By the same token, misconduct, for example not paying back debts, is easily detected in this tightly knit community and entails high social—and eventually financial—costs. People living outside the village do not have access to the credit and banking system, and it is not common among Ninh Hiệp traders to offer non-village customers to purchase on credit. Most rules in the village have a strong moral character and do not only guide people how to behave, but also contribute to individuals having certain expectations about the actions of others and thus are helpful to make decisions, for example whether to give someone a credit.

Shared moral values as an informal agreement of how to behave properly are important to structure interactions in the community. As I have shown in Chap. 8, moral norms circulate in discourses and are buttressed by social practices. On the one hand, these shared ideas of morality, especially the notions of fairness (honesty discourse) and modesty (peasantry discourse), guide the actions of individuals and thereby lead to a smooth functioning of the market and the village life more broadly. Traders, who do not abide by these rules, are criticised and, if they continue to disrespect the rules, excluded from social networks that are essential for obtaining information and accessing commonly organised business trips. As mentioned earlier, having a good reputation—not only as trustworthy, but also as morally upright—is crucial in the village. These norms also target wealth and the use of money: by spending money in a "traditional way", that is not wasting money for "unnecessary" things but instead in a way that is worth the hard work needed to earn it, the peasant discourse is being reinforced. On the other hand, committing to a set of shared values is important to create a moral community. The performance of a moral identity, not only on the individual but also on the village level, is used as a strategy to invoke the right to make a living.

Besides the creation of social networks and the performance of a moral identity, applying illegal practices is another way of dealing with uncertainties, especially those stemming from incoherence and lack of transparency of the state. In regard of the transition period, the domain of the not-yet-(il)legal is of importance as the boundaries of what is considered as legal and illegal are shifting. In the first years after Đổi mới, and to some extent until the present day, legal uncertainty in the realm of commerce has been prevalent. While this threatens the stability of the traders' position, it also enables them to exploit uncertain situations to their advantage, as uncertainty allows for negotiations and flexible adjustments. For instance, constantly changing and vaguely formulated regulations are not necessarily enforced, but implemented as the person in charge sees fit, and in this vein leave space for manoeuvre for the involved actors.

In order to understand why Ninh Hiệp was able to adjust successfully to the reform era, it is necessary to look at the time prior to the launch of Đổi mới. The fact that Ninh Hiệp is a village with longstanding trading experience, as documented in Chaps. 2 and 3, is crucial, especially when compared to other villages in the Red River Delta that have not relied on their traditional trade after the introduction of Đổi mới but have switched to new ones. Not only particular trading skills and knowledge were pivotal for Ninh Hiệp villagers, but also their way of exploring novel situations and learning from others. Many traders emphasised the relevance of an entrepreneurial spirit, in the sense of not being risk-averse but instead seize new opportunities. Furthermore, a decisive factor for Ninh Hiệp's success was its continuous engagement with commerce during the subsidy period and the dense social networks traders cultivated. As a way to cope with the many uncertainties they faced at that time, merchants established close social bonds with one another and especially with local officials. As I described in Chap. 3, the support of these local cadres prior to Đổi mới and the creation of a unified system of commerce was extremely important for trade to flourish and gave Ninh Hiệp a head start over other villages. In the aftermath of Đổi mới, these arrangements between villagers and local cadres were needed much less and slowly suspended. This does not mean, however, that the relation between villagers and local cadres is insignificant nowadays. Even if local authorities are not the main actors in large market projects, they fulfil a crucial intermediary role between the state and the people. While they need to be respectful and carry out their duties towards higher levels of the state, in interactions with locals, they first and foremost need to gain the people's trust. As the new mode of governance implies greater distance between the state and the people, trust is more difficult to enhance, even more so when the state is perceived as acting in an intransparent and ambiguous manner. Thus, the effort one has to put into creating and constantly renewing relations of trust—like Mr. Thắng, who emphasised the importance of openness and transparent planning—seems to have become even greater in the post-reform period.

Marketisation or Alternative Economy?

In Ninh Hiệp, most people choose the model of the family business because it allows them to reconcile financial, social and emotional needs. Although some of the inhabitants of Ninh Hiệp have earned university degrees or have had well-paid jobs outside the village, many have decided to come back and establish a trade business. Yet, commerce has still not fully lost the connotation of a low-status occupation, and in the attempt to give the country a modern look, the state enacted decrees to restrict trading activities and relegate traders away from public places into private commercialised spaces. This undertaking is formulated as though it would satisfy the demands of the people, as, for example, in the recent statement of the Vice Chairman of the People's Committee of Gia Lâm district. He justified the approval of a new market project on the grounds that his district has not yet built commercial centres (*trung tâm thương mại*), only areas for commerce and services (*khu dịch vụ thương mại*), areas for entertainment, parks and parking lots, and that commercial centres would serve the people and advance the upgrade of Ninh Hiệp into a town Châu Anh (2014). His statement is not only inaccurate regarding the fact that Ninh Hiệp already *has* two commercial centres, but it also misrepresents the opinion of many Ninh Hiệp people who clearly say that commercial centres do not suit their needs. Quite the contrary: the trend to private markets—paid to a substantial degree indirectly by traders in the form of very high stall rental fees—results in the marginalisation of traders who do not have the means to acquire a stall. While at the beginning, the expansion of Ninh Hiệp's markets offered chances to many villagers to participate in clothing trade, this development has reached a point where villagers perceive growing inequalities and fear not being able to keep up with the pace of marketisation. In contrast to the 1990s and early 2000s, when the local economy was primarily driven by the needs and initiative of villagers, powerful state and private actors heavily influence recent marketisation processes. The trend to more privately owned markets does not only mean increasing competition and more pronounced inequalities, but also the loss of communal land and the displacement of public institutions, if they happen to be on that land.

While Ninh Hiệp villagers have managed to adapt successfully to changing conditions in the past by creating social networks, the current situation is rather challenging, especially because the local state's ability to support the traders' needs vis-à-vis the district and provincial government is limited. Villagers criticise local officials for not keeping them up to date and instead concealing important information about the markets. Thus, many traders, especially those at the old market, feel a measure of discomfort about the idea that higher echelons of the government get to make decisions that may not necessarily be in their interest..

However, Ninh Hiệp traders are not at the mercy of an all-powerful state, but actively seek strategies to continue their business and make their claims heard. The social networks of traders are not only important to conduct business, but also to create solidarity and a moral community among traders. When common interests are threatened, these ties can be activated to organise collective actions as happened in the recent past. By publicly debunking the inconsistency between the rhetoric of social justice and benefit-for-all versus the actual practice of take over of land and deprivation of people's livelihood, Ninh Hiệp traders exert strong pressure on the state. This case stands in contrast to successfully accomplished renovations of marketplaces in other parts of Vietnam. While vendors often react with protests when confronted with market renovation, these protests usually dissolve when a group of traders give in to promises of a stall in the transient or the renewed marketplace. As a result, the ties of solidarity among traders that were used to initiate the protest are cut and resisting renovation projects becomes much more difficult for those traders who did not accept the deal. In Ninh Hiệp, protests have taken place several times in the past 5 years, each time drawing on a few hundred to a thousand people. Unlike in other cases of market renovation, in Ninh Hiệp the sense of solidarity is constantly reproduced in the context of the moral community. Also, comparisons with other renovated or newly built markets may lead traders to think that even if they were given a stall in an upgraded market, their businesses would not thrive as much as they do now. Therefore, apart from solidarity, many traders recognise the keeping of the old market in the current state as much a communal as their individual interest and readily participate in collective actions. In many ways, Ninh Hiệp represents a typical case for the redevelopment of markets, an ongoing process throughout the country for more than a decade as well as in the region more broadly. But it is also particular in that the traders form a very strong moral community and organise collective actions that generated the pressure needed to force the government to reassess the project.

Throughout the course of this book, it has been my goal not only to provide a lens into the complex functioning of a marketplace, but also to embed it into the larger political-economic context in a manner Brenner and Theodore (2002) have dubbed an ethnography of "actually existing neoliberalism". As I have argued, the neoliberal logic is only one—albeit an increasingly potent—element of the new mode of governance in Vietnam. The normalisation of the middle class needs to be seen in the wider context of a class-making that is spurred in large part by neoliberal practices. In this sense, framing neoliberalism as an exception to today's rule in Vietnam is not entirely accurate. But at the same time, this neoliberal order is not unchallenged either. Nationwide protests against the privatisation of public goods and the seizure of land are clear signs that the new mode of governance and the implications of the state's particular vision of modernity have not been received well by all. In Ninh Hiệp, where the book's ethnographic thrust is drawn from, the moralising of spending practices, resulting in the rejection of middle-class consumerism, is but one way to refute neoliberal ideals while withstanding the power that is exerted from afar.

The calls for social equality in Vietnam have become louder and more widespread. The developments I witnessed during my time in Ninh Hiệp reflect this trend. At the same time, propositions about how to create an economy that serves the human need in general are hotly discussed by anthropologists (Hart 2008; Hart et al. 2010). What alternatives to the current system can be imagined to build an economic democracy? How could a human economy look like? In the foreseeable future, these will be the most pressing questions, both for academics *and* policy circles alike, since the neoliberal ideology is proving ever more illusory not only in levelling the playing field in society, but also in shoring up economic and political stability.

References

Brenner, Neil, and Nik Theodore. 2002. Cities and the Geographies of Actually Existing Neoliberalism. *Antipode* 34 (3): 349–379.

Châu Anh. 2014. 'Chợ Vải Nổi Tiếng Ninh Hiệp đang Bị "bức Tử"? [Is the Famous Cloth Market in Ninh Hiệp Forced to Commit Suicide?]'. *BizLIVE*, March 18. http://bizlive.vn/du-an/cho-vai-noi-tieng-ninh-hiep-dang-bi-buc-tu-120997.html.

Hart, Keith. 2008. The Human Economy. *Association of Social Anthropologists of the UK and Commonwealth* 1 (1): 1–12.

Hart, Keith, Jean-Louis Laville, and Antonio D. Cattani. 2010. *The Human Economy: A Citizen's Guide*. Cambridge: Polity Press.

Leshkowich, Ann Marie. 2014. *Essential Trade: Vietnamese Women in a Changing Marketplace*. Honolulu: University of Hawaii Press.

Bibliography

Leshkowich, Ann Marie. 2012. Rendering Infant Abandonment Technical and Moral: Expertise, Neoliberal Logics, and Class Differentiation in Ho Chi Minh City. *Positions* 20 (2): 497–526.

Nguyễn Tuấn Anh. 2010. Kinship as Social Capital: Economic, Social and Cultural Dimensions of Changing Kinship Relations in a Northern Vietnamese Village. PhD Thesis. Amsterdam: VU University Amsterdam.

UBND xã Ninh Hiệp. 2012. Báo Cáo: Kết Quả Thực Hiện Công Tác Dân Số—KHHGĐ Năm 2012. Nhiệm vụ Trọng Tâm Năm 2013 [Report: Results].

E. Horat, *Trading in Uncertainty*,
DOI 10.1007/978-3-319-55648-2

Index

E. Horat, *Trading in Uncertainty*,
DOI 10.1007/978-3-319-55648-2

Kolibri 360 GmbH
Ferdinand-Jühlke-Straße 7
99095 Erfurt, Deutschland
produktsicherheit@kolibri360.de